THE COMPUTER TUTOR

Little, Brown Computer Systems Series

Gerald M. Weinberg, *Editor*

Barnett, Michael P., and Graham K. Barnett
Personal Graphics for Profit and Pleasure on the Apple II® Plus Computer

Basso, David T., and Ronald D. Schwartz
Programming with FORTRAN/WATFOR/WATFIV

Chattergy, Rahul, and Udo W. Pooch
Top-down, Modular Programming in FORTRAN with WATFIV

Coats, R. B., and A. Parkin
Computer Models in the Social Sciences

Conway, Richard, and David Gries
An Introduction to Programming: A Structured Approach Using PL/I and PL/C, Third Edition

Conway, Richard, and David Gries
Primer on Structured Programming: Using PL/I, PL/C, and PL/CT

Conway, Richard, David Gries, and E. Carl Zimmerman
A Primer on Pascal, Second Edition

Cripps, Martin
An Introduction to Computer Hardware

Easley, Grady M.
Primer for Small Systems Management

Finkenaur, Robert G.
COBOL for Students: A Programming Primer

Freedman, Daniel P., and Gerald M. Weinberg
Handbook of Walkthroughs, Inspections, and Technical Reviews: Evaluating Programs, Projects, and Products, Third Edition

Graybeal, Wayne, and Udo W. Pooch
Simulation: Principles and Methods

Greenfield, S. E.
The Architecture of Microcomputers

Greenwood, Frank
Profitable Small Business Computing

Healey, Martin, and David Hebditch
The Microcomputer in On-Line Systems: Small Computers in Terminal-Based Systems and Distributed Processing Networks

Lemone, Karen A., and Martin E. Kaliski
Assembly Language Programming for the VAX-11

Lias, Edward J.
Future Mind: The Microcomputer—New Medium, New Mental Environment

Lines, M. Vardell, and Boeing Computer Services Company
Minicomputer Systems

Mashaw, B. J.
Programming Byte by Byte: Structured FORTRAN 77

Mills, Harlan D.
Software Productivity

Monro, Donald M.
Basic BASIC: An Introduction to Programming

Morrill, Harriet
Mini and Micro BASIC: Introducing Applesoft®, Microsoft®, and BASIC Plus

Mosteller, William S.
Systems Programmer's Problem Solver

Nahigian, J. Victor, and William S. Hodges
Computer Games for Businesses, Schools, and Homes

Nahigian, J. Victor, and William S. Hodges
Computer Games for Business, School, and Home for TRS-80® Level II BASIC

Orwig, Gary W., and William S. Hodges
The Computer Tutor: Learning Activities for Homes and Schools

Parikh, Girish
Techniques of Program and System Maintenance

Parkin, Andrew
Data Processing Management

Parkin, Andrew
Systems Analysis

Pizer, Stephen M., with Victor L. Wallace
To Compute Numerically: Concepts and Strategies

Pooch, Udo W., William H. Greene, and Gary G. Moss
Telecommunications and Networking

Reingold, Edward M., and Wilfred J. Hansen
Data Structures

Savitch, Walter J.
Abstract Machines and Grammars

Shneiderman, Ben
Software Psychology: Human Factors in Computer and Information Systems

Simpson, Tom, and Shaffer & Shaffer Applied Research & Development, Inc.
VisiCalc® Programming: No Experience Necessary

Walker, Henry M.
Problems for Computer Solutions Using FORTRAN

Walker, Henry M.
Problems for Computer Solutions Using BASIC

Weinberg, Gerald M.
Rethinking Systems Analysis and Design

Weinberg, Gerald M.
Understanding the Professional Programmer

Windeknecht, Thomas G.
6502 Systems Programming

THE COMPUTER TUTOR

Learning Activities for Homes and Schools

GARY W. ORWIG
University of Central Florida

WILLIAM S. HODGES

LITTLE, BROWN and COMPANY   Boston

Library of Congress Catalog Card No. 82-21673

ISBN 0-316-66500-2

Cover and interior illustrations by Jesse Clay

10 9 8 7 6 5 4 3

CONTENTS

FOREWORD

Here is a book for parents who are growing with their children, who care about their learning, and who like to be involved with them in new and exciting ways. It is a book for parents who would like to play with their children while their children play with computers, or play with their computers while their children play with those same computers. And it is a book for teachers who want computer-assisted instructional exercise material for the classroom microcomputer. In short, here is a book for almost anyone who is interested in children, in education, in computers.

Americans have always been interested in children and in education. They've also been interested in applying technology in education and play, as in other areas of their lives. When necessary, they've been prepared to study at home, no matter what feeble technology they had at their disposal. This Great American Tradition of self-education is exemplified by young Abraham Lincoln studying by firelight, writing in charcoal on a shovel.

Today, of course, learning is more complex, so it is easy to leave the schools in charge of the whole job. But the home computer revolution has given today's Honest Abe a new kind of shovel. This new "shovel" isn't quite as easy to use as the old kind—and that's where Orwig and Hodges come in. They've assembled a book of practical computer-assisted instruction (CAI) for real people with real ideas about what they want to learn, or want their children or students to learn.

More sophisticated programs for computer-assisted instruction certainly exist. But the beauty of the shovel wasn't its sophistication, but its accessibility. *Learners* want to be able to understand CAI programs when they decide to get inside and make a few custom changes.

Chesterfield once said, "There are three classes of people in the world. The first learn from their own experience—these are wise; the second learn from the experience of others—these are happy; the third neither learn from their own experience nor the experience of others—these are fools." The person who programs a home computer for self-education is both wise and happy when using a book like *The Computer Tutor.* There is the very direct learning obtained from interacting with the programs, but perhaps even more important is the *learning about learning* that comes from getting behind the scenes through sharing the authors' experience.

If you already own a computer, you know what a powerful teacher it can be, but perhaps you don't suspect its full power or know how to harness it to your own learning goals. If so, you're likely to be receptive to Orwig and Hodges. You'll undoubtedly be able to think of hundreds of lessons which can be created along the lines of one of this book's model programs.

If you don't already own a computer, I can think of no better reason for investing in one than as a self-education device. And I can think of no better place to start than with one of the programs in this book. I don't promise you'll become The Great Emancipator, or even just an ordinary President of the United States. But I will promise that you'll be taking part in The Great American Tradition—and it's easier than splitting rails!

Gerald M. Weinberg

Series Editor

PREFACE

Thomas Jefferson, a member of the original group of architects of the United States government and third U.S. President, once stated that in order to have an informative, cohesive society, the masses must be educated. In his day and time Jefferson was speaking about the 3 R's of reading, writing, and arithmetic. He never dreamed that a 4th R would develop in the future that would be just as important to the continued evolution of an informed society as were the original basic disciplines of education.

It has been predicted that this 4th R in education will be (or already is) the need for individuals to develop fundamental computer literacy. Digital computers and computer programming have been in existence for decades; however, with the appearance of microcomputers in the 1970's, the importance of computer literacy was dramatically magnified. Educators could no longer ignore the computer as an important tool, especially when they discovered that many of their students had microcomputers in their own homes. It has been predicted that the 1980's will be the beginning of computer education for the entire world on a mass marketing basis, and that anyone not computer literate will be as lost in society as those who neither read nor write today.

Educators who have worked with microcomputers in programmed instruction (PI) classrooms unanimously agree that microcomputers motivate students (especially in remedial training) more than any other single instructional tool. Computer-assisted instruction (CAI) teaches students logical thinking, allows for individualized review and practice (drill and practice), provides immediate feedback on performance, and in many cases gives a student a chance to demonstrate his or her creativity. Automatic interaction and instant feedback gives CAI a tremendous advantage over other audio/visual classroom techniques.

Although some critics charge that CAI is "mechanical" and impersonal, this rarely is the case. In fact, a student in need of remedial instruction can often obtain more personalized, "humanistic" attention from well designed CAI programs than he or she can get from a classroom with 34 other students in it. Most instructors using CAI feel that they become consultants instead of lecturers. These teachers are not hardware or software experts, but they do know enough to instruct students on how to use microcomputers and peripherals such as cassette tapes, disks, and printers.

Complete teacher acceptance and training in CAI is essential for the predicted computer literacy evolution of the 1980's to take place. The lack of high-quality, portable CAI courseware has slowed the computer literacy movement; to help fill this courseware void we have created a book intended to make CAI programs easily accessible to educators worldwide.

The Computer Tutor was written to be both educational and entertaining to teachers, parents, and students alike. Our courseware and the explanation of programming techniques cover a variety of subjects such as mathematics, science, social studies, etc. The courseware also includes a discussion on the insertion of graphic subroutines into the program listings. At the same time we have tried to maintain a tone designed to exploit the excitement and challenge of CAI.

We realize that without computer hardware our courseware cannot be utilized. With increasing distribution of low-cost microcomputers into educational systems, more hardware is becoming available to educators. However, greater efforts must be directed toward establishing computer literacy in the minds of taxpayers (parents) and local, state, and federal government officials. Computer awareness groups can be formed to educate taxpayers and school board officials of the educational and practical usefulness of CAI in their school systems. School seminars can also be given at PTA (Parent/Teacher Association) meetings to inform the public of the need for computer hardware and software as teaching tools for students.

CAI will never replace teachers as human factors in classrooms. However, it will give educators an excellent opportunity to enhance their teaching techniques. For example, it might give instructors time away from lecture and other "mass education" delivery methods in order to devote more personal time to both remedial and gifted students in the classroom.

We hope *The Computer Tutor* will provide a vehicle to assist the educator in CAI and to act as a stimulus toward a better understanding of computers and computer literacy by the general public. The task will not be an easy one and, like most worthwhile things, it will take time. However, with the help of teachers, parents, officials, and students working together, we believe that computer literacy on the part of the public will eventually be achieved. And we suspect that Thomas Jefferson would be very pleased.

Gary W. Orwig

William S. Hodges

THE COMPUTER TUTOR

INTRODUCTION

Computer-assisted instruction (CAI) can be traced back to a machine invented in 1924 by Dr. Sidney Pressey that was used to grade multiple-choice examinations. However, CAI's real roots are associated with B. F. Skinner, a behavioral psychologist who in 1954 published an article in the *Harvard Education Review* titled "The Science of Learning and the Art of Teaching." Programmed instruction (PI) in education was made more prominent as a direct result of this article. Also, terms such as linear programming, drill and practice, branching, and simulation became a part of an educator's vocabulary. CAI is nothing more than programmed instruction (PI) using computer hardware and software to carry out the teaching techniques. The main value of CAI is that it is an effective teaching tool for *individual* instruction rather than by the *group* lecturing method.

The Computer Tutor is a guide for developing CAI in elementary and secondary schools as well as in the home environment. Twenty-five computer programs teaching mathematics, science, vocabulary, and social studies by use of *linear, branching,* and *simulation* programmed instruction (PI) techniques have been included in the book. All program listings and their sample runs were written and operated on an APPLE II microcomputer using 16K Floating Point BASIC (APPLESOFT*) computer programming language. The CAI programs can also be operated on TRS-80 Level II, Commodore Pet with floating point BASIC, and any other computer using standard floating point BASIC 16K memory and above.

Graphic subroutines for pictorial displays are included at the back of the book to be used as suggested guides for adding graphics to the programs. Only the APPLE II, TRS-80 Level II, and the Commodore Pet microcomputers are mentioned in the graphic subroutines section.

Programming techniques and suggestions for modifying and/or personalizing the programs included in the text are mentioned after each program description. Also, a *glossary* covering some computer hardware and software words, CAI terms, and graphic definitions is included in the back of the book. The glossary should assist the reader or instructor in understanding some of the terms used in the explanations of the programs and elsewhere in the book.

All of the program listings are easily entered into the computer's memory by following the programming instructions described in each individual computer hardware owner's

---

* APPLESOFT is a registered trademark of Apple Computer, Inc.

manual. The REM (Remarks) statements in the program listings do not need to be typed or entered into the computer's memory. These statements are only comments to the reader or instructor in modifying the programs.

PROGRAM DISCUSSION

The programs which follow have been written in a standard floating point BASIC which allows undimensioned strings and dimensioned string arrays. All programs will run directly on an Apple II floating point computer, and they will also run on most other computers with only minor changes. The most frequent (and simple to correct) change occurs in randomization routines. These areas are pointed out within the programs.

A few computers (most notably the popular Atari 800) utilize a floating point BASIC which does not allow standard string arrays. This is a major deviation from the "norm," and it will complicate many of these program listings. With patience and some programing skills, there are still methods of creating the equivalent of string arrays. In the case of Atari, however, there are indications that an Extended BASIC which will correct this problem will soon be available.

The programs presented here contain the following components:

A. Program Description

B. Program Notes

C. Program Listing

D. Sample Run

It should be noted that the sample runs have been condensed (blank lines removed) to save space (ie. reduce cost). In many cases, the programs are very active, with information constantly scrolling on and off the video screen. One of the shorter programs, with all scrolling lines left in, produced over 20 feet of print-out on a sample run! In addition, some of the sample runs, such as the Spelling Quiz, don't seem to make a lot of sense. You must keep in mind that the print-out is permanent, while the actual video image can come and go very rapidly.

Finally, the program listings follow very definite patterns. You will notice that the same line numbers perform the same functions whenever possible. It is wise to develop this habit because you will find that subroutines can often be memorized if they are repeated frequently. For variety, though, the same function has sometimes been performed several different ways. This was not an accident — it is intended to allow you to select your favorite methods.

Happy CAI!

Hello! My name is Arthur. I have been selected as your guide to lead you through an exciting and rewarding adventure! Follow me as I demonstrate to you how fun and easy it is to learn mathematical and verbal skills with the use of personal computers.

LINEAR PROGRAMS

Linear programming is the most common form of programmed instruction (PI). It is presented in a logical (fixed) sequence of small steps or frames. When used with a computer, linear programming becomes a form of *drill and practice* computer-assisted instruction (CAI). The fifteen program listings and sample runs were chosen as a representative sample of linear programs that provide instruction in basic mathematics, vocabulary, science, memory enhancement, and social studies.

CAPITALS OF NATIONS

PROGRAM DESCRIPTION

A geography lesson is presented in this program. For this "trip around the world," the computer asks you a series of multiple-choice questions either to select the correct capital of a nation or the nation with a given capital. The computer will ask you the questions you missed at a later time during the test. You must answer all of the questions correctly in order to complete the program.

PROGRAM NOTES

1. This program may need occasional updating. Nations and capitals do have a tendency to change!

2. By changing the data base you could use this program to teach any sets of matched pairs like English/French, event/date, author/title, etc.

PROGRAM LISTING

```
100  REM  CAPITALS OF NATIONS BY GARY ORWIG
1000 REM  INITIALIZATION
1010 TL = 114
1020 DIM N(4),CA$(TL),NA$(TL)
1030 REM    READ IN NATION & CAPITAL ARRAYS
1040 FOR I = 1 TO TL
1050 READ NA$(I),CA$(I)
1060 NEXT I
1070 G = 0
1080 BL = TL
```

```
1090 N = 0
2000 REM  INTRODUCTION
2010 L = 12
2020 GOSUB 18000
2030 PRINT "     NATIONS AND CAPITALS"
2040 GOSUB 18000
2050 DE = 1000
2060 GOSUB 19000
2070 GOSUB 18000
2080 PRINT "THIS IS A PROGRAM WHICH WILL TEST YOUR"
2090 PRINT "KNOWLEDGE OF NATIONS AND THEIR"
2100 PRINT "CAPITALS."
2110 PRINT
2120 PRINT "YOU WILL BE GIVEN MULTIPLE CHOICE"
2130 PRINT "QUESTIONS WHICH HAVE FOUR ANSWERS EACH."
2140 PRINT
2150 PRINT "YOU SHOULD ANSWER WITH A '1,' '2,'"
2160 PRINT "'3,' OR '4.'"
2170 PRINT
2180 PRINT "TO STOP AT ANY TIME, TYPE IN A '0'"
2190 PRINT "FOR AN ANSWER."
2200 PRINT
2210 PRINT "YOU HAVE A CHOICE:"
2220 PRINT "   1. BE GIVEN THE NATION"
2230 PRINT "      AND ANSWER WITH THE CAPITAL"
2240 PRINT
2250 PRINT "   2. BE GIVEN THE CAPITAL"
2260 PRINT "      AND ANSWER WITH THE NATION"
2270 PRINT
2280 PRINT "PICK '1' OR '2'"
2290 INPUT SE
2300 IF SE < 1 OR SE > 2 THEN 2280
2310 L = 18
2320 GOSUB 18000
2330 L = 9
4000 REM  MAIN PROGRAM - CHANGE RND(1) TO RND(0) FOR TRS-80 AND
   PET
4010 GOSUB 10000
4020 REM  C IS POSITION OF CORRECT ANSWER
4030 C = INT ( RND (1) * 4) + 1
4040 REM  PICK THREE NUMBERS
4050 FOR I = 1 TO 3
4060 N(I) = INT ( RND (1) * TL) + 1
4070 NEXT I
4080 N(4) = N(C)
4090 N(C) = R
4100 REM  MAKE CERTAIN ALL FOUR NUMBERS DIFFER
4110 IF N(1) = N(2) OR N(1) = N(3) OR N(1) = N(4) THEN 4050
4120 IF N(2) = N(3) OR N(2) = N(4) OR N(3) = N(4) THEN 4050
4130 IF SE = 2 THEN 4230
4140 REM  PRINT CAPITALS
4150 GOSUB 18000
4160 PRINT "1.";CA$(N(1))
4170 PRINT "2.";CA$(N(2))
4180 PRINT "3.";CA$(N(3))
4190 PRINT "4.";CA$(N(4))
```

```
4200  GOSUB 18000
4210  PRINT "THE CAPITAL OF ";NA$(R);" IS";
4220  GOTO 4310
4230  REM  PRINT NATIONS
4240  GOSUB 18000
4250  PRINT "1.";NA$(N(1))
4260  PRINT "2.";NA$(N(2))
4270  PRINT "3.";NA$(N(3))
4280  PRINT "4.";NA$(N(4))
4290  GOSUB 18000
4300  PRINT CA$(R);" IS THE CAPITAL OF ";
4310  INPUT SA
4320  IF SA < 1 OR SA > 4 THEN 4610
4330  IF SA = C THEN 4430
4340  PRINT
4350  PRINT "WRONG!"
4360  IF SE = 2 THEN  GOTO 4400
4370  PRINT
4380  PRINT "THE CAPITAL OF ";NA$(R);" IS ";CA$(R);"."
4390  GOTO 4560
4400  PRINT
4410  PRINT CA$(R);" IS THE CAPITAL OF ";NA$(R);"."
4420  GOTO 4560
4430  REM
4440 N = N + 1
4450  PRINT
4460  PRINT "RIGHT! YOU HAVE ";N;" CORRECT!"
4470  REM  REMOVE CORRECT ANSWER FROM LIST
4480 S$ = CA$(R)
4490 CA$(R) = CA$(BL)
4500 CA$(BL) = S$
4510 S$ = NA$(R)
4520 NA$(R) = NA$(BL)
4530 NA$(BL) = S$
4540 BL = BL - 1
4550  IF BL = 0 THEN  GOTO 4670
4560 DE = 1000
4570  GOSUB 19000
4580 G = G + 1
4590  GOTO 4010
4600  REM  STOP?
4610  PRINT "DO YOU WANT TO STOP";
4620  INPUT SA$
4630  IF SA$ = "Y" OR SA$ = "YES" THEN 4680
4640  PRINT "WHAT WAS YOUR ANSWER"
4650  PRINT "TO THE LAST PROBLEM";
4660  GOTO 4310
4670 G = G + 1
4680  PRINT "YOU GOT ";N;" RIGHT IN ";G;" GUESSES"
4690  PRINT
4700  PRINT "WOULD YOU LIKE TO TRY AGAIN";
4710  INPUT SA$
4720  PRINT
4730  IF SA$ = "Y" OR SA$ = "YES" THEN  GOTO 1070
4740  END
```

```
10000 REM  RANDOMIZATION - CHANGE 'RND (1)' TO 'RND (0)' FOR TRS
      -80 AND PET!
10010 R = INT ( RND (1) * BL) + 1
10020 RETURN
18000 REM  SCROLLING
18010 FOR I = 1 TO L
18020 PRINT
18030 NEXT I
18040 RETURN
19000 REM  DELAY
19010 FOR I = 1 TO DE
19020 NEXT I
19030 RETURN
21000 REM  DATA
21010 DATA "AFGHANISTAN","KABUL","ALBANIA","TIRANA","ALGERIA","AL
      GIERS"
21020 DATA "ANGOLA","LUANDA","ARGENTINA","BUENOS AIRES","AUSTRALI
      A","CANBERRA"
21030 DATA "AUSTRIA","VIENNA","THE BAHAMAS","NASSAU","BANGLADESH"
      ,"DACCA"
21040 DATA "BARBADOS","BRIDGETOWN","BELGIUM","BRUSSELS","BOLIVIA"
      ,"SUCRE"
21050 DATA "BOTSWANA","GABORONE","BRAZIL","BRASILIA","BULGARIA","
      SOFIA"
21060 DATA "BURMA","RANGOON","CAMBODIA","PHNOM PENH","CANADA","OT
      TAWA"
21070 DATA "CHILE","SANTIAGO","PEOPLE'S REPUBLIC OF CHINA","PEKIN
      G"
21080 DATA "REPUBLIC OF CHINA","TAIPEI","COLOMBIA","BOGOTA","COST
      A RICA","SAN JOSE"
21090 DATA "CUBA","HAVANA","CYPRUS","NICOSIA","CZECHOSLOVAKIA","P
      RAGUE"
21100 DATA "DENMARK","COPENHAGEN","DOMINICAN REPUBLIC","SANTO DOM
      INGO"
21110 DATA "ECUADOR","QUITO","EGYPT","CAIRO","EL SALVADOR","SAN S
      ALVADOR"
21120 DATA "ETHIOPIA","ADDIS ABABA","FIJI","SUVA","FINLAND","HELS
      INKI"
21130 DATA "FRANCE","PARIS","GERMANY","BERLIN","GHANA","ACCRA","G
      REECE","ATHENS"
21140 DATA "GUATEMALA","GUATEMALA CITY","HAITI","PORT-AU-PRINCE",
      "HONDURAS","TEGUCIGALPA"
21150 DATA "HUNGARY","BUDAPEST","ICELAND","REYKJAVIK","INDIA","NE
      W DELHI"
21160 DATA "INDONESIA","JAKARTA","IRAN","TEHRAN","IRAQ","BAGHDAD"

21170 DATA "IRELAND","DUBLIN","ISRAEL","JERUSALEM","ITALY","ROME"

21180 DATA "JAMAICA","KINGSTON","JAPAN","TOKYO","JORDON","AMMAN",
      "KENYA","NAIROBI"
21190 DATA "SOUTH KOREA","SEOUL","KUWAIT","KUWAIT CITY","LAOS","V
      IENTIANE"
21200 DATA "LEBANON","BEIRUT","LIBERIA","MONROVIA","LIBYA","TRIPO
      LI"
21210 DATA "LIECHTENSTEIN","VADUZ","MADAGASCAR","TANANARIVE","MAL
      AYSIA","KUALA LUMPUR"
```

```
21220  DATA "MALI","BAMAKO","MALTA","VALETTA","MAURITANIA","NOUAKC
       HOTT"
21230  DATA "MEXICO","MEXICO CITY","MONGOLIA","ULAN BATOR","MOROCC
       O","RABAT"
21240  DATA "MOZAMBIQUE","MAPUTO","NEPAL","KATMANDU","THE NETHERLA
       NDS","AMSTERDAM"
21250  DATA "NEW ZEALAND","WELLINGTON","NICARAGUA","MANAGUA","NIGE
       R","NIAMEY"
21260  DATA "NIGERIA","LAGOS","NORWAY","OSLO","OMAN","MUSCAT","PAK
       ISTAN","ISLAMBAD"
21270  DATA "PANAMA","PANAMA","PARAGUAY","ASUNCION","PERU","LIMA"
21280  DATA "PHILIPPINES","QUEZON CITY","POLAND","WARSAW","PORTUGA
       L","LISBON"
21290  DATA "RHODESIA","SALISBURY","ROMANIA","BUCHAREST","SAUDI AR
       ABIA","RIYADH"
21300  DATA "SENEGAL","DAKAR","SIERRA LEONE","FREETOWN","SOMALIA",
       "MOGADISHU"
21310  DATA "REPUBLIC OF SOUTH AFRICA","PRETORIA AND CAPE TOWN","S
       PAIN","MADRID"
21320  DATA "SRI LANKA","COLOMBO","SUDAN","KHARTOUM","SWEDEN","STO
       CKHOLM"
21330  DATA "SWITZERLAND","BERN","SYRIA","DAMASCUS","TANZANIA","DA
       R ES SALAAM"
21340  DATA "THAILAND","BANGKOK","TOGO","LOME","TONGA","NUKUALOFA"

21350  DATA "TRINIDAD & TOBAGO","PORT OF SPAIN","TUNISIA","TUNIS",
       "TURKEY","ANKARA"
21360  DATA "UGANDA","KAMPALA","RUSSIA (USSR)","MOSCOW","UNITED AR
       AB EMIRATES","ABU DHABI"
21370  DATA "UNITED KINGDOM","LONDON","URUGUAY","MONTEVIDEO","VENE
       ZUELA","CARACAS"
21380  DATA "VIETNAM","HANOI","YUGOSLAVIA","BELGRADE","ZAIRE","KIN
       SHASA","ZAMBIA","LUSAKA"
```

                 * -->TABLE OF VARIABLES<--

BL - BOTTOM OF LIST MARKER
1080 4490 4500 4520 4530 4540 4540 4550 10010

C - POSITION OF CORRECT ANSWER
4030 4080 4090 4330

CA$(*) - CAPITALS LIST
1020 1050 4160 4170 4180 4190 4300 4380 4410 4480 4490
4490 4500

DE - DELAY
2050 4560 19010

G - NUMBER OF GUESSES
1070 4580 4580 4670 4670 4680

I - COUNTER
1040 1050 1050 1060 4050 4060 4070 18010 18030 19010 19020

L - LINES OF SCROLLING
2010 2310 2330 18010

N - NUMBER CORRECT
1090 4440 4440 4460 4680

N(*) - ANSWER ARRAY
1020 4060 4080 4080 4090 4110 4110 4110 4110 4110 4110
4120 4120 4120 4120 4120 4120 4160 4170 4180 4190 4250
4260 4270 4280

NA$(*) - NATIONS LIST
1020 1050 4210 4250 4260 4270 4280 4380 4410 4510 4520
4520 4530

R - RANDOM NUMBER
4090 4210 4300 4380 4380 4410 4410 4480 4490 4510 4520
10010

S$ - TRANSFER VARIABLE
4480 4500 4510 4530

SA - STUDENT ANSWER
4310 4320 4320 4330

SA$ - STUDENT ANSWER
4620 4630 4630 4710 4730 4730

SE - PRESENTATION MODE
2290 2300 2300 4130 4360

TL - NUMBER OF PAIRS IN LIST
1010 1020 1020 1040 1080 4060

END OF VAR. LIST

SAMPLE RUN

```
]RUN
     NATIONS AND CAPITALS
THIS IS A PROGRAM WHICH WILL TEST YOUR
KNOWLEDGE OF NATIONS AND THEIR
CAPITALS.
YOU WILL BE GIVEN MULTIPLE CHOICE
QUESTIONS WHICH HAVE FOUR ANSWERS EACH.
YOU SHOULD ANSWER WITH A '1,' '2,'
'3,' OR '4,'
TO STOP AT ANY TIME, TYPE IN A '0'
FOR AN ANSWER.
YOU HAVE A CHOICE:
   1. BE GIVEN THE NATION
      AND ANSWER WITH THE CAPITAL
   2. BE GIVEN THE CAPITAL
      AND ANSWER WITH THE NATION
PICK '1' OR '2'
?1
1.OSLO
2.ASUNCION
3.SANTO DOMINGO
4.PARIS
```

```
THE CAPITAL OF PARAGUAY IS?1
WRONG!
THE CAPITAL OF PARAGUAY IS ASUNCION.
1.MUSCAT
2.ADDIS ABABA
3.SALISBURY
4.VIENTIANE
THE CAPITAL OF OMAN IS?1
RIGHT! YOU HAVE 1 CORRECT!
1.CAIRO
2.RANGOON
3.SALISBURY
4.TEHRAN
THE CAPITAL OF RHODESIA IS?3
RIGHT! YOU HAVE 2 CORRECT!
1.JERUSALEM
2.DACCA
3.TEGUCIGALPA
4.PEKING
THE CAPITAL OF ISRAEL IS?

]
```

GUESS THE NUMBERS

PROGRAM DESCRIPTION

All the skills of addition, subtraction, multiplication, and division are tested in this program. The computer picks two numbers and adds, subtracts, multiplies, and divides them. The answers which are a result of the two numbers being added, subtracted, multiplied, or divided, are displayed. You are to try and guess which two numbers were used to obtain the list of answers shown to you.

PROGRAM NOTES

1. For a less complicated game, always present the four "results" in the same order.

2. Line 10080 eliminates number pairs which don't divide evenly. What happens if you remove it?

PROGRAM LISTING

```
100  REM  GUESS THE NUMBERS BY GARY ORWIG
1000 REM  INITIALIZATION
1010 DIM P(4)
2000 REM    INTRODUCTION - USE 'RND (0)' IN PLACE OF 'RND (1)' FO
     R TRS-80 AND PET!
2010 FOR I = 1 TO 200
2020 PRINT INT ( RND (1) * 10000);"  ";
2030 NEXT I
2040 FOR I = 1 TO 3000
2050 NEXT I
2060 FOR I = 1 TO 25
2070 PRINT
```

```
2080  NEXT I
2090  PRINT "      GUESS THE NUMBERS"
2100  FOR I = 1 TO 10
2110  PRINT
2120  NEXT I
2130  PRINT "WHAT IS YOUR NAME?"
2140  INPUT NA$
2150  PRINT
2160  PRINT "IT'S NICE TO MEET YOU, ";NA$;"."
2170  PRINT
2180  PRINT
2190  PRINT "I WILL THINK OF TWO NUMBERS AND"
2200  PRINT "ADD, SUBTRACT, MULTIPLY, AND"
2210  PRINT "DIVIDE THEM.  I WILL THEN MIX UP"
2220  PRINT "THE ANSWERS AND SHOW THEM TO YOU."
2230  PRINT
2240  PRINT "IT WILL BE YOUR JOB TO FIGURE OUT"
2250  PRINT "THE ORIGINAL TWO NUMBERS!"
2260  PRINT
2270  PRINT
2280  PRINT "WHAT IS THE LARGEST NUMBER YOU"
2290  PRINT "WANT TO WORK WITH, ";NA$
2300  INPUT MX
2310  PRINT
2320  PRINT "OK, I WILL TRY NOT TO GIVE YOU"
2330  PRINT "PROBLEMS THAT HAVE ANSWERS OVER ";MX;"."
2340  FOR I = 1 TO 2000
2350  NEXT I
2360  PRINT
2370  PRINT
2380  PRINT "HERE WE GO!"
2390  PRINT
2400  PRINT
4000  REM  MAIN PROGRAM
4010 I = 0
4020  GOSUB 10000
4030  GOSUB 10500
4040 P(1) = E
4050  GOSUB 10500
4060  IF E = P(1) THEN 4050
4070 P(2) = E
4080  GOSUB 10500
4090  IF E = P(1) OR E = P(2) THEN 4080
4100 P(3) = E
4110 P(4) = 10 - (P(1) + P(2) + P(3))
4120 I = I + 1
4130  IF I = 5 THEN 4230
4140  ON P(I) GOTO 4150,4170,4190,4210
4150  PRINT A + B;"   ";
4160  GOTO 4120
4170  PRINT A - B;"   ";
4180  GOTO 4120
4190  PRINT A * B;"   ";
4200  GOTO 4120
4210  PRINT A / B;"   ";
4220  GOTO 4120
```

```
4230  PRINT
4240  PRINT "WHAT DO YOU THINK THE TWO"
4250  PRINT "NUMBERS ARE?  TYPE THEM IN"
4260  PRINT "LIKE THIS: 6,7"
4270  INPUT S1,S2
4280 TR = TR + 1
4290  GOSUB 11000
4300  IF HT = 1 THEN 4340
4310  GOSUB 14000
4320 I = 0
4330  GOTO 4120
4340 HT = 0
4350  GOSUB 12000
10000  REM   RANDOMIZATION - USE 'RND (0)' IN PLACE OF 'RND (1)' F
   OR TRS-80 AND PET!
10010 A =  INT ( RND (1) * MX) + 1
10020 B =  INT ( RND (1) * MX) + 1
10030  IF A < B THEN 10050
10040  GOTO 10080
10050 D = B
10060 B = A
10070 A = D
10080  IF A / B > INT (A / B) THEN 10010
10090  RETURN
10500  REM   PRESENTATION ORDER - USE 'RND (0)' IN PLACE OF 'RND (
   1)' FOR TRS-80 AND PET!
10510 E =  INT ( RND (1) * 4) + 1
10520  RETURN
11000  REM  JUDGE ANSWERS
11010  IF S1 = A GOTO 11040
11020  IF S1 = B THEN 11060
11030  GOTO 11100
11040  IF S2 = B THEN 11080
11050  GOTO 11100
11060  IF S2 = A GOTO 11080
11070  GOTO 11100
11080 HT = 1
11090  RETURN
11100 HT = 0
11110 I = 0
11120  RETURN
12000  REM  REWARD
12010  FOR I = 1 TO 50
12020  PRINT "     YOU FOUND THEM!";
12030  NEXT I
12040  GOTO 15000
14000  REM  WRONG ANSWER
14010  PRINT
14020  PRINT "SORRY!  TRY AGAIN!"
14030  PRINT
14040  RETURN
15000  PRINT
15010  PRINT
15020  PRINT
15030  PRINT "IT TOOK ";TR;" TRIES!"
15040  PRINT
```

```
15050  PRINT
15060  PRINT
15070  PRINT "DO YOU WANT ANOTHER PROBLEM?"
15080  PRINT "(YES OR NO)
15090  INPUT S$
15100  IF S$ = "YES" THEN 15130
15110  PRINT "BYE FOR NOW!"
15120  END
15130 TR = 0
15140 HT = 0
15150 I = 0
15160  GOTO 4000
```

* -->TABLE OF VARIABLES<--

A - ONE NUMBER
4150 4170 4190 4210 10010 10030 10060 10070 10080 10080
11010 11060

B - THE OTHER NUMBER
4150 4170 4190 4210 10020 10030 10050 10060 10080 10080
11020 11040

D - TRANSFER VARIABLE
10050 10070

E - PRESENTATION ORDER
4040 4060 4070 4090 4090 4100 10510

HT - HIT
4300 4340 11080 11100 15140

I - COUNTER
2010 2030 2040 2050 2060 2080 2100 2120 2340 2350 4010
4120 4120 4130 4140 4320 11110 12010 12030 15150

MX - MAXIMUM SIZE
2300 2330 10010 10020

NA$ - NAME
2140 2160 2290

P(*) - PRESENTATION ORDER
1010 4040 4060 4070 4090 4090 4100 4110 4110 4110 4110
4140

S$ - STUDENT ANSWER
15090 15100

S1 - STUDENT ANSWER
4270 11010 11020

S2 - STUDENT ANSWER
4270 11040 11060

TR - NUMBER OF TRIES
4280 4280 15030 15130

END OF VAR. LIST

SAMPLE RUN

```
]RUN
        GUESS THE NUMBERS
WHAT IS YOUR NAME?
?GARY
IT'S NICE TO MEET YOU, GARY.
I WILL THINK OF TWO NUMBERS AND
ADD, SUBTRACT, MULTIPLY, AND
DIVIDE THEM.  I WILL THEN MIX UP
THE ANSWERS AND SHOW THEM TO YOU.
IT WILL BE YOUR JOB TO FIGURE OUT
THE ORIGINAL TWO NUMBERS!
WHAT IS THE LARGEST NUMBER YOU
WANT TO WORK WITH, GARY
?20
OK, I WILL TRY NOT TO GIVE YOU
PROBLEMS THAT HAVE ANSWERS OVER 20.
HERE WE GO!
80   16   24   5
WHAT DO YOU THINK THE TWO
NUMBERS ARE?  TYPE THEM IN
LIKE THIS: 6,7
?4,6
SORRY!  TRY AGAIN!
80   16   24   5
WHAT DO YOU THINK THE TWO
NUMBERS ARE?  TYPE THEM IN
LIKE THIS: 6,7
?20,4
        YOU FOUND THEM!     YOU FOUND THEM!
IT TOOK 2 TRIES!
DO YOU WANT ANOTHER PROBLEM?
(YES OR NO)
?NO
BYE FOR NOW!
]
```

GUESS THE WORD

PROGRAM DESCRIPTION

Spelling skills and word recognition are practiced in this program. The computer selects a word from an instructor-made data file and then presents an appropriate number of blanks to be filled by letters. You try and guess the letters that make up the selected word. At any point, you may enter an "!" which will allow you to guess the whole word and reduce the number of times it takes you to guess the word. The computer also gives you one hint when you enter a " ? ".

PROGRAM NOTES

If you are a real graphics whiz, develop a subroutine which will gradually "hang" a man and slip it into the 14000 section of the program. If you prefer less violence, draw a robot that gradually walks off a cliff!

Of course, you can enter your own words in the data section (lines 21000...). Just enter each word followed by its hint. Set TL equal to the number of words.

PROGRAM LISTING

```
100  REM   GUESS THE WORD BY GARY ORWIG
1000 REM   INITIALIZATION – SET 'TL' TO TOTAL NUMBER OF WORDS IN
     YOUR DATA SET.
1010 TL = 20
1020 BL = TL
1030 DIM A$(20),B$(20),FL$(TL),HN$(TL)
1040 FOR I = 1 TO TL
```

```
1050  READ FL$(I),HN$(I)
1060  NEXT I
2000  REM  INTRODUCTION
2010  FOR I = 1 TO 12
2020  PRINT
2030  NEXT I
2040  PRINT "    GUESS THE WORD"
2050  FOR I = 1 TO 12
2060  PRINT
2070  NEXT I
2080  FOR I = 1 TO 1000
2090  NEXT I
2100  PRINT "WHAT IS YOUR NAME";
2110  INPUT NA$
2120  PRINT "I AM HAPPY TO MEET YOU, ";NA$;"."
2130  PRINT
2140  PRINT
2150  PRINT
2160  PRINT "I AM GOING TO THINK OF A WORD,"
2170  PRINT "AND IT WILL BE YOUR JOB TO"
2180  PRINT "GUESS IT.  YOU DO THIS BY"
2190  PRINT "GUESSING ONE LETTER AT A TIME."
2200  PRINT
2210  PRINT "AT ANY TIME YOU CAN TYPE IN"
2220  PRINT "AN '!' AND THEN GUESS THE WHOLE"
2230  PRINT "WORD.  IF YOU NEED A HINT, TYPE"
2240  PRINT "IN A '?' AND I WILL TRY TO HELP YOU."
2250  PRINT
2260  PRINT
2270  PRINT "HERE WE GO!"
2280  PRINT
2290  PRINT
4000  REM  MAIN PROGRAM
4010  GOSUB 10000
4020  C$ = FL$(R)
4030  L =  LEN (C$)
4040  FOR I = 1 TO L
4050  A$(I) =  MID$ (C$,I,1)
4060  B$(I) = "*"
4070  NEXT I
4080  GOSUB 18000
4090  PRINT
4100  PRINT
4110  PRINT
4120  PRINT "GUESS A LETTER (OR '?' OR '!'),"
4130  HT = 0
4140  INPUT S$
4150  IF  LEN (S$) = 1 THEN 4180
4160  PRINT "TYPE IN ONLY ONE LETTER!"
4170  GOTO 4140
4180  GOSUB 11000
4190  IF HT = 2 THEN 4120
4200  TR = TR + 1
4210  IF HT = 1 THEN 4250
4220  GOSUB 14000
4230  GOSUB 18000
```

```
4240  GOTO 4090
4250  HT = 0
4260  GOSUB 12000
4270  GOSUB 18000
4280  GOSUB 15000
4290  GOTO 4090
10000 REM   RANDOMIZATION - CHANGE 'RND (1)' TO 'RND (0)' FOR TR
      S-80 AND PET!
10010 R = INT ( RND (1) * BL) + 1
10020 RETURN
11000 REM  JUDGE ANSWER
11010 IF S$ = "?" THEN 16000
11020 IF S$ = "!" THEN 17000
11030 FOR I = 1 TO L
11040 IF A$(I) = S$ THEN 11070
11050 NEXT I
11060 RETURN
11070 HT = 1
11080 B$(I) = S$
11090 NEXT I
11100 RETURN
12000 REM  REWARD
12010 PRINT "GOOD GUESS, ";NA$;"!"
12020 RETURN
14000 REM  WRONG GUESS
14010 PRINT "THERE ARE NO ";S$;"'S IN"
14020 PRINT "THE WORD, ";NA$;"."
14030 RETURN
15000 REM  SCORE KEEPING
15010 IF WD$ = C$ THEN 15030
15020 RETURN
15030 PRINT "YOU FOUND THE WORD IN ";TR;" TRIES!"
15040 GOTO 20000
16000 REM  HINT
16010 PRINT
16020 PRINT HN$(R)
16030 HN$(R) = "NO MORE HINTS!"
16040 HT = 2
16050 RETURN
17000 REM  SEE IF STUDENT KNOWS WORD
17010 PRINT "WHAT DO YOU THINK THE WORD IS";
17020 INPUT S$
17030 IF S$ = C$ THEN 15030
17040 PRINT "SORRY--KEEP TRYING"
17050 HT = 2
17060 GOTO 14000
18000 REM  PRINT ROUTINE
18010 WD$ = ""
18020 FOR I = 1 TO L
18030 WD$ = WD$ + B$(I)
18040 NEXT I
18050 GS$ = GS$ + S$
18060 PRINT
18070 PRINT WD$
18080 PRINT
18090 PRINT "LETTERS GUESSED: ";GS$
```

```
18100  RETURN
20000  REM  CLOSING
20010  PRINT "WOULD YOU LIKE ANOTHER WORD (YES OR NO)";
20020  INPUT S$
20030  IF S$ = "NO" THEN 20170
20040 TR = 0
20050 HT = 0
20060 WD$ = ""
20070 GS$ = ""
20080 S$ = ""
20090  REM  DELETE CORRECT WORD FROM LIST
20100 FL$(R) = FL$(BL)
20110 HN$(R) = HN$(BL)
20120 BL = BL - 1
20130  IF BL = 0 THEN  GOTO 20150
20140  GOTO 4010
20150  PRINT "SORRY! YOU HAVE USED ALL THE"
20160  PRINT "WORDS I KNOW, ";NA$;"!"
20170  END
21000  REM  DATA
21010  DATA  EVENING,DARK,COMPUTER,DIGITAL
21020  DATA  RHYTHM,MUSIC,QUIZ,TEST,LYNX,CAT,KNOCK,TAP,UGLY,MONSTE
       R
21030  DATA  VULTURE,BIRD,YAWN,MOUTH,ERUPT,VOLCANO,FUDGE,CANDY,HUSK
       ,CORN
21040  DATA  PLUTO,PLANET,GYPSY,TRAVELER,HOLY,CHURCH,HUGE,BIG,INJU
       RY,HURT
21050  DATA  MUMPS,ILLNESS,ZERO,NONE,ZINC,METAL,OXYGEN,BREATHE,DUT
       Y,JOB
```

* -->TABLE OF VARIABLES<--

A$(*) - WORD BROKEN INTO LETTERS
1030 4050 11040

B$(*) - ARRAY HOLDING *'S OR GUESSED LETTERS
1030 4060 11080 18030

BL - BOTTOM OF LIST
1020 10010 20100 20110 20120 20120 20130

C$ - CORRECT WORD
4020 4030 4050 15010 17030

FL$(*) - WORD LIST
1030 1050 4020 20100 20100

GS$ - LETTERS GUESSED
18050 18050 18090 20070

HN$(*) - HINT LIST
1030 1050 16020 16030 20110 20110

HT - HIT
4130 4190 4210 4250 11070 16040 17050 20050

I - COUNTER
1040 1050 1050 1060 2010 2030 2050 2070 2080 2090 4040
4050 4050 4060 4070 11030 11040 11050 11080 11090 18020
18030 18040

L - LENGTH OF WORD
4030 4040 11030 18020

NA$ - NAME
2110 2120 12010 14020 20160

R - RANDOM NUMBER
4020 10010 16020 16030 20100 20110

S$ - STUDENT ANSWER
4140 4150 11010 11020 11040 11080 14010 17020 17030 18050
20020 20030 20080

TL - NUMBER OF WORDS IN LIST
1010 1020 1030 1030 1040

TR - NUMBER OF TRIES
4200 4200 15030 20040

WD$ - ASSEMBLED WORD WITH MISSING LETTERS
15010 18010 18030 18030 18070 20060

END OF VAR. LIST

SAMPLE RUN

```
]RUN
    GUESS THE WORD
WHAT IS YOUR NAME?JOYCE
I AM HAPPY TO MEET YOU, JOYCE.
I AM GOING TO THINK OF A WORD,
AND IT WILL BE YOUR JOB TO
GUESS IT.  YOU DO THIS BY
GUESSING ONE LETTER AT A TIME.
AT ANY TIME YOU CAN TYPE IN
AN '!' AND THEN GUESS THE WHOLE
WORD.  IF YOU NEED A HINT, TYPE
IN A '?' AND I WILL TRY TO HELP YOU.
HERE WE GO!
****
LETTERS GUESSED:
GUESS A LETTER (OR '?' OR '!').
?E
THERE ARE NO E'S IN
THE WORD, JOYCE.
****
LETTERS GUESSED: E
GUESS A LETTER (OR '?' OR '!').
?I
GOOD GUESS, JOYCE!
```

22

```
*I**
LETTERS GUESSED: EI
GUESS A LETTER (OR '?' OR '!').
?O
THERE ARE NO O'S IN
THE WORD, JOYCE.
*I**
LETTERS GUESSED: EIO
GUESS A LETTER (OR '?' OR '!').
?U
THERE ARE NO U'S IN
THE WORD, JOYCE.
*I**
LETTERS GUESSED: EIOU
GUESS A LETTER (OR '?' OR '!').
?A
THERE ARE NO A'S IN
THE WORD, JOYCE.
*I**
LETTERS GUESSED: EIOUA
GUESS A LETTER (OR '?' OR '!').
??
METAL
GUESS A LETTER (OR '?' OR '!').
?Z
GOOD GUESS, JOYCE!
ZI**
LETTERS GUESSED: EIOUAZ
GUESS A LETTER (OR '?' OR '!').
?!
WHAT DO YOU THINK THE WORD IS?ZINC
YOU FOUND THE WORD IN 6 TRIES!
WOULD YOU LIKE ANOTHER WORD (YES OR NO)?NO
]
```

MATH TUTOR

PROGRAM DESCRIPTION

In this program the computer presents problems on simple addition, subtraction, multiplication, and division. You select which math category you want and the number of problems in that category you want to work. The computer also asks you the largest set of numbers (digits) you want to work with in the category selected, and in the case of division, the computer allows you to choose whether you want to have remainders in your division problems or no remainders. Correct answers and wrong answers are acknowledged, and after you have finished the number of problems that you originally selected to decipher, the computer tells you how many problems you did correctly.

PROGRAM NOTES

1. After a pre-set number of wrong answers to a problem, give the correct answer, and then go on to another problem.

2. See if you can come up with a "mixed" selection where all types of problems will appear at random.

3. If you have a printer, consider saving any "missed" problems during the program. Print these problems out as a "homework" assignment at the end of the program. Three arrays could be set up to cover the two numbers and the arithmetic process (+, −, *, or /).

```
100  REM  MATH TUTOR BY GARY ORWIG
2000 REM  INTRODUCTION
2010 PRINT
2020 PRINT "*******************************************"
2030 PRINT
2040 PRINT "             MATH TUTOR"
2050 PRINT
2060 PRINT "*******************************************"
2070 FOR DE = 1 TO 1000
2080 NEXT DE
2090 PRINT "WHAT IS YOUR NAME";
2100 INPUT NA$
2110 PRINT
2120 PRINT
2130 PRINT "I AM HAPPY TO MEET YOU, ";NA$;"."
2140 PRINT "WE ARE GOING TO PRACTICE SOME"
2150 PRINT "MATH PROBLEMS."
2160 REM  OPERATING PARAMETERS
2170 PRINT
2180 PRINT
2190 PRINT "WOULD YOU LIKE TO PRACTICE:"
2200 PRINT "1. ADDITION"
2210 PRINT "2. SUBTRACTION"
2220 PRINT "3. MULTIPLICATION"
2230 PRINT "4. DIVISION"
2240 PRINT
2250 PRINT "(TYPE IN THE NUMBER YOU WANT)"
2260 INPUT SA$
2270 IF SA$ = "1" THEN 2350
2280 IF SA$ = "2" THEN 2350
2290 IF SA$ = "3" THEN 2350
2300 IF SA$ = "4" THEN 2350
2310 PRINT
2320 PRINT "PLEASE PAY ATTENTION, "NA$
2330 PRINT "TYPE IN ONLY A 1,2,3, OR 4!"
2340 GOTO 2200
2350 PRINT
2360 PRINT "HOW MANY PROBLEMS DO YOU"
2370 PRINT "WANT, ";NA$;
2380 INPUT NU
2390 PRINT
2400 PRINT "VERY GOOD, ";NU;" IT WILL BE!"
2410 PRINT
2420 PRINT "WHAT IS THE LARGEST NUMBER"
2430 PRINT "YOU WANT TO WORK WITH ";NA$;
2440 INPUT MX
2450 PRINT
2460 PRINT "GREAT!  I WILL TRY NOT TO GIVE YOU"
2470 PRINT "ANY NUMBERS OVER ";MX;"."
2480 IF SA$ = "4" THEN 2620
2490 PRINT
2500 PRINT "I AM NOW READY TO START!"
2510 PRINT
2520 FOR DE = 1 TO 500
```

```
2530  NEXT DE
2540  PRINT "HERE WE GO!!"
2550  FOR DE = 1 TO 500
2560  NEXT DE
2570  PRINT
2580  PRINT
2590  PRINT
2600  PRINT
2610  GOTO 4000
2620  PRINT
2630  PRINT "DO YOU WANT DIVISION PROBLEMS"
2640  PRINT "WITH REMAINDERS (YES OR NO)";
2650  INPUT RE$
2660  IF RE$ = "YES" THEN 2720
2670  IF RE$ = "NO" THEN 2720
2680  PRINT
2690  PRINT "JUST TYPE A 'YES' OR 'NO' PLEASE"
2700  PRINT
2710  GOTO 2620
2720  GOTO 2490
4000  REM  MAIN PROGRAM
4010  IF SA$ = "1" THEN 4730
4020  IF SA$ = "2" THEN 4570
4030  IF SA$ = "3" THEN 4470
4040  IF RE$ = "YES" THEN 4220
4050  REM  DIVISION WITHOUT REMAINDER
4060  GOSUB 10000
4070 HT = 1
4080  IF A < B THEN 4110
4090 C = A / B
4100  GOTO 4150
4110 D = B
4120 B = A
4130 A = D
4140  GOTO 4090
4150  IF C - INT (C) > 0 THEN 4060
4160  PRINT A;" DIVIDED BY ";B;" EQUALS";
4170  INPUT SA
4180  GOSUB 11000
4190  GOSUB 12000
4200  GOSUB 15000
4210  GOTO 4050
4220  REM  DIVISION WITH REMAINDER
4230  GOSUB 10000
4240 HT = 1
4250  IF A < B THEN 4290
4260 C = INT (A / B)
4270 RE = A - (C * B)
4280  GOTO 4330
4290 D = B
4300 B = A
4310 A = D
4320  GOTO 4260
4330  PRINT
4340  PRINT A;" DIVIDED BY ";B;" EQUALS?"
4350  PRINT "WHAT IS THE WHOLE NUMBER";
```

26

```
4360  INPUT SA
4370  GOSUB 11000
4380  GOSUB 12000
4390  PRINT "AND WHAT IS THE REMAINDER?"
4400  PRINT "TYPE IN 0 IF THERE IS NONE."
4410  INPUT SA
4420 C = RE
4430  GOSUB 11000
4440  GOSUB 12000
4450  GOSUB 15000
4460  GOTO 4220
4470  REM  MULTIPLICATION
4480  GOSUB 10000
4490 HT = 1
4500 C = A * B
4510  PRINT A;" TIMES ";B;" EQUALS";
4520  INPUT SA
4530  GOSUB 11000
4540  GOSUB 12000
4550  GOSUB 15000
4560  GOTO 4470
4570  REM  SUBTRACTION
4580  GOSUB 10000
4590 HT = 1
4600  IF A < B THEN 4630
4610 C = A - B
4620  GOTO 4670
4630 D = B
4640 B = A
4650 A = D
4660  GOTO 4610
4670  PRINT A;" MINUS ";B;" EQUALS";
4680  INPUT SA
4690  GOSUB 11000
4700  GOSUB 12000
4710  GOSUB 15000
4720  GOTO 4570
4730  REM  ADDITION
4740  GOSUB 10000
4750 HT = 1
4760 C = A + B
4770  PRINT A;" PLUS ";B;" EQUALS";
4780  INPUT SA
4790  GOSUB 11000
4800  GOSUB 12000
4810  GOSUB 15000
4820  GOTO 4730
10000  REM  RANDOMIZING - USE 'RND (0)' IN PLACE OF 'RND (1)' FOR
    TRS-80 AND PET!
10010 A = INT (MX * RND (1)) + 1
10020 B = INT (MX * RND (1)) + 1
10030  RETURN
11000  REM  JUDGE ANSWER
11010  IF SA = C THEN 11070
11020  GOSUB 14000
11030  PRINT
```

```
11040  PRINT "TRY AGAIN!"
11050  INPUT SA
11060  GOTO 11010
11070  RETURN
12000  REM  REWARDS - USE 'RND(0)' IN PLACE OF 'RND(1)' FOR TRS-80
    AND PET!
12010  PRINT
12020 I =  INT (5 * RND (1)) + 1
12030  ON I GOTO 12050,12070,12090,12110,12130
12040  REM  REWARDS
12050  PRINT "GREAT!"
12060  RETURN
12070  PRINT "SUPER!"
12080  RETURN
12090  PRINT "FANTASTIC!"
12100  RETURN
12110  PRINT "YOU'RE REALLY GOING NOW, ";NA$
12120  RETURN
12130  PRINT "THAT'S GREAT, ";NA$
12140  RETURN
14000  REM  WRONG - USE 'RND(0)' IN PLACE OF 'RND(1)' FOR TRS-80
    AND PET!
14010  PRINT
14020  IF HT = 0 THEN 14050
14030 WR = WR + 1
14040 HT = 0
14050 I =  INT (5 * RND (1)) + 1
14060  ON I GOTO 14080,14100,14120,14140,14160
14070  REM  WRONGS
14080  PRINT "OOPS!"
14090  RETURN
14100  PRINT "LOOK CLOSER, ";NA$
14110  RETURN
14120  PRINT "NO...."
14130  RETURN
14140  PRINT "ARE YOU PAYING ATTENTION, ";NA$
14150  RETURN
14160  PRINT "SORRY!"
14170  RETURN
15000  REM  SCORE KEEPING
15010 TL = TL + 1
15020  IF TL = NU THEN 20000
15030  RETURN
20000  REM  CLOSING
20010  PRINT
20020  PRINT "THAT'S ALL!"
20030  PRINT
20040  PRINT "I HOPE YOU HAD FUN, ";NA$
20050  PRINT
20060  PRINT
20070  PRINT
20080  PRINT "YOU HAD ";NU - WR;" OUT OF "
20090  PRINT NU;" PROBLEMS CORRECT!"
20100  END
```

```
        *  -->TABLE OF VARIABLES<--

A - ONE OF THE NUMBERS
4080 4090 4120 4130 4160 4250 4260 4270 4300 4310 4340
4500 4510 4600 4610 4640 4650 4670 4760 4770 10010

B - THE OTHER NUMBER
4080 4090 4110 4120 4160 4250 4260 4270 4290 4300 4340
4500 4510 4600 4610 4630 4640 4670 4760 4770 10020

C - CORRECT ANSWER
4090 4150 4150 4260 4270 4420 4500 4610 4760 11010

D - TRANSFER VARIABLE
4110 4130 4290 4310 4630 4650

DE - DELAY
2070 2080 2520 2530 2550 2560

HT - HIT (CORRECT ANSWER)
4070 4240 4490 4590 4750 14020 14040

I - COUNTER
12020 12030 14050 14060

MX - MAXIMUM SIZE OF A AND B
2440 2470 10010 10020

NA$ - NAME
2100 2130 2320 2370 2430 12110 12130 14100 14140 20040

NU - NUMBER OF PROBLEMS
2380 2400 15020 20080 20090

RE - REMAINDER
4270 4420

RE$ - REMAINDER FLAG FOR DIVISION
2650 2660 2670 4040

SA - STUDENT ANSWER
4170 4360 4410 4520 4680 4780 11010 11050

SA$ - STUDENT ANSWER
2260 2270 2280 2290 2300 2480 4010 4020 4030

TL - NUMBER OF PROBLEMS PRESENTED
15010 15010 15020

WR - NUMBER WRONG
14030 14030 20080

END OF VAR. LIST
```

SAMPLE RUN

```
]RUN
*******************************************
          MATH TUTOR
*******************************************
WHAT IS YOUR NAME?CHRIS
I AM HAPPY TO MEET YOU, CHRIS.
WE ARE GOING TO PRACTICE SOME
MATH PROBLEMS.
WOULD YOU LIKE TO PRACTICE:
1. ADDITION
2. SUBTRACTION
3. MULTIPLICATION
4. DIVISION
(TYPE IN THE NUMBER YOU WANT)
?3
HOW MANY PROBLEMS DO YOU
WANT, CHRIS?3
VERY GOOD, 3 IT WILL BE!
WHAT IS THE LARGEST NUMBER
YOU WANT TO WORK WITH CHRIS?10
GREAT!  I WILL TRY NOT TO GIVE YOU
ANY NUMBERS OVER 10.
I AM NOW READY TO START!
HERE WE GO!!
3 TIMES 3 EQUALS?9
YOU'RE REALLY GOING NOW, CHRIS
6 TIMES 8 EQUALS?47
SORRY!
TRY AGAIN!
?48
SUPER!
4 TIMES 6 EQUALS?24
GREAT!
THAT'S ALL!
I HOPE YOU HAD FUN, CHRIS
YOU HAD 2 OUT OF
3 PROBLEMS CORRECT!
]
```

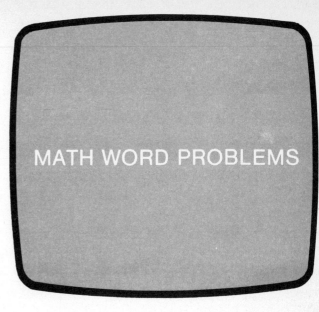

MATH WORD PROBLEMS

PROGRAM DESCRIPTION

Word problems in math are presented in this program. The computer displays a word problem and if you don't want to work that particular problem you have the option of receiving a new and different problem by entering in a "0" in to the computer. When giving the answer to a problem use only numbers; not units such as $, liters, or other words.

PROGRAM NOTES

1. Consider providing the answer after a certain number of wrong guesses.

2. You can enter your own problems in place of the ones that are there. Start each problem with the correct answer, and use several lines to enter the problem. End each problem with a RETURN command. Be sure to maintain the proper sequence of line numbers to start each problem!

PROGRAM LISTING

```
100  REM  MATH WORD PROBLEMS BY GARY ORWIG
1000 REM  INITIALIZATION - MAKE 'TL' EQUAL TO THE NUMBER OF PROBL
     EMS IN YOUR DATA STATEMENTS
1010 TL = 10
1020 DIM C(TL)
1030 FOR I = 1 TO TL
1040 C(I) = 0
1050 NEXT I
```

```
2000  REM  INTRODUCTION
2010 D = 25
2020 L = 24
2030  GOSUB 18000
2040  FOR J = 1 TO 30
2050  PRINT "MATH"
2060  GOSUB 19000
2070  NEXT J
2080  FOR J = 1 TO 30
2090  PRINT "    WORD"
2100  GOSUB 19000
2110  NEXT J
2120  FOR J = 1 TO 30
2130  PRINT "        PROBLEMS"
2140  GOSUB 19000
2150  NEXT J
2160  D = 1000
2170  GOSUB 19000
2180 L = 24
2190  GOSUB 18000
2200  PRINT "HI!  I'M GLAD TO SEE YOU."
2210  PRINT "WHAT IS YOUR NAME?"
2220 L = 11
2230  GOSUB 18000
2240  INPUT NA$
2250 L = 12
2260  GOSUB 18000
2270  PRINT "I'M HAPPY TO MEET YOU, ";NA$;"."
2280  PRINT "I AM GOING TO GIVE YOU SOME WORD"
2290  PRINT "PROBLEMS.  IF YOU DON'T WANT TO TRY"
2300  PRINT "ANY PARTICULAR PROBLEM, TYPE IN A '0'"
2310  PRINT "FOR THE ANSWER AND I WILL GIVE YOU "
2320  PRINT "ANOTHER.  "
2330  PRINT
2340  PRINT "WHEN YOU TYPE IN AN ANSWER, TYPE IN"
2350  PRINT "ONLY THE NUMBER (DON'T TYPE IN"
2360  PRINT "'$', LITERS, OR OTHER WORDS)."
2370  PRINT
2380  PRINT "PUSH THE 'RETURN' OR 'ENTER' KEY"
2390  PRINT "WHEN YOU ARE READY TO START.": REM  FOR PET PRESS ANY
     LETTER BEFORE PRESSING RETURN
2400 L = 6
2410  GOSUB 18000
2420  INPUT SA$
4000  REM  MAIN PROGRAM
4010 WR = 0
4020  FOR I = 1 TO TL
4030  IF C(I) = 0 THEN  GOTO 4060
4040  NEXT I
4050  GOTO 20120
4060  GOSUB 10000
4070  IF C(R) = 1 THEN 4060
4080  C(R) = 1
4090 L = 24
4100  GOSUB 18000
```

```
4110  ON R GOSUB 21000,21050,21100,21150,21200,21250,21300,21350,2
        1400,21450
4120 L = 10
4130  GOSUB 18000
4140  INPUT SA
4150  GOSUB 11000
4160  ON HT GOTO 4200,4170,4000
4170  GOSUB 12000
4180  GOSUB 15000
4190  GOTO 4000
4200  GOSUB 14000
4210  GOSUB 15000
4220  GOTO 4090
10000  REM  RANDOMIZATION - CHANGE 'RND (1)' TO 'RND (0)' FOR TRS
        -80 AND PET!
10010 R = INT ( RND (1) * TL) + 1
10020  RETURN
11000  REM  JUDGE ANSWER
11010  IF SA = 0 THEN 11070
11020  IF SA = C THEN 11050
11030 HT = 1
11040  RETURN
11050 HT = 2
11060  RETURN
11070 HT = 3
11080  RETURN
12000  REM  REWARD
12010 L = 24
12020  GOSUB 18000
12030  PRINT "         VERY GOOD!"
12040 L = 12
12050  GOSUB 18000
12060 D = 500
12070  GOSUB 19000
12080  RETURN
14000  REM  WRONG
14010 L = 24
14020  GOSUB 18000
14030  PRINT "         SORRY!"
14040 L = 12
14050  GOSUB 18000
14060 D = 500
14070  GOSUB 19000
14080  RETURN
15000  REM  SCORE KEEPING
15010  IF HT = 1 THEN 15030
15020  GOTO 20000
15030 WR = WR + 1
15040  RETURN
18000  REM  SCROLLING
18010  FOR I = 1 TO L
18020  PRINT
18030  NEXT I
18040  RETURN
19000  REM  DELAY
19010  FOR I = 1 TO D
```

```
19020  NEXT I
19030  RETURN
20000  REM  CLOSING
20010  IF WR = 0 THEN 20050
20020  PRINT "IT TOOK ";WR + 1;" TRIES TO GET THIS"
20030  PRINT "PROBLEM RIGHT, ";NA$;"."
20040  GOTO 20060
20050  PRINT "YOU GOT IT ON THE FIRST TRY, ";NA$;"!"
20060  PRINT "DO YOU WANT ANOTHER PROBLEM?"
20070  INPUT SA$
20080  IF SA$ = "NO" THEN 20100
20090  GOTO 4000
20100  PRINT "BYE FOR NOW"
20110  END
20120  PRINT "SORRY, I'M OUT OF PROBLEMS."
20130  END
21000  REM  PROBLEM SUBROUTINES
21010  C = 244.2
21020  PRINT "MR. JONES AVERAGES 22.2 MILES PER GAL."
21030  PRINT "OF GAS. HOW FAR CAN HE GO ON 11 GALLONS?"
21040  RETURN
21050  C = 9
21060  PRINT "JANE EARNS $1.25 AN HOUR MOWING THE"
21070  PRINT "LAWN. HOW MANY HOURS DID SHE WORK"
21080  PRINT "TO EARN $11.25?"
21090  RETURN
21100  C = 5
21110  PRINT "HOW MANY WHOLE BOXES OF ICE CREAM BARS"
21120  PRINT "CAN BE BOUGHT FOR $3.75, IF "
21130  PRINT "EACH BOX COSTS $.69
21140  RETURN
21150  C = 8
21160  PRINT "JANICE HAS SAVED 3 QUARTERS EACH WEEK"
21170  PRINT "FOR 3 WEEKS. FOR HOW MANY MORE WEEKS"
21180  PRINT "MUST SHE SAVE TO BUY AN $8.25 ALBUM?"
21190  RETURN
21200  C = 30
21210  PRINT "DICK SPELLED 70% OF 100 WORDS"
21220  PRINT "CORRECTLY. HOW MANY WORDS DID HE"
21230  PRINT "MISS?"
21240  RETURN
21250  C = 10.50
21260  PRINT "MARTHA BOUGHT SOME JEANS WHICH WERE 25%"
21270  PRINT "OFF THE MARKED PRICE OF $14.00."
21280  PRINT "HOW MUCH DID SHE PAY?"
21290  RETURN
21300  C = 10
21310  PRINT "A PUNCH RECIPE CALLS FOR 5 PARTS GRAPE"
21320  PRINT "JUICE TO 2 PARTS GINGER ALE. HOW MUCH"
21330  PRINT "ALE GOES WITH 25 LITERS OF GRAPE JUICE?"
21340  RETURN
21350  C = 24
21360  PRINT "25% OF A CLASS OF 32 STUDENTS WERE"
21370  PRINT "ABSENT. HOW MANY STUDENTS WERE "
21380  PRINT "IN CLASS?"
21390  RETURN
```

```
21400 C = 132
21410  PRINT "A MARCHING BAND HAS 22 ROWS WITH"
21420  PRINT "6 PEOPLE IN EACH ROW.  HOW"
21430  PRINT "MANY PEOPLE DOES THIS MAKE?"
21440  RETURN
21450 C = 72
21460  PRINT "I FERRIS WHEEL HAS 24 CARS.  EACH"
21470  PRINT "CAN HOLD 3 PEOPLE.  WHAT IS THE"
21480  PRINT "MAXIMUM CAPACITY OF THE FERRIS WHEEL?"
21490  RETURN
```

* -->TABLE OF VARIABLES<--

C - CORRECT ANSWER
11020 21010 21050 21100 21150 21200 21250 21300 21350 21400
21450

C(*) - PROBLEMS ANSWERED CORRECTLY
1020 1040 4030 4070 4080

D - DELAY
2010 2160 12060 14060 19010

HT - HIT
4160 11030 11050 11070 15010

I - COUNTER
1030 1040 1050 4020 4030 4040 18010 18030 19010 19020

J - COUNTER
2040 2070 2080 2110 2120 2150

L - LINES FOR SCROLLING
2020 2180 2220 2250 2400 4090 4120 12010 12040 14010 14040
18010

NA$ - NAME
2240 2270 20030 20050

R - RANDOM NUMBER
4070 4080 4110 10010

SA - STUDENT ANSWER
4140 11010 11020

SA$ - STUDENT ANSWER
2420 20070 20080

TL - NUMBER OF PROBLEMS
1010 1020 1030 4020 10010

WR - NUMBER OF TRIES
4010 15030 15030 20010 20020

END OF VAR. LIST

SAMPLE RUN

```
]RUN
MATH WORD PROBLEMS
HI!  I'M GLAD TO SEE YOU.
WHAT IS YOUR NAME?
?EARL
I'M HAPPY TO MEET YOU, EARL.
I AM GOING TO GIVE YOU SOME WORD
PROBLEMS.  IF YOU DON'T WANT TO TRY
ANY PARTICULAR PROBLEM, TYPE IN A '0'
FOR THE ANSWER AND I WILL GIVE YOU
ANOTHER.
WHEN YOU TYPE IN AN ANSWER, TYPE IN
ONLY THE NUMBER (DON'T TYPE IN
'$', LITERS, OR OTHER WORDS).
PUSH THE 'RETURN' OR 'ENTER' KEY
WHEN YOU ARE READY TO START.
?
JANICE HAS SAVED 3 QUARTERS EACH WEEK
FOR 3 WEEKS.  FOR HOW MANY MORE WEEKS
MUST SHE SAVE TO BUY AN $8.25 ALBUM?
?4
        SORRY!
JANICE HAS SAVED 3 QUARTERS EACH WEEK
FOR 3 WEEKS.  FOR HOW MANY MORE WEEKS
MUST SHE SAVE TO BUY AN $8.25 ALBUM?
?8
        VERY GOOD!
IT TOOK 2 TRIES TO GET THIS
PROBLEM RIGHT, EARL.
DO YOU WANT ANOTHER PROBLEM?
?NO
BYE FOR NOW
]
```

MEMORY TEST - LETTERS

PROGRAM DESCRIPTION

This program enables you to test the power of your memory. The computer rapidly scrolls letters randomly at different time intervals and you try to remember the letters for the correct answer. You may choose which time interval (either short, medium, or long) you want the computer to display the letters depending on the skill level that you feel is most comfortable. The more you guess correctly, the more difficult the memory test becomes. The computer increases the letters in the series scrolled as you answer correctly each time.

PROGRAM NOTES

This program is very much like the Memory Test — Numbers program. Consider combining them, with an option for presenting numbers, letters, or a mixture!

PROGRAM LISTING

```
100  REM  MEMORY TEST-LETTERS BY GARY ORWIG
2000 REM  INTRODUCTION
2010 FOR I = 1 TO 40
2020 GOSUB 10000
2030 PRINT AB$
2040 NEXT I
2050 FOR I = 1 TO 2000
2060 NEXT I
2070 FOR I = 1 TO 12
2080 PRINT
```

```
2090  NEXT I
2100  PRINT "     MEMORY TEST - LETTERS"
2110  FOR I = 1 TO 12
2120  PRINT
2130  NEXT I
2140  PRINT "HI!  I AM A FRIENDLY COMPUTER!"
2150  PRINT "WHAT IS YOUR NAME";
2160  INPUT NA$
2170  PRINT
2180  PRINT
2190  PRINT "IT'S NICE TO MEET YOU, ";NA$;"."
2200  PRINT
2210  PRINT
2220  PRINT "THIS IS A GAME DESIGNED TO TEST"
2230  PRINT "YOUR MEMORY FOR LETTERS."
2240  PRINT
2250  PRINT "I WILL SHOW YOU SOME LETTERS"
2260  PRINT "AND YOU WILL"
2270  PRINT "TRY TO REMEMBER THEM LONG ENOUGH"
2280  PRINT "TO TYPE THEM BACK TO ME."
2290  PRINT
2300  PRINT
2310  PRINT "I CAN SHOW YOU THE LETTERS FOR:"
2320  PRINT
2330  PRINT "1. A SHORT TIME"
2340  PRINT "2. A MEDIUM TIME"
2350  PRINT "3. A LONG TIME"
2360  PRINT
2370  PRINT
2380  PRINT "WHICH DO YOU WANT (1, 2, OR 3)"
2390  PRINT "YOU CAN USE A DECIMAL (LIKE.5)"
2400  PRINT "OR A LARGER NUMBER IF YOU WANT."
2410  INPUT T
2420  T = T * 200
2430  FOR I = 1 TO 12
2440  PRINT
2450  NEXT I
2460  PRINT "OK!  HERE WE GO!"
2470  AB$ = ""
2480  FOR I = 1 TO 12
2490  PRINT
2500  NEXT I
2510  FOR I = 1 TO 2000
2520  NEXT I
4000  REM  MAIN PROGRAM
4010  GOSUB 10000
4020  FOR I = 1 TO 25
4030  PRINT
4040  NEXT I
4050  PRINT AB$
4060  FOR I = 1 TO T
4070  NEXT I
4080  FOR I = 1 TO 25
4090  PRINT
4100  NEXT I
4110  PRINT "WHAT WAS THE LETTER SET?"
```

```
4120  INPUT SA$
4130  GOSUB 11000
4140  IF HT = 0 THEN 4180
4150  GOSUB 12000
4160  GOSUB 15000
4170  GOTO 4010
4180  GOSUB 14000
4190  GOTO 20000
10000  REM    RANDOMIZATION - CHANGE 'RND (1)' TO 'RND (0)' FOR TR
   S-80 AND PET!
10010 A =  INT ( RND (1) * 26) + 65
10020 A$ =  CHR$ (A)
10030 AB$ = AB$ + A$
10040  RETURN
11000  REM  JUDGE ANSWER
11010  IF SA$ = AB$ GOTO 11040
11020 HT = 0
11030  RETURN
11040 HT = 1
11050  RETURN
12000  REM  REWARDS
12010 HT = 0
12020  PRINT "GREAT!"
12030  FOR I = 1 TO 1000
12040  NEXT I
12050  RETURN
14000  REM  WRONG
14010  FOR I = 1 TO 12
14020  PRINT
14030  NEXT I
14040  PRINT "SORRY!"
14050  FOR I = 1 TO 10
14060  PRINT
14070  NEXT I
14080  RETURN
15000  REM  SCORE KEEPING
15010 C = C + 1
15020  RETURN
20000  REM  CLOSING
20010  PRINT "YOUR ANSWER WAS:"
20020  PRINT SA$
20030  PRINT
20040  PRINT "THE CORRECT LETTER SET WAS:"
20050  PRINT AB$
20060  PRINT
20070  PRINT
20080  PRINT "YOU REMEMBERED A SET"
20090  PRINT C;" LETTERS LONG!"
20100  PRINT "DO YOU WANT TO TRY AGAIN?"
20110  PRINT "(YES OR NO)";
20120  INPUT SA$
20130  IF SA$ = "YES" THEN 20160
20140  PRINT "BYE FOR NOW!"
20150  END
20160 SA$ = ""
```

```
20170 AB$ = ""
20180 C = 0
20190  GOTO 2290
```

                    * -->TABLE OF VARIABLES<--

A - RANDOM NUMBER
10010 10020

A$ - RANDOM LETTER
10020 10030

AB$ - RANDOM LETTER STRING
2030 2470 4050 10030 10030 11010 20050 20170

C - LENGTH OF STRING
15010 15010 20090 20180

HT - HIT
4140 11020 11040 12010

I - COUNTER
2010 2040 2050 2060 2070 2090 2110 2130 2430 2450 2480
2500 2510 2520 4020 4040 4060 4070 4080 4100 12030 12040
14010 14030 14050 14070

NA$ - NAME
2160 2190

SA$ - STUDENT ANSWER
4120 11010 20020 20120 20130 20160

T - DELAY
2410 2420 2420 4060

END OF VAR. LIST

SAMPLE RUN

```
JRUN
MEMORY TEST-LETTERS
HI! I AM A FRIENDLY COMPUTER!
WHAT IS YOUR NAME?LINDA
IT'S NICE TO MEET YOU, LINDA.
THIS IS A GAME DESIGNED TO TEST
YOUR MEMORY FOR LETTERS.
I WILL SHOW YOU SOME LETTERS
AND YOU WILL
TRY TO REMEMBER THEM LONG ENOUGH
TO TYPE THEM BACK TO ME.
I CAN SHOW YOU THE LETTERS FOR:
1. A SHORT TIME
2. A MEDIUM TIME
3. A LONG TIME
WHICH DO YOU WANT (1, 2, OR 3)
YOU CAN USE A DECIMAL (LIKE.5)
OR A LARGER NUMBER IF YOU WANT.
```

```
?2
OK!  HERE WE GO!
S
WHAT WAS THE LETTER SET?
?S
GREAT!
SI
WHAT WAS THE LETTER SET?
?SI
GREAT!
SIY
WHAT WAS THE LETTER SET?
?SIY
GREAT!
SIYJ
WHAT WAS THE LETTER SET?
?SIYJ
GREAT!
SIYJN
WHAT WAS THE LETTER SET?
?SIYJN
GREAT!
SIYJNR
WHAT WAS THE LETTER SET?
?SIYJNR
GREAT!
SIYJNRP
WHAT WAS THE LETTER SET?
?SIYJRNP
SORRY!
YOUR ANSWER WAS:
SIYJRNP
THE CORRECT LETTER SET WAS:
SIYJNRP
YOU REMEMBERED A SET
6 LETTERS LONG!
DO YOU WANT TO TRY AGAIN?
(YES OR NO)?NO
BYE FOR NOW!
]
```

MEMORY TEST - NUMBERS

PROGRAM DESCRIPTION

This program is very similar to Memory Test — Letters, except that it is easier to perform. The computer rapidly scrolls numbers randomly at different time intervals and you try to remember the numbers for the correct answer. You may choose which time interval (either short, medium, or long) you want the computer to display the numbers depending on the skill level that you feel is most comfortable. Again, as in Memory Test — Letters, the more you guess correctly, the more difficult the memory test becomes. The computer increases the digits in the number scrolled as you answer correctly each time.

PROGRAM NOTES

1. The scrolling process can be built into a subroutine of its own. See line 18000 of some of the other programs.

2. If your computer allows it, consider "flashing" the numbers on the screen through a series of clear screen, print, and clear screen commands.

3. Depending on your computer, you may want to adjust line 2410 to get suitable delay times.

PROGRAM LISTING

```
100 REM MEMORY TEST-NUMBERS BY GARY ORWIG
2000 REM INTRODUCTION
2010 FOR I = 1 TO 40
```

```
2020 GOSUB 10000
2030 PRINT AB$
2040 NEXT I
2050 FOR I = 1 TO 2000
2060 NEXT I
2070 FOR I = 1 TO 12
2080 PRINT
2090 NEXT I
2100 PRINT "    MEMORY TEST - NUMBERS"
2110 FOR I = 1 TO 12
2120 PRINT
2130 NEXT I
2140 PRINT "HI! I AM A FRIENDLY COMPUTER!"
2150 PRINT "WHAT IS YOUR NAME";
2160 INPUT NA$
2170 PRINT
2180 PRINT
2190 PRINT "IT'S NICE TO MEET YOU, ";NA$;"."
2200 PRINT
2210 PRINT
2220 PRINT "THIS IS A GAME DESIGNED TO TEST"
2230 PRINT "YOUR MEMORY FOR NUMBERS."
2240 PRINT
2250 PRINT "I WILL SHOW YOU A NUMBER, AND YOU WILL"
2260 PRINT "TRY TO REMEMBER IT LONG ENOUGH"
2270 PRINT "TO TYPE IT BACK TO ME."
2280 PRINT
2290 PRINT
2300 PRINT "I CAN SHOW YOU THE NUMBER FOR:"
2310 PRINT
2320 PRINT "1. A SHORT TIME"
2330 PRINT "2. A MEDIUM TIME"
2340 PRINT "3. A LONG TIME"
2350 PRINT
2360 PRINT
2370 PRINT "WHICH DO YOU WANT (1, 2, OR 3)"
2380 PRINT "YOU CAN USE A DECIMAL (LIKE.5)"
2390 PRINT "OR A LARGER NUMBER IF YOU WANT."
2400 INPUT DE
2410 DE = DE * 500
2420 FOR I = 1 TO 12
2430 PRINT
2440 NEXT I
2450 PRINT "OK! HERE WE GO!"
2460 AB$ = ""
2470 FOR I = 1 TO 12
2480 PRINT
2490 NEXT I
2500 FOR I = 1 TO 2000
2510 NEXT I
4000 REM  MAIN PROGRAM
4010 GOSUB 10000
4020 FOR I = 1 TO 25
4030 PRINT
4040 NEXT I
4050 PRINT AB$
```

```
4060  FOR I = 1 TO DE
4070  NEXT I
4080  FOR I = 1 TO 25
4090  PRINT
4100  NEXT I
4110  PRINT "WHAT WAS THE NUMBER?"
4120  INPUT SA$
4130  GOSUB 11000
4140  IF HT = 0 THEN 4180
4150  GOSUB 12000
4160  GOSUB 15000
4170  GOTO 4010
4180  GOSUB 14000
4190  GOTO 20000
10000  REM   RANDOMIZATION - CHANGE 'RND (1)' TO 'RND (0)' FOR TRS
       -80 AND PET!
10010  A$ = STR$ ( INT ( RND (1) * 10))
10020  AB$ = AB$ + A$
10030  RETURN
11000  REM  JUDGE ANSWER
11010  IF SA$ = AB$ GOTO 11040
11020  HT = 0
11030  RETURN
11040  HT = 1
11050  RETURN
12000  REM  REWARDS
12010  HT = 0
12020  PRINT "GREAT!"
12030  FOR I = 1 TO 1000
12040  NEXT I
12050  RETURN
14000  REM  WRONG
14010  FOR I = 1 TO 12
14020  PRINT
14030  NEXT I
14040  PRINT "SORRY!"
14050  FOR I = 1 TO 10
14060  PRINT
14070  NEXT I
14080  RETURN
15000  REM  SCORE KEEPING
15010  C = C + 1
15020  RETURN
20000  REM  CLOSING
20010  PRINT "YOUR ANSWER WAS:"
20020  PRINT SA$
20030  PRINT
20040  PRINT "THE CORRECT NUMBER WAS:"
20050  PRINT AB$
20060  PRINT
20070  PRINT
20080  PRINT "YOU REMEMBERED A NUMBER"
20090  PRINT C;" DIGITS LONG!"
20100  PRINT "DO YOU WANT TO TRY AGAIN?"
20110  PRINT "(YES OR NO)";
20120  INPUT SA$
```

```
20130  IF SA$ = "YES" THEN 20160
20140  PRINT "BYE FOR NOW!"
20150  END
20160 SA$ = ""
20170 AB$ = ""
20180 C = 0
20190  GOTO 2280
```

                    * -->TABLE OF VARIABLES<--

A$ - SINGLE DIGIT
10010 10020

AB$ - SET OF DIGITS
2030 2460 4050 10020 10020 11010 20050 20170

C - CORRECT RESPONSES
15010 15010 20090 20180

DE - DELAY
2400 2410 2410 4060

HT - HIT
4140 11020 11040 12010

I - COUNTER
2010 2040 2050 2060 2070 2090 2110 2130 2420 2440 2470
2490 2500 2510 4020 4040 4060 4070 4080 4100 12030 12040
14010 14030 14050 14070

NA$ - NAME
2160 2190

SA$ - STUDENT ANSWER
4120 11010 20020 20120 20130 20160

END OF VAR. LIST

SAMPLE RUN

```
]RUN
     MEMORY TEST - NUMBERS
HI!  I AM A FRIENDLY COMPUTER!
WHAT IS YOUR NAME?SAM
IT'S NICE TO MEET YOU, SAM.
THIS IS A GAME DESIGNED TO TEST
YOUR MEMORY FOR NUMBERS.
I WILL SHOW YOU A NUMBER, AND YOU WILL
TRY TO REMEMBER IT LONG ENOUGH
TO TYPE IT BACK TO ME.
I CAN SHOW YOU THE NUMBER FOR:
1. A SHORT TIME
2. A MEDIUM TIME
3. A LONG TIME
WHICH DO YOU WANT (1, 2, OR 3)
YOU CAN USE A DECIMAL (LIKE.5)
OR A LARGER NUMBER IF YOU WANT.
```

```
?2
OK!  HERE WE GO!
5
WHAT WAS THE NUMBER?
?5
GREAT!
52
WHAT WAS THE NUMBER?
?52
GREAT!
525
WHAT WAS THE NUMBER?
?525
GREAT!
5258
WHAT WAS THE NUMBER?
?5258
GREAT!
52586
WHAT WAS THE NUMBER?
?52586
GREAT!
525864
WHAT WAS THE NUMBER?
?525864
GREAT!
5258645
WHAT WAS THE NUMBER?
?5258645
GREAT!
52586457
WHAT WAS THE NUMBER?
?52586457
GREAT!
525864575
WHAT WAS THE NUMBER?
?525865475
SORRY!
YOUR ANSWER WAS:
525865475
THE CORRECT NUMBER WAS:
525864575
YOU REMEMBERED A NUMBER
8 DIGITS LONG!
DO YOU WANT TO TRY AGAIN?
(YES OR NO)?NO
BYE FOR NOW!
]
```

SCRAMBLED WORDS

PROGRAM DESCRIPTION

In this program the computer selects words from an instructor-made data file and scrambles the letters in the words. The computer displays a scrambled word on the screen and asks you to identify it. By entering in a "?", the computer provides you hints about the word. This program is an excellent drill for both spelling and reading.

PROGRAM NOTES

1. Consider setting a letter in place each time a cue (like "*") is typed in. It would probably be best to start from the end of the word, and to work toward the beginning. This could be accomplished by randomizing a shorter length of the word each time the "*" is typed in.

2. Be careful of using words whose letters make up other words (snake, sneak). While some of these are likely to get into your list, too many can be frustrating.

PROGRAM LISTING

```
100  REM  SCRAMBLED WORDS BY GARY ORWIG
1000 REM  INITIALIZATION - SET 'TL' EQUAL TO TOTAL NUMBER OF WORD
     S IN YOUR DATA SET,
1010 TL = 20
1020 BL = TL
1030 DIM FL$(TL),HN$(TL),B$(20)
1040 FOR I = 1 TO TL
1050 READ FL$(I),HN$(I)
```

```
1060  NEXT I
2000  REM  INTRODUCTION
2010  FOR I = 1 TO 200
2020  PRINT "WORD SCRAMBLE ";
2030  NEXT I
2040  FOR I = 1 TO 3000
2050  NEXT I
2060  FOR I = 1 TO 24
2070  PRINT
2080  NEXT I
2090  PRINT "HI!  I'M YOUR FRIENDLY COMPUTER!"
2100  PRINT
2110  PRINT
2120  PRINT "WHAT IS YOUR NAME?"
2130  INPUT NA$
2140  PRINT
2150  PRINT "I'M GLAD TO MEET YOU, ";NA$;"."
2160  PRINT
2170  PRINT
2180  PRINT "WE ARE GOING TO PLAY A WORD GAME."
2190  PRINT "I WILL THINK OF A WORD AND"
2200  PRINT "SCRAMBLE UP THE LETTERS."
2210  PRINT
2220  PRINT "I WILL SHOW YOU THE LETTERS,"
2230  PRINT "AND YOU HAVE TO GUESS THE WORD!"
2240  PRINT "IF YOU TYPE IN A '?' I WILL"
2250  PRINT "GIVE YOU A HINT."
2260  PRINT
2270  PRINT "HERE WE GO!"
4000  REM  MAIN PROGRAM
4010  GOSUB 10000
4020  C$ = FL$(R)
4030  L = LEN (C$)
4040  T$ = ""
4050  FOR I = 1 TO L
4060  B$(I) = "#"
4070  NEXT I
4080  FOR I = 1 TO L
4090  D$ = MID$ (C$,I,1)
4100  J = INT ( RND (1) * L) + 1: REM  MIX POSITION
4110  IF B$(J) = "#" THEN 4130
4120  GOTO 4100
4130  B$(J) = D$
4140  NEXT I
4150  FOR I = 1 TO L
4160  T$ = T$ + B$(I)
4170  NEXT I
4180  IF T$ = C$ THEN 4040
4190  PRINT
4200  PRINT "HERE IS THE SCRAMBLED WORD."
4210  PRINT
4220  PRINT T$
4230  PRINT
4240  PRINT "WHAT DO YOU THINK THE WORD IS?"
4250  PRINT "TYPE IN A '?' FOR A HINT."
4260  INPUT S$
```

```
4270  GOSUB 11000
4280  IF HT = 1 THEN 15000
4290  GOTO 4200
10000 REM   RANDOMIZATION - CHANGE 'RND (1)' TO 'RND (0)' FOR TR
   S-80 AND PET!
10010 R =  INT ( RND (1) * BL) + 1
10020 RETURN
11000 REM  JUDGE ANSWER
11010 IF S$ = "?" THEN 16000
11020 TR = TR + 1
11030 IF S$ = C$ THEN 12000
11040 GOTO 14000
12000 REM  REWARD
12010 HT = 1
12020 PRINT "GOOD GUESS, ";NA$;"!"
12030 RETURN
14000 REM  WRONG GUESS
14010 PRINT "SORRY, ";NA$;". ";S$
14020 PRINT "IS NOT THE WORD. TRY AGAIN!"
14030 RETURN
15000 REM  SCORE KEEPING
15010 HT = 0
15020 PRINT "YOU FOUND THE WORD IN"
15030 IF TR = 1 THEN 15060
15040 PRINT TR;" TRIES!"
15050 GOTO 20000
15060 PRINT "ONE TRY!"
15070 GOTO 20000
16000 REM  HINT
16010 PRINT
16020 PRINT HN$(R)
16030 HN$(R) = "NO MORE HINTS!"
16040 PRINT
16050 RETURN
20000 REM  CLOSING
20010 PRINT "WOULD YOU LIKE ANOTHER WORD (YES OR NO)";
20020 INPUT S$
20030 IF S$ = "YES" THEN 20060
20040 PRINT "BYE FOR NOW!"
20050 END
20060 S$ = ""
20070 TR = 0
20080 HT = 0
20090 REM  DELETE CORRECT WORD FROM LIST
20100 FL$(R) = FL$(BL)
20110 HN$(R) = HN$(BL)
20120 BL = BL - 1
20130 IF BL = 0 THEN 20150
20140 GOTO 4010
20150 PRINT "SORRY, YOU HAVE USED ALL MY WORDS!"
20160 GOTO 20040
21000 REM  DATA
21010 DATA  CHAIR,SIT,BREAKFAST,MORNING,PICTURE,WALL,MONEY,PAY,GR
   ASS,GREEN
21020 DATA  DRIVEWAY,CEMENT,LIBRARY,BOOKS,RASPBERRY,FRUIT,PILLOW,
   SLEEP,CLOTHES,WEAR
```

21030 DATA BICYCLE,RIDE,DESSERT,CAKE,TELEPHONE,TALK,PIANO,MUSIC,
     PENCIL,WRITE
21040 DATA SLEIGH,SNOW,OCEAN,WATER,AIRPLANE,FLY,EXERCISE,JOG,GIR
     AFFE,ANIMAL

* -->TABLE OF VARIABLES<--

B$(*) - SCRAMBLED WORD ARRAY
1030 4060 4110 4130 4160

BL - BOTTOM OF LIST MARKER
1020 10010 20100 20110 20120 20120 20130

C$ - CORRECT WORD
4020 4030 4090 4180 11030

D$ - SINGLE LETTER OF WORD
4090 4130

FL$(*) - WORD LIST
1030 1050 4020 20100 20100

HN$(*) - HINT LIST
1030 1050 16020 16030 20110 20110

HT - HIT
4280 12010 15010 20080

I - COUNTER
1040 1050 1050 1060 2010 2030 2040 2050 2060 2080 4050
4060 4070 4080 4090 4140 4150 4160 4170

J - RANDOM NUMBER FOR POSITION
4100 4110 4130

L - LENGTH OF WORD
4030 4050 4080 4100 4150

NA$ - NAME
2130 2150 12020 14010

R - RANDOM NUMBER
4020 10010 16020 16030 20100 20110

S$ - STUDENT ANSWER
4260 11010 11030 14010 20020 20030 20060

T$ - SCRAMBLED WORD
4040 4160 4160 4180 4220

TL - NUMBER OF WORDS IN LIST
1010 1020 1030 1030 1040

TR - NUMBER OF TRIES
11020 11020 15030 15040 20070

END OF VAR. LIST

SAMPLE RUN

```
]RUN
SCRAMBLED WORDS
HI!  I'M YOUR FRIENDLY COMPUTER!
WHAT IS YOUR NAME?
?KIM
I'M GLAD TO MEET YOU, KIM.
WE ARE GOING TO PLAY A WORD GAME.
I WILL THINK OF A WORD AND
SCRAMBLE UP THE LETTERS.
I WILL SHOW YOU THE LETTERS,
AND YOU HAVE TO GUESS THE WORD!
IF YOU TYPE IN A '?' I WILL
GIVE YOU A HINT.
HERE WE GO!
HERE IS THE SCRAMBLED WORD.
EYNOM
WHAT DO YOU THINK THE WORD IS?
TYPE IN A '?' FOR A HINT.
?MONKEY
SORRY, KIM.  MONKEY
IS NOT THE WORD.  TRY AGAIN!
HERE IS THE SCRAMBLED WORD.
EYNOM
WHAT DO YOU THINK THE WORD IS?
TYPE IN A '?' FOR A HINT.
??
PAY
HERE IS THE SCRAMBLED WORD.
EYNOM
WHAT DO YOU THINK THE WORD IS?
TYPE IN A '?' FOR A HINT.
?MONEY
GOOD GUESS, KIM!
YOU FOUND THE WORD IN
2 TRIES!
WOULD YOU LIKE ANOTHER WORD (YES OR NO)?NO
BYE FOR NOW!
]
```

SPELLING QUIZ

PROGRAM DESCRIPTION

This program selects spelling words from an instructor-made data file. The computer rapidly scrolls a word at different time intervals and then asks you to spell the selected word. You may choose which time interval (either short, medium, or long) you want the computer to display the word to be spelled. At the end of the data word file, the computer will repeat any words that were missed until all of the words in the file are spelled correctly.

PROGRAM NOTES

1. If your computer allows clearing of the screen, you can "flash" the words instead of scrolling them.

2. If you can control an audio tape player from your computer, you can present the words over the player. You will not be able to randomize, and it would be difficult to repeat improperly spelled words.

PROGRAM LISTING

```
100  REM  SPELLING QUIZ BY GARY ORWIG
1000 REM  INITIALIZATION - SET 'TL' TO TOTAL NUMBER OF WORDS IN Y
     OUR DATA SET.
1010 TL = 20
1020 BL = TL
1030 DIM A$(TL)
1040 FOR I = 1 TO TL
1050 READ A$(I)
```

```
1060  NEXT I
2000  REM  INTRODUCTION
2010 L = 12
2020  GOSUB 18000
2030  PRINT "          SPELLING QUIZ"
2040  GOSUB 18000
2050 D = 2000
2060  GOSUB 19000
2070  PRINT "HELLO!  I'M GLAD YOU COULD MAKE IT!"
2080  PRINT "WHAT'S YOUR NAME?"
2090  INPUT NA$
2100  PRINT
2110  PRINT "IT'S NICE TO MEET YOU, ";NA$;"."
2120 L = 4
2130  GOSUB 18000
2140  PRINT "THIS IS A GAME WHERE I WILL"
2150  PRINT "GIVE YOU WORDS TO PRACTICE SPELLING."
2160  PRINT "SINCE I CAN'T TALK, I WILL FLASH"
2170  PRINT "A WORD ON THE SCREEN FOR JUST A"
2180  PRINT "MOMENT, THEN I WILL WAIT FOR YOU"
2190  PRINT "TO TYPE IT BACK IN."
2200  PRINT
2210  PRINT "I CAN LET YOU SEE THE WORDS FOR:"
2220  PRINT "     1. A SHORT TIME"
2230  PRINT "     2. A MEDIUM TIME"
2240  PRINT "     3. A LONG TIME"
2250  PRINT
2260  PRINT "WHICH WOULD YOU PREFER (TYPE 1,2,OR 3)"
2270  INPUT T
2280 T = T * 200
2290  PRINT "VERY GOOD, HERE WE GO!"
2300  GOSUB 19000
4000  REM  MAIN PROGRAM
4010  GOSUB 10000
4020 L = 12
4030  GOSUB 18000
4040  PRINT "          ";A$(R)
4050  GOSUB 18000
4060 D = T
4070  GOSUB 19000
4080  GOSUB 18000
4090  PRINT "WHAT WAS THE WORD"
4100  INPUT S$
4110  GOSUB 15000
4120  GOSUB 11000
4130  IF HT = 1 THEN 4190
4140  GOSUB 14000
4150  PRINT "WE WILL TRY THAT ONE AGAIN LATER!"
4160 D = 2000
4170  GOSUB 19000
4180  GOTO 4010
4190  GOSUB 12000
4200 D = 2000
4210  GOSUB 19000
4220  REM  DELETE CORRECT ANSWER FROM LIST OF WORDS
4230 A$(R) = A$(BL)
```

```
4240 BL = BL - 1
4250  IF BL = 0 THEN 20000
4260  GOTO 4010
10000  REM   RANDOMIZATION - CHANGE 'RND (1)' TO 'RND (0)' FOR TR
    S-80 AND PET!
10010 R =  INT ( RND (1) * BL) + 1
10020  RETURN
11000  REM  JUDGE ANSWER
11010  IF S$ = A$(R) THEN 11040
11020 HT = 0
11030  RETURN
11040 HT = 1
11050  RETURN
12000  REM  REWARDS
12010  FOR I = 1 TO 100
12020  PRINT "GREAT!   ";
12030  NEXT I
12040  RETURN
14000  REM  WRONG
14010  FOR I = 1 TO 100
14020  PRINT "SORRY!  ";
14030  NEXT I
14040 L = 3
14050  GOSUB 18000
14060  RETURN
15000  REM  SCORE KEEPING
15010 N = N + 1
15020  RETURN
18000  REM  SCROLLING
18010  FOR I = 1 TO L
18020  PRINT
18030  NEXT I
18040  RETURN
19000  REM  TIME DELAY
19010  FOR I = 1 TO D
19020  NEXT I
19030  RETURN
20000  REM  CLOSING
20010  PRINT "WE ARE FINISHED, ";NA$;"!"
20020  PRINT "IT TOOK YOU ";N;" TRIES"
20030  PRINT "TO SPELL THE ";TL;" WORDS."
21000  REM  DATA
21010  DATA  FEBRUARY,GHOST,ALUMINUM,PRECEDE,RECEIVE,JUDGEMENT,KNO
    WLEDGE,FRAGILE,NINETY,GUARANTEE
21020  DATA  JEWELRY,NUCLEAR,OMITTED,OCCURRENCE,MANAGEABLE,TECHNIC
    AL,GRIEVANCE,EXCUSABLE,DEVELOPMENT,COMPETENT
```

                    * —>TABLE OF VARIABLES<--

A$(*) - SPELLING WORD ARRAY
1030 1050 4040 4230 4230 11010

BL - BOTTOM OF LIST MARKER
1020 4230 4240 4240 4250 10010

D - DELAY TIMER
2050 4060 4160 4200 19010

HT – HIT (RIGHT ANSWER)
4130 11020 11040

I – GENERAL PURPOSE COUNTER
1040 1050 1060 12010 12030 14010 14030 18010 18030 19010
19020

L – NUMBER OF SCROLLING LINES
2010 2120 4020 14040 18010

N – SCORE KEEPER
15010 15010 20020

NA$ – STUDENT'S NAME
2090 2110 20010

R – RANDOM NUMBER
4040 4230 10010 11010

S$ – STUDENT'S ANSWER
4100 11010

T – DISPLAY TIME
2270 2280 2280 4060

TL – NUMBER OF WORDS IN LIST
1010 1020 1030 1040 20030

END OF VAR. LIST

SAMPLE RUN

```
]RUN
        SPELLING QUIZ
HELLO!  I'M GLAD YOU COULD MAKE IT!
WHAT'S YOUR NAME?
?JOHNNY
IT'S NICE TO MEET YOU, JOHNNY.
THIS IS A GAME WHERE I WILL
GIVE YOU WORDS TO PRACTICE SPELLING.
SINCE I CAN'T TALK, I WILL FLASH
A WORD ON THE SCREEN FOR JUST A
MOMENT, THEN I WILL WAIT FOR YOU
TO TYPE IT BACK IN.
I CAN LET YOU SEE THE WORDS FOR:
    1. A SHORT TIME
    2. A MEDIUM TIME
    3. A LONG TIME
WHICH WOULD YOU PREFER (TYPE 1,2,OR 3)
?2
VERY GOOD, HERE WE GO!
        JEWELRY
WHAT WAS THE WORD
?JEWELRY
GREAT!  GREAT!  GREAT!  GREAT!  GREAT!
        DEVELOPMENT
```

```
WHAT WAS THE WORD
?DEVELOPMENT
GREAT!   GREAT!   GREAT!   GREAT!   GREAT!
        GUARANTEE
WHAT WAS THE WORD
?GARUNTEE
SORRY!  SORRY!  SORRY!  SORRY!  SORRY!
WE WILL TRY THAT ONE AGAIN LATER!
        NUCLEAR
WHAT WAS THE WORD
?NUCLEAR
GREAT!   GREAT!   GREAT!   GREAT!   GREAT!
        FRAGILE
WHAT WAS THE WORD
?
```

STORY TELLER

PROGRAM DESCRIPTION

This program is an excellent drill for developing speed reading skills. The computer prints out an instructor-made data file story and you are requested to read the story as it is printed. You may adjust the speed of the printed material depending on which reading level you feel is most comfortable.

PROGRAM NOTES

1. This program is formatted for 40 characters per line. If you can print longer lines on your computer, simply allow each data statement to be longer.

2. The quotation marks in the data statements are needed by most computers. Otherwise commas in the sentences will confuse the computer!

3. Consider breaking the story at points and inserting questions to test for reading comprehension.

4. The "999" at the end of the data is commonly called an "EOF" (end of file) signal. It tells the computer that there is no more data.

5. Consider adding a comprehension test at the end of the story that you type in.

```
100  REM  STORY TELLER BY GARY ORWIG
500  DATA "'WILL YOU WALK INTO MY PARLOR?' SAID"
502  DATA "THE SPIDER TO THE FLY -"
504  DATA "'TIS THE PRETTIEST LITTLE PARLOR THAT"
506  DATA "EVER YOU DID SPY."
508  DATA "THE WAY INTO MY PARLOR IS UP A WINDING"
510  DATA "STAIR;"
512  DATA "AND I HAVE MANY CURIOUS THINGS TO SHOW"
514  DATA "YOU WHEN YOU'RE THERE.'"
516  DATA " "
518  DATA "'OH,NO,NO,'SAID THE LITTLE FLY;"
520  DATA "'TO ASK ME IS IN VAIN;"
522  DATA "FOR WHO GOES UP YOUR WINDING STAIR"
524  DATA "CAN NE'ER COME DOWN AGAIN.'"
526  DATA " "
528  DATA "'I'M SURE YOU MUST BE WEARY, DEAR,"
530  DATA "WITH SOARING UP SO HIGH;"
532  DATA "WILL YOU NOT REST UPON MY LITTLE BED?'"
534  DATA "SAID THE SPIDER TO THE FLY."
536  DATA "'THERE ARE PRETTY CURTAINS DRAWN AROUND;"
538  DATA "THE SHEETS ARE FINE AND THIN;"
540  DATA "AND IF YOU LIKE TO REST AWHILE,"
542  DATA "I'LL SNUGLY TUCK YOU IN!'"
544  DATA " "
546  DATA "'OH, NO, NO,' SAID THE LITTLE FLY;"
548  DATA "'FOR I'VE OFTEN HEARD IT SAID,"
550  DATA "THEY NEVER, NEVER WAKE AGAIN,"
552  DATA "WHO SLEEP UPON YOUR BED!'"
554  DATA " "
556  DATA "SAID THE CUNNING SPIDER TO THE FLY -"
558  DATA "'DEAR FRIEND, WHAT CAN I DO"
560  DATA "TO PROVE THE WARM AFFECTION I'VE ALWAYS"
562  DATA "FELT FOR YOU?'"
564  DATA " "
566  DATA "'I THANK YOU, GENTLE SIR,' SHE SAID,"
568  DATA "'FOR WHAT YOU'RE PLEASED TO SAY,"
570  DATA "AND BIDDING YOU GOOD MORNING NOW,"
572  DATA "I'LL CALL ANOTHER DAY.'"
574  DATA " "
576  DATA "THE SPIDER TURNED HIM ROUND ABOUT"
578  DATA "AND WENT INTO HIS DEN,"
580  DATA "FOR WELL HE KNEW THE SILLY FLY"
582  DATA "WOULD SOON COME BACK AGAIN;"
584  DATA "SO HE WOVE A SUBTLE WEB"
586  DATA "IN A LITTLE CORNER SLY,"
588  DATA "AND SET HIS TABLE READY, TO DINE"
590  DATA "UPON THE FLY."
592  DATA " "
594  DATA "THEN HE CAME OUT TO HIS DOOR AGAIN,"
596  DATA "AND MERRILY DID SING -"
598  DATA "'COME HITHER, HITHER, PRETTY FLY,"
600  DATA "WITH THE PEARL AND SILVER WING;"
602  DATA "YOUR ROBES ARE GREEN AND PURPLE -"
604  DATA "THERE'S A CREST UPON YOUR HEAD!"
```

```
606 DATA "YOUR EYES ARE LIKE THE DIAMOND BRIGHT"
608 DATA "BUT MINE ARE DULL AS LEAD!'"
610 DATA " "
612 DATA "ALAS! ALAS! HOW VERY SOON"
614 DATA "THIS SILLY LITTLE FLY,"
616 DATA "HEARING HIS WILY, FLATTERING WORDS"
618 DATA "CAME SLOWLY FLITTING BY,"
620 DATA "WITH BUZZING WINGS SHE HUNG ALOFT,"
622 DATA "THEN NEAR AND NEARER DREW;"
624 DATA "THINKING ONLY OF HER BRILLIANT EYES,"
626 DATA "HER GREEN AND PURPLE HUE -"
628 DATA "THINKING ONLY OF HER CRESTED HEAD -"
630 DATA "POOR FOOLISH THING!  AT LAST,"
632 DATA "UP JUMPED THE CUNNING SPIDER,"
634 DATA "AND FIRMLY HELD HER FAST!"
636 DATA " "
638 DATA "HE DRAGGED HER UP HIS WINDING STAIR,"
640 DATA "INTO HIS DISMAL DEN,"
642 DATA "WITHIN HIS LITTLE PARLOR -"
644 DATA "BUT SHE NE'ER CAME OUT AGAIN!"
646 DATA " "
648 DATA " "
650 DATA "AND NOW, DEAR LITTLE CHILDREN,"
652 DATA "WHO MAY THIS STORY READ,"
654 DATA "TO IDLE, SILLY, FLATTERING WORDS,"
656 DATA "I PRAY YOU NE'ER GIVE HEED;"
658 DATA "UNTO AN EVIL COUNSELOR CLOSE HEART,"
660 DATA "AND EAR, AND EYE,"
662 DATA "AND TAKE A LESSON FROM THIS TALE"
664 DATA "OF THE SPIDER AND THE FLY!"
666 DATA 999
2000 REM  INTRODUCTION
2010 L = 24
2020 GOSUB 18000
2030 PRINT "          STORY TELLER"
2040 L = 12
2050 GOSUB 18000
2060 D = 1000
2070 GOSUB 19000
2080 GOSUB 18000
2090 PRINT "THIS IS A PROGRAM WHICH TELLS"
2100 PRINT "YOU A STORY.  DO YOU WANT TO READ"
2110 PRINT
2120 PRINT "    1. FAST"
2130 PRINT "    2. MEDIUM"
2140 PRINT "    3. SLOW"
2150 PRINT
2160 PRINT "TYPE IN A NUMBER AND PRESS"
2170 PRINT "THE 'RETURN' OR 'ENTER' KEY"
2180 L = 8
2190 GOSUB 18000
2200 INPUT SA
2210 SP = SA * 25
2220 PRINT
2230 PRINT "OK! HERE WE GO!"
2240 D = 1000
```

```
2250  GOSUB 19000
2260 L = 24
2270  GOSUB 18000
4010  READ A$
4020  IF A$ = "999" THEN 20000
4030 LE =  LEN (A$)
4040  FOR I = 1 TO LE
4050  PRINT  MID$ (A$,I,1);
4060  FOR J = 1 TO SP
4070  NEXT J
4080  NEXT I
4090  PRINT
4100  GOTO 4010
18000  REM  SCROLL
18010  FOR I = 1 TO L
18020  PRINT
18030  NEXT I
18040  RETURN
19000  REM  DELAY
19010  FOR I = 1 TO D
19020  NEXT I
19030  RETURN
20000  REM  CLOSING
20010  PRINT
20020  PRINT "THE END"
20030  END
```

                  * -->TABLE OF VARIABLES<--

A$ - ONE LINE OF STORY
4010 4020 4030 4050

D - DELAY
2060 2240 19010

I - COUNTER
4040 4050 4080 18010 18030 19010 19020

J - COUNTER
4060 4070

L - LINES OF SCROLLING
2010 2040 2180 2260 18010

LE - LENGTH OF LINE A$
4030 4040

SA - STUDENT ANSWER
2200 2210

SP - SPEED OF PRINT
2210 4060

END OF VAR. LIST

SAMPLE RUN

]RUN
          STORY TELLER
THIS IS A PROGRAM WHICH TELLS
YOU A STORY. DO YOU WANT TO READ
     1. FAST
     2. MEDIUM
     3. SLOW
TYPE IN A NUMBER AND PRESS
THE 'RETURN' OR 'ENTER' KEY
?1
OK! HERE WE GO!
'WILL YOU WALK INTO MY PARLOR?' SAID
THE SPIDER TO THE FLY -
'TIS THE PRETTIEST LITTLE PARLOR THAT
EVER YOU DID SPY.
THE WAY INTO MY PARLOR IS UP A WINDING
STAIR;
AND I HAVE MANY CURIOUS THINGS TO SHOW
YOU WHEN YOU'RE THERE.'

'OH,NO,NO,'SAID THE LITTLE FLY;
'TO ASK ME IS IN VAIN;
FOR WHO GOES UP YOUR WINDING STAIR
CAN NE'ER COME DOWN AGAIN.'

'I'M SURE YOU MUST BE WEARY, DEAR,
WITH SOARING UP SO HIGH;
WILL YOU NOT REST UPON MY LITTLE BED?'
SAID THE SPIDER TO THE FLY.
'THERE ARE PRETTY CURTAINS DRAWN AROUND;
THE SHEETS ARE FINE AND THIN;
AND IF YOU LIKE TO REST AWHILE,
I'LL SNUGLY TUCK YOU IN!'

'OH, NO, NO,' SAID THE LITTLE FLY;
'FOR I'VE OFTEN HEARD IT SAID,
THEY NEVER, NEVER WAKE AGAIN,
WHO SLEEP UPON YOUR BED!'

SAID THE CUNNING SPIDER TO THE FLY -
'DEAR FRIEND, WHAT CAN I DO
TO PROVE THE WARM AFFECTION I'VE ALWAYS
FELT FOR YOU?'

'I THANK YOU, GENTLE SIR,' SHE SAID,
'FOR WHAT YOU'RE PLEASED TO SAY,
AND BIDDING YOU GOOD MORNING NOW,
I'LL CALL ANOTHER DAY.'

THE SPIDER TURNED HIM ROUND ABOUT
AND WENT INTO HIS DEN,
FOR WELL HE KNEW THE SILLY FLY
WOULD SOON COME BACK AGAIN;
SO HE WOVE A SUBTLE WEB

IN A LITTLE CORNER SLY,
AND SET HIS TABLE READY, TO DINE
UPON THE FLY.

THEN HE CAME OUT TO HIS DOOR AGAIN,
AND MERRILY DID SING -
'COME HITHER, HITHER, PRETTY FLY,
WITH THE PEARL AND SILVER WING;
YOUR ROBES ARE GREEN AND PURPLE -
THERE'S A CREST UPON YOUR HEAD!
YOUR EYES ARE LIKE THE DIAMOND BRIGHT
BUT MINE ARE DULL AS LEAD!'

ALAS! ALAS! HOW VERY SOON
THIS SILLY LITTLE FLY,
HEARING HIS WILY, FLATTERING WORDS
CAME SLOWLY FLITTING BY.
WITH BUZZING WINGS SHE HUNG ALOFT,
THEN NEAR AND NEARER DREW;
THINKING ONLY OF HER BRILLIANT EYES,
HER GREEN AND PURPLE HUE -
THINKING ONLY OF HER CRESTED HEAD -
POOR FOOLISH THING! AT LAST,
UP JUMPED THE CUNNING SPIDER,
AND FIRMLY HELD HER FAST!

HE DRAGGED HER UP HIS WINDING STAIR,
INTO HIS DISMAL DEN,
WITHIN HIS LITTLE PARLOR -
BUT SHE NE'ER CAME OUT AGAIN!

AND NOW, DEAR LITTLE CHILDREN,
WHO MAY THIS STORY READ,
TO IDLE, SILLY, FLATTERING WORDS,
I PRAY YOU NE'ER GIVE HEED;
UNTO AN EVIL COUNSELOR CLOSE HEART,
AND EAR, AND EYE,
AND TAKE A LESSON FROM THIS TALE
OF THE SPIDER AND THE FLY!
THE END
]

SYNONYMS/ANTONYMS

PROGRAM DESCRIPTION

This program is a word game to learn the differences between synonyms and antonyms. The computer will first define a synonym and an antonym for the purposes of the program. Then a list of words is chosen by the computer with synonyms or antonyms mixed in with the selected words. The computer does not tell you whether there are synonyms or antonyms in the list of words; however, you do have the option of selecting the number of paired words (synonyms or antonyms) within the list. By using multiple-choice questions, the computer asks you to select either synonyms or antonyms that are hidden in the list of words. You need to know the definitions of all the words in the list, because you have to answer all of the questions correctly in order to finish the program.

PROGRAM NOTES

1. If you prefer, you can announce whether the student should look for a synonym or an antonym. This would require another array which would contain the necessary information for each problem.

2. Consider adding homonyms to the program.

PROGRAM LISTING

```
100 REM SYNONYMS-ANTONYMS BY GARY ORWIG
1000 REM  INITIALIZATION - SET 'TL' EQUAL TO THE NUMBER OF PROBL
     EMS IN YOUR DATA SET.
1010 TL = 20
```

```
1020 BL = TL
1030 DIM Q$(TL),A1$(TL),A2$(TL),A3$(TL),A4$(TL),KE(TL)
1040 FOR I = 1 TO TL
1050 READ Q$(I),A1$(I),A2$(I),A3$(I),A4$(I),KE(I)
1060 NEXT I
2000 REM  INTRODUCTION
2010 FOR I = 1 TO 50
2020 FOR J = 1 TO 50
2030 NEXT J
2040 PRINT "SYNONYMS - ANTONYMS        ";
2050 NEXT I
2060 D = 2500
2070 GOSUB 19000
2080 L = 12
2090 GOSUB 18000
2100 PRINT "WHAT IS YOUR NAME?"
2110 GOSUB 18000
2120 INPUT NA$
2130 PRINT
2140 PRINT
2150 PRINT "I'M HAPPY TO MEET YOU, ";NA$;"."
2160 PRINT
2170 PRINT
2180 PRINT "THIS IS A GAME OF SYNONYMS"
2190 PRINT "AND ANTONYMS."
2200 PRINT
2210 PRINT "DO YOU NEED INSTRUCTIONS?"
2220 PRINT "TYPE IN A YES OR A NO."
2230 INPUT S$
2240 IF S$ = "NO" THEN 3060
2250 GOSUB 18000
2260 PRINT "THIS IS REALLY PRETTY EASY, ";NA$;"."
2270 PRINT
2280 PRINT "A 'SYNONYM' IS A WORD WHICH MEANS"
2290 PRINT "ABOUT THE SAME THING AS ANOTHER WORD."
2300 PRINT "FOR EXAMPLE, 'FAST' AND 'SWIFT' "
2310 PRINT "ARE SYNONYMS.  THEY MEAN ABOUT THE"
2320 PRINT "SAME THING."
2330 PRINT
2340 PRINT "ANTONYMS, ON THE OTHER HAND, ARE"
2350 PRINT "OPPOSITES.  FOR EXAMPLE, 'FAST' AND"
2360 PRINT "'SLOW' ARE ANTONYMS.  THEY MEAN"
2370 PRINT "OPPOSITE THINGS."
3000 PRINT
3010 PRINT
3020 PRINT "LET'S TRY SOME GROUPS OF WORDS."
3030 PRINT "FOR EACH WORD AT THE TOP, TRY TO"
3040 PRINT "PICK A SYNONYM OR ANTONYM FROM THE"
3050 PRINT "LIST. "
3060 PRINT
3070 PRINT "READY?  PUSH THE 'RETURN' OR 'ENTER'"
3080 PRINT "KEY TO BEGIN.": REM  FOR PET PRESS ANY LETTER BEFORE
     PRESSING RETURN
3090 INPUT S$
4000 REM  MAIN PROGRAM
4010 GOSUB 10000
```

```
4020  GOSUB 17000
4030  PRINT "TYPE IN A 1, 2, 3, OR 4";
4040  INPUT SA
4050  IF SA < 1 OR SA > 4 THEN 4030
4060  GOSUB 15000
4070  GOSUB 11000
4080  IF HT = 1 THEN 4140
4090  GOSUB 14000
4100  PRINT "WE WILL TRY THAT ONE AGAIN LATER!"
4110 D = 2000
4120  GOSUB 19000
4130  GOTO 4010
4140  GOSUB 12000
4150 D = 2000
4160  GOSUB 19000
4170  REM  DELETE CORRECT WORDS FROM LIST
4180 Q$(R) = Q$(BL)
4190 A1$(R) = A1$(BL)
4200 A2$(R) = A2$(BL)
4210 A3$(R) = A3$(BL)
4220 A4$(R) = A4$(BL)
4230 KE(R) = KE(BL)
4240 BL = BL - 1
4250  IF BL = 0 THEN  GOTO 20000
4260  GOTO 4010
10000  REM    RANDOMIZATION - CHANGE 'RND (1)' TO 'RND (0)' FOR TR
    S-80 AND PET!
10010 R =  INT ( RND (1) * BL) + 1
10020  RETURN
11000  REM  JUDGE ANSWER
11010  IF SA = KE(R) THEN 11040
11020 HT = 0
11030  RETURN
11040 HT = 1
11050  RETURN
12000  REM  REWARD
12010  PRINT
12020  PRINT "GREAT!"
12030  PRINT
12040  RETURN
14000  REM  WRONG
14010  PRINT
14020  PRINT "SORRY!"
14030  PRINT
14040  RETURN
15000  REM  SCORE KEEPING
15010 N = N + 1
15020  RETURN
17000  REM  PRINT OUT PROBLEM
17010 L = 12
17020  GOSUB 18000
17030  PRINT Q$(R)
17040  PRINT
17050  PRINT "    1. ";A1$(R)
17060  PRINT "    2. ";A2$(R)
17070  PRINT "    3. ";A3$(R)
```

```
17080 PRINT "    4, ";A4$(R)
17090 L = 8
17100 GOSUB 18000
17110 RETURN
18000 REM  PRINT LINES
18010 FOR I = 1 TO L
18020 PRINT
18030 NEXT I
18040 RETURN
19000 REM  DELAY
19010 FOR I = 1 TO D
19020 NEXT I
19030 RETURN
20000 REM  CLOSING
20010 L = 12
20020 GOSUB 18000
20030 PRINT "IT TOOK ";N;" TRIES TO GET"
20040 PRINT TL;" PROBLEMS CORRECT!"
20050 END
21000 REM  DATA
21010 DATA  SHORT, LONG,OPEN,HEAVY,CLOSE,1
21020 DATA  SLY,CUNNING,TIRED,PRETTY,GENTLE,1
21030 DATA  SHARP,DULL,HOT,AWFUL,FAST,1
21040 DATA  SMART,TERRIBLE,CLEVER,HUGE,RAPID,2
21050 DATA  ODD,HARSH,EVEN,CORRECT,SMALL,2
21060 DATA  ERECT,SLOW,BUILD,REPORT,SOFT,2
21070 DATA  SOFT,SWIFT,THICK,FAT,HARD,4
21080 DATA  QUICK,GENTLE,CRUEL,SUBTLE,FAST,4
21090 DATA  YOUNG,SMART,HAPPY,GAWKY,OLD,4
21100 DATA  KIND,BLUNT,GRACIOUS,REGULAR,SWIFT,2
21110 DATA  LITTLE,COLD,ENORMOUS,BULKY,STRONG,2
21120 DATA  SLENDER,GENTLE,OBVIOUS,THIN,IDLE,3
21130 DATA  HEAVY,SKILLFUL,COMMON,LIGHT,LAME,3
21140 DATA  MILD,GHOSTLY,SPACIOUS,CALM,CRAFTY,3
21150 DATA  FAR,NEAR,DARK,HOLLOW,AFTER,1
21160 DATA  DECREASE,APPROACH,TREMBLE,REST,DIMINISH,4
21170 DATA  POOR,SICK,EASY,DOWDY,WEALTHY,4
21180 DATA  AWKWARD,CLUMSY,AMIABLE,BIG,SLENDER,1
21190 DATA  REMEMBER,CLEAR,APPROACH,FORGET,ATTACK,3
21200 DATA  PROGRESS,BEWITCH,ADVANCE,SCATTER,DISGUISE,2
21210 DATA  LAZY,LITTLE,ACTIVE,DIFFICULT,PRETTY,2
```

               * -->TABLE OF VARIABLES<--

A1$(*) – ANSWERS 1
1030 1050 4190 4190 17050

A2$(*) – ANSWERS 2
1030 1050 4200 4200 17060

A3$(*) – ANSWERS 3
1030 1050 4210 4210 17070

A4$(*) – ANSWERS 4
1030 1050 4220 4220 17080

BL – BOTTOM OF LIST MARKER
1020 4180 4190 4200 4210 4220 4230 4240 4240 4250 10010

D – DELAY
2060 4110 4150 19010

HT – HIT
4080 11020 11040

I – COUNTER
1040 1050 1050 1050 1050 1050 1050 1060 2010 2050 18010
18030 19010 19020

J – COUNTER
2020 2030

KE(*) – KEYS
1030 1050 4230 4230 11010

L – LINES OF SCROLLING
2080 17010 17090 18010 20010

N – NUMBER OF GUESSES
15010 15010 20030

NA$ – NAME
2120 2150 2260

Q$(*) – QUESTIONS
1030 1050 4180 4180 17030

R – RANDOM NUMBER
4180 4190 4200 4210 4220 4230 10010 11010 17030 17050
17060 17070 17080

S$ – STUDENT ANSWER
2230 2240 3090

SA – STUDENT ANSWER
4040 4050 4050 11010

TL – QUESTIONS IN LIST
1010 1020 1030 1030 1030 1030 1030 1030 1040 20040

END OF VAR. LIST

SAMPLE RUN

]RUN
SYNONYMS – ANTONYMS   SYNONYMS – ANTONYMS
WHAT IS YOUR NAME?
?MELISSA
I'M HAPPY TO MEET YOU, MELISSA.
THIS IS A GAME OF SYNONYMS
AND ANTONYMS.
DO YOU NEED INSTRUCTIONS?

```
TYPE IN A YES OR A NO,
?YES
THIS IS REALLY PRETTY EASY, MELISSA,
A 'SYNONYM' IS A WORD WHICH MEANS
ABOUT THE SAME THING AS ANOTHER WORD,
FOR EXAMPLE, 'FAST' AND 'SWIFT'
ARE SYNONYMS, THEY MEAN ABOUT THE
SAME THING,
ANTONYMS, ON THE OTHER HAND, ARE
OPPOSITES, FOR EXAMPLE, 'FAST' AND
'SLOW' ARE ANTONYMS, THEY MEAN
OPPOSITE THINGS,
LET'S TRY SOME GROUPS OF WORDS,
FOR EACH WORD AT THE TOP, TRY TO
PICK A SYNONYM OR ANTONYM FROM THE
LIST,
READY?  PUSH THE 'RETURN' OR 'ENTER'
KEY TO BEGIN,
?
AWKWARD
    1, CLUMSY
    2, AMIABLE
    3, BIG
    4, SLENDER
TYPE IN A 1, 2, 3, OR 4?1
GREAT!
POOR
    1, SICK
    2, EASY
    3, DOWDY
    4, WEALTHY
TYPE IN A 1, 2, 3, OR 4?1
SORRY!
WE WILL TRY THAT ONE AGAIN LATER!
SHORT
    1, LONG
    2, OPEN
    3, HEAVY
    4, CLOSE
TYPE IN A 1, 2, 3, OR 4?1
GREAT!
PROGRESS
    1, BEWITCH
    2, ADVANCE
    3, SCATTER
    4, DISGUISE
TYPE IN A 1, 2, 3, OR 4?2
GREAT!
```

TEST TUTOR

PROGRAM DESCRIPTION

This program provides an instructor-made data base for developing a review test on any subject. The instructor can insert multiple-choice questions, answers, and explanations to the answers. If you answer a question correctly you have a choice either to go on to the next question or receive an explanation of the answer. However, if you answer the question incorrectly, you automatically receive an explanation of the answer and the computer will ask you the same question again at a later time during the review test. You must complete all of the questions correctly before you can finish the program.

PROGRAM NOTES

1. The large spaces in the data statements are due to the 40 character per line spacing of the computer. If your computer uses a different format (like 64 characters per line), space over the 64th character. Otherwise, a word will "break" over two lines.

2. Consider using A, B, C, or D for the multiple-choice answers.

3. Once again, you can enter your own questions. Just look at the data statements. There are three for each problem: the question, the selections (with key), and the explanations.

PROGRAM LISTING

```
100  REM  TEST TUTOR BY GARY ORWIG
1000  REM   INITIALIZATION - SET 'TL' EQUAL TO THE NUMBER OF PROBL
      EMS IN YOUR DATA SET.
1010 TL = 10
1020  DIM Q$(TL),A1$(TL),A2$(TL),A3$(TL),A4$(TL),KE(TL),EX$(TL)
1030  FOR I = 1 TO TL
1040  READ Q$(I),A1$(I),A2$(I),A3$(I),A4$(I),KE(I),EX$(I)
1050  NEXT I
2000  REM  INTRODUCTION
2010  FOR I = 1 TO 50
2020  FOR J = 1 TO 50
2030  NEXT J
2040  PRINT "        TEST TUTOR ";
2050  NEXT I
2060 D = 2500
2070  GOSUB 19000
2080 L = 12
2090  GOSUB 18000
2100  PRINT "WHAT IS YOUR NAME?"
2110  GOSUB 18000
2120  INPUT NA$
2130  PRINT
2140  PRINT
2150  PRINT "I'M HAPPY TO MEET YOU, ";NA$;"."
2160  PRINT
2170  PRINT
2180  PRINT "THIS IS A PROGRAM WHICH WILL HELP"
2190  PRINT "YOU STUDY FOR YOUR TEST!  "
2200  PRINT "I WILL ASK YOU QUESTIONS, AND YOU PICK"
2210  PRINT "THE NUMBER OF THE CORRECT ANSWER."
2220 L = 8
2230  GOSUB 18000
2240  PRINT "READY?  PUSH THE 'RETURN' OR 'ENTER'"
2250  PRINT "KEY TO BEGIN.": REM  FOR PET PRESS ANY KEY BEFORE PRE
      SSING RETURN
2260  INPUT S$
4000  REM  MAIN PROGRAM
4010  GOSUB 10000
4020  IF KE(NX) = 5 THEN 4060
4030 C = 0
4040  GOSUB 17000
4050  GOTO 4090
4060 C = C + 1
4070  IF C = TL + 1 THEN 20000
4080  GOTO 4010
4090  PRINT "TYPE IN A 1, 2, 3, OR 4";
4100  INPUT SA
4110  IF SA < 1 OR SA > 4 THEN 4090
4120  GOSUB 15000
4130  GOSUB 11000
4140  IF HT = 1 THEN 4230
4150  GOSUB 14000
4160 D = 1000
4170  GOSUB 19000
```

```
4180  GOSUB 6000
4190  PRINT "WE WILL TRY THAT ONE AGAIN LATER!"
4200 D = 1000
4210  GOSUB 19000
4220  GOTO 4010
4230  GOSUB 12000
4240 D = 1000
4250  GOSUB 19000
4260  PRINT "WOULD YOU LIKE AN EXPLANATION?"
4270  PRINT "(TYPE IN 'YES' OR 'NO')"
4280  INPUT S$
4290  IF S$ = "YES" THEN  GOSUB 6000
4300  GOTO 4010
6000  REM  EXPLANATION
6010 L = 24
6020  GOSUB 18000
6030  PRINT EX$(NX)
6040 L = 12
6050  GOSUB 18000
6060  PRINT "PRESS 'RETURN' OR 'ENTER'.": REM  FOR PET PRESS ANY L
     ETTER BEFORE PRESSING RETURN
6070  INPUT S$
6080  RETURN
10000  REM  SEQUENCE QUESTIONS
10010 NX = NX + 1
10020  IF NX < TL + 1 THEN 10050
10030 NX = 0
10040  GOTO 10010
10050  RETURN
11000  REM  JUDGE ANSWER
11010  IF SA = KE(NX) THEN 11040
11020 HT = 0
11030  RETURN
11040 HT = 1
11050 KE(NX) = 5
11060  RETURN
12000  REM  REWARD
12010  PRINT
12020  PRINT "GREAT!"
12030  PRINT
12040  RETURN
14000  REM  WRONG
14010  PRINT
14020  PRINT "SORRY!"
14030  PRINT
14040  RETURN
15000  REM  SCORE KEEPING
15010 N = N + 1
15020  RETURN
17000  REM  PRINT OUT PROBLEM
17010 L = 12
17020  GOSUB 18000
17030  PRINT Q$(NX)
17040  PRINT
17050  PRINT "    1. ";A1$(NX)
17060  PRINT "    2. ";A2$(NX)
```

```
17070  PRINT "    3. ";A3$(NX)
17080  PRINT "    4. ";A4$(NX)
17090  L = 8
17100  GOSUB 18000
17110  RETURN
18000  REM  PRINT LINES
18010  FOR I = 1 TO L
18020  PRINT
18030  NEXT I
18040  RETURN
19000  REM  DELAY
19010  FOR I = 1 TO D
19020  NEXT I
19030  RETURN
20000  REM  CLOSING
20010  L = 12
20020  GOSUB 18000
20030  PRINT "IT TOOK ";N;" TRIES TO GET"
20040  PRINT TL;" PROBLEMS CORRECT!"
20050  END
21000  REM  DATA
21010  DATA "THE VOLTAGE ACROSS A 5.0 OHM RESISTANCE IS MEASURED T
       O BE 10.0 VOLTS.  WHAT IS  THE CURRENT THROUGH THE RESISTANCE
       ?"
21020  DATA .5 AMPS,2 AMPS,50 AMPS,15 AMPS,2
21030  DATA "V=I*R, SO I=V/R; I=10/5 = 2 AMPS"
21040  DATA "THE CURRENT THROUGH A 10.0 OHM      RESISTANCE IS
       MEASURED TO BE 11.0 AMPS. WHAT VOLTAGE IS BEING APPLIED TO T
       HE   RESISTANCE?"
21050  DATA 21 VOLTS,1.1 VOLTS,110 VOLTS,.9 VOLTS,3
21060  DATA "V=I*R, SO V = 11 * 10, WHICH EQUALS    110 VOLTS
21070  DATA "HOW MUCH POWER IS USED BY A CIRCUIT    WHICH DRAWS
       5.0 AMPS OF CURRENT WHEN   20.0 VOLTS ARE APPLIED?"
21080  DATA 4.0 WATTS,.25 WATTS,25 WATTS,100 WATTS,4
21090  DATA "P=VI, SO P = 20 * 5, WHICH IS 100 WATTS."
21100  DATA "WHAT IS THE MINIMUM SIZE FUSE REQUIRED  TO SUPPLY CUR
       RENT TO A CIRCUIT WHICH    USES 300 WATTS AT 10.0 VOLTS?"
21110  DATA 3000 AMPS,3 AMPS,.33 AMPS,30 AMPS,4
21120  DATA "P=VI, SO I=P/V; I = 300/10, WHICH IS    30 AMPS.  ANY
       SMALLER FUSE WILL BURN   OUT."
21130  DATA "WHAT IS THE MINIMUM SIZE FUSE REQUIRED  TO SUPPLY CUR
       RENT TO A CIRCUIT WHICH    USES 300 WATTS AT 100 VOLTS?"
21140  DATA 3000 AMPS,3 AMPS,.33 AMPS,30 AMPS,2
21150  DATA "I=P/V, SO I = 300/100 WHICH EQUALS    3 AMPS.  AS V
       OLTAGE INCREASES, LESS    CURRENT IS REQUIRED TO SUPPLY THE
       SAME  AMOUNT OF POWER."
21160  DATA "WHAT AMOUNT OF POWER IS CONSUMED BY A   RESISTANCE OF
       100 OHMS WHEN A CURRENT   OF 3 AMPS IS PASSING THROUGH IT?"
21170  DATA 33 WATTS, 300 WATTS,900 WATTS,3000 WATTS,3
21180  DATA "P=I^2*R, SO P=3 * 3 * 100, WHICH IS 900 WATTS."
21190  DATA "HOW MUCH POWER IS CONSUMED BY A CABLE   WHICH HAS A R
       ESISTANCE OF 2.0 OHMS WHEN A VOLTAGE DROP OF 20 VOLTS OCCURS
       ACROSS IT?"
21200  DATA 40 WATTS,10 WATTS,22 WATTS,200 WATTS,4
21210  DATA "P=V^2/R, SO P = (20 *20)/2, WHICH IS    200 WATTS."
```

21220 DATA "WHAT IS THE VOLTAGE SUPPLIED TO A MOTOR IF THE TOTAL
    RESISTANCE OF THE SUPPLY   CABLE IS 2.0 OHMS AND THE CURRENT
    IS   10.0 AMPS. THE VOLTAGE AT THE POWER   SOURCE IS 120 V
    OLTS."
21230 DATA 20 VOLTS,80 VOLTS, 100 VOLTS, 120 VOLTS,3
21240 DATA "V=IR, SO V=10 * 2 WHICH IS 20 VOLTS - - THE VOLTAGE L
    OST IN THE CABLE.   120 - 20 = 100 VOLTS, THE VOLTAGE
       SUPPLIED TO THE MOTOR."
21250 DATA "WHAT IS THE TOTAL RESISTANCE OF 3, 30   OHM RESISTORS
    CONNECTED IN SERIES?"
21260 DATA 3 OHMS,10 OHMS,33 OHMS,90 OHMS,4
21270 DATA "RT=R1+R2+R3, SO RT = 30 + 30 + 30,   WHICH IS 90 O
    HMS."
21280 DATA "WHAT IS THE TOTAL RESISTANCE OF 3, 30   OHM RESISTORS
    CONNECTED IN PARALLEL?"
21290 DATA 3 OHMS, 10 OHMS, 33 OHMS, 90 OHMS,2
21300 DATA "1/RT=1/R1 + 1/R2 + 1/R3, SO   1/RT=1/30 + 1
    /30 + 1/30; RT=10."

```
             * -->TABLE OF VARIABLES<--
```

A1$(*) - ANSWER 1
1020 1040 17050

A2$(*) - ANSWER 2
1020 1040 17060

A3$(*) - ANSWER 3
1020 1040 17070

A4$(*) - ANSWER 4
1020 1040 17080

C - NUMBER OF QUESTIONS ANSWERED
4030 4060 4060 4070

D - DELAY
2060 4160 4200 4240 19010

EX$(*) - EXPLANATIONS
1020 1040 6030

HT - HIT
4140 11020 11040

I - COUNTER
1030 1040 1040 1040 1040 1040 1040 1040 1050 2010 2050
18010 18030 19010 19020

J - COUNTER
2020 2030

KE(*) - KEYS
1020 1040 4020 11010 11050

L - LINES OF SCROLLING
2080 2220 6010 6040 17010 17090 18010 20010

N - NUMBER OF TRIES
15010 15010 20030

NA$ - NAME
2120 2150

NX - NUMBER IN SEQUENCE
4020 6030 10010 10010 10020 10030 11010 11050 17030 17050
17060 17070 17080

Q$(*) - QUESTIONS
1020 1040 17030

S$ - STUDENT ANSWER
2260 4280 4290 6070

SA - STUDENT ANSWER
4100 4110 4110 11010

TL - QUESTIONS IN LIST
1010 1020 1020 1020 1020 1020 1020 1020 1030 4070 10020
20040

END OF VAR. LIST

SAMPLE RUN

]RUN
       TEST TUTOR   TEST TUTOR
WHAT IS YOUR NAME?
?AMY
I'M HAPPY TO MEET YOU, AMY.
THIS IS A PROGRAM WHICH WILL HELP
YOU STUDY FOR YOUR TEST!
I WILL ASK YOU QUESTIONS, AND YOU PICK
THE NUMBER OF THE CORRECT ANSWER.
READY? PUSH THE 'RETURN' OR 'ENTER'
KEY TO BEGIN.
?
THE VOLTAGE ACROSS A 5.0 OHM RESISTANCE
IS MEASURED TO BE 10.0 VOLTS. WHAT IS
THE CURRENT THROUGH THE RESISTANCE?
    1. .5 AMPS
    2. 2 AMPS
    3. 50 AMPS
    4. 15 AMPS
TYPE IN A 1, 2, 3, OR 4?3
SORRY!
V=I*R, SO I=V/R; I=10/5 = 2 AMPS
PRESS 'RETURN' OR 'ENTER'.
?
WE WILL TRY THAT ONE AGAIN LATER!
THE CURRENT THROUGH A 10.0 OHM
RESISTANCE IS MEASURED TO BE 11.0 AMPS.
WHAT VOLTAGE IS BEING APPLIED TO THE
RESISTANCE?

        1. 21 VOLTS
        2. 1.1 VOLTS
        3. 110 VOLTS
        4. .9 VOLTS
TYPE IN A 1, 2, 3, OR 4?3
GREAT!
WOULD YOU LIKE AN EXPLANATION?
(TYPE IN 'YES' OR 'NO')
?NO
HOW MUCH POWER IS USED BY A CIRCUIT
WHICH DRAWS 5.0 AMPS OF CURRENT WHEN
20.0 VOLTS ARE APPLIED?
        1. 4.0 WATTS
        2. .25 WATTS
        3. 25 WATTS
        4. 100 WATTS
TYPE IN A 1, 2, 3, OR 4?4
GREAT!
WOULD YOU LIKE AN EXPLANATION?
(TYPE IN 'YES' OR 'NO')
?YES
P=VI, SO P = 20 * 5, WHICH IS 100 WATTS.
PRESS 'RETURN' OR 'ENTER'.
?
WHAT IS THE MINIMUM SIZE FUSE REQUIRED
TO SUPPLY CURRENT TO A CIRCUIT WHICH
USES 300 WATTS AT 10.0 VOLTS?
        1. 3000 AMPS
        2. 3 AMPS
        3. .33 AMPS
        4. 30 AMPS
TYPE IN A 1, 2, 3, OR 4?

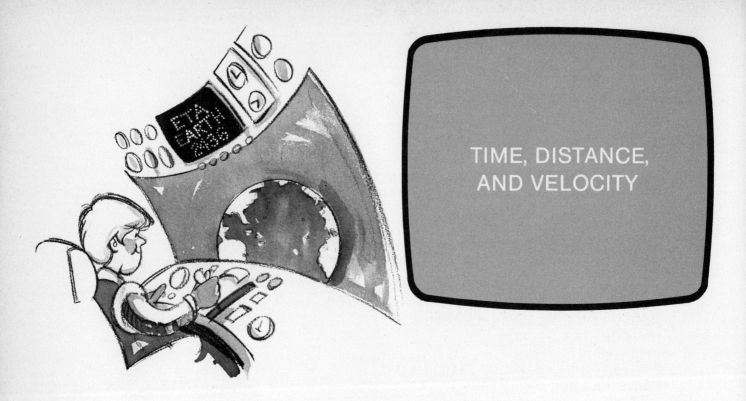

TIME, DISTANCE,
AND VELOCITY

PROGRAM DESCRIPTION

This program studies the mathematical relationships between time, distance, and velocity. It allows the user to enter values for any two variables, and it will then calculate the value of the third variable.

PROGRAM NOTES

This is only a shell to work around. Depending on your particular application, you may want to use only the conversion routines, or you may want to add more instruction and de-emphasize these routines.

If you are really into program writing, try to allow for the input of mixed units such as 3 hours 15 minutes and 25 seconds!

PROGRAM LISTING

```
100  REM  TIME DISTANCE AND VELOCITY BY GARY ORWIG
1000  REM  INITIALIZATION
1010  DIM A$(5),A(5,5),B$(6),B(6,6)
1020  FOR I = 1 TO 5
1030  FOR J = 1 TO 5
1040  READ A(I,J)
1050  NEXT J
1060  NEXT I
1070  FOR I = 1 TO 5
1080  READ A$(I)
1090  NEXT I
1100  FOR I = 1 TO 6
```

```
1110  FOR J = 1 TO 6
1120  READ B(I,J)
1130  NEXT J
1140  NEXT I
1150  FOR I = 1 TO 6
1160  READ B$(I)
1170  NEXT I
2000  REM  INTRODUCTION
2010  D = 20
2020  FOR I = 1 TO 25
2030  FOR J = 1 TO I
2040  PRINT " ";
2050  NEXT J
2060  PRINT "TIME"
2070  GOSUB 19000
2080  NEXT I
2090  FOR I = 1 TO 25
2100  FOR J = 1 TO I
2110  PRINT " ";
2120  NEXT J
2130  PRINT "DISTANCE"
2140  GOSUB 19000
2150  NEXT I
2160  FOR I = 1 TO 25
2170  FOR J = 1 TO I
2180  PRINT " ";
2190  NEXT J
2200  PRINT "VELOCITY"
2210  GOSUB 19000
2220  NEXT I
2230  D = 1000
2240  GOSUB 19000
2250  L = 24
2260  GOSUB 18000
2270  PRINT "HI! I'M HAPPY TO SEE YOU."
2280  PRINT
2290  PRINT "WHAT IS YOUR NAME?"
2300  L = 12
2310  GOSUB 18000
2320  INPUT NA$
2330  PRINT "IT'S NICE TO MEET YOU, ";NA$;"."
2340  PRINT
2350  PRINT
2360  PRINT "IN THIS PROGRAM WE ARE GOING TO"
2370  PRINT "STUDY TIME, DISTANCE, AND"
2380  PRINT "VELOCITY.
2390  PRINT
2400  PRINT
2410  PRINT "FIRST, LET'S WORK WITH TIME."
2420  PRINT "TIME CAN BE MEASURED IN A VARIETY"
2430  PRINT "OF UNITS, INCLUDING SECONDS,"
2440  PRINT "MINUTES, HOURS, AND SO FORTH."
2450  PRINT
2460  PRINT "WE WILL PRACTICE CONVERTING"
2470  PRINT "VALUES FROM ONE TO ANOTHER FOR"
2480  PRINT "A BIT JUST TO GET USED TO THEM."
```

```
2490  PRINT
2500  PRINT
2510  PRINT "PRESS THE 'RETURN' OR 'ENTER' KEY"; REM  FOR PET PRES
      S ANY LETTER BEFORE PRESSING RETURN
2520  INPUT S$
2530 L = 24
2540  GOSUB 18000
4000  REM  MAIN PROGRAM
4010  PRINT
4020  PRINT "TYPE IN ONE VALUE AND I WILL CONVERT"
4030  PRINT "IT FOR YOU!"
4040  PRINT
4050  PRINT "TYPE IN A '0' TO GO ON."
4060  PRINT
4070  PRINT
4080  PRINT "CHANGE FROM (PICK A NUMBER)"
4090  PRINT
4100  GOSUB 9010
4110  INPUT TU
4120  IF TU = 0 THEN 5000
4130  PRINT
4140  PRINT "CHANGE FROM ";A$(TU);" TO"
4150  PRINT "(PICK A NUMBER)"
4160  PRINT
4170  GOSUB 9010
4180  INPUT T2
4190  PRINT
4200  PRINT "CHANGE FROM ";A$(TU);" TO"
4210  PRINT A$(T2);"."
4220  PRINT
4230  PRINT "HOW MANY ";A$(TU);"?"
4240  INPUT TM
4250 TX = TM * A(TU,T2)
4260  PRINT
4270  PRINT TM;" ";A$(TU);" EQUALS ";TX;" ";A$(T2);"."
4280  GOTO 4040
5000  REM  DISTANCE
5010 L = 24
5020  GOSUB 18000
5030  PRINT "DISTANCE IS ALSO MEASURED IN"
5040  PRINT "A VARIETY OF UNITS."
5050  PRINT "AMONG THEM ARE METRIC UNITS"
5060  PRINT "SUCH AS CENTIMETERS, METERS, AND"
5070  PRINT "KILOMETERS.  IN ADDITION, THERE"
5080  PRINT "ARE ENGLISH UNITS SUCH AS FEET"
5090  PRINT "AND MILES.
5100  PRINT
5110  PRINT
5120  PRINT "LET'S PRACTICE CONVERTING SOME"
5130  PRINT "DISTANCES BETWEEN THE VARIOUS UNITS."
5140  PRINT
5150  PRINT "ALTHOUGH IT ISN'T TOO GOOD OF AN"
5160  PRINT "IDEA TO CONVERT BETWEEN ENGLISH AND"
5170  PRINT "METRIC UNITS, I WILL INCLUDE THEM BOTH"
5180  PRINT "FOR YOU TO WORK WITH."
5190  PRINT
```

```
5200  PRINT "PUSH 'RETURN' OR 'ENTER'"; REM  FOR PET PRESS ANY LET
      TER BEFORE PRESSING RETURN
5210  INPUT S$
5220 L = 24
5230  GOSUB 18000
5240  PRINT
5250  PRINT "TYPE IN A '0' TO GO ON."
5260  PRINT
5270  PRINT
5280  PRINT "CHANGE FROM (PICK A NUMBER)"
5290  PRINT
5300  GOSUB 9080
5310  PRINT
5320  INPUT DU
5330  IF DU = 0 THEN 6000
5340  PRINT
5350  PRINT "CHANGE FROM ";B$(DU);" TO"
5360  PRINT "(PICK A NUMBER)"
5370  PRINT
5380  GOSUB 9080
5390  PRINT
5400  INPUT D2
5410  PRINT
5420  PRINT "CHANGE FROM ";B$(DU);" TO"
5430  PRINT B$(D2);"."
5440  PRINT
5450  PRINT "HOW MANY ";B$(DU);"?"
5460  INPUT DI
5470 DX = DI * B(DU,D2)
5480  PRINT
5490  PRINT DI;" ";B$(DU);" EQUALS ";DX;" ";B$(D2);"."
5500  GOTO 5240
6000  REM  VELOCITY
6010 L = 24
6020  GOSUB 18000
6030  PRINT "NOW LETS WORK WITH VELOCITY."
6040  PRINT
6050  PRINT "VELOCITY IS THE DISTANCE COVERED"
6060  PRINT "IN A GIVEN UNIT OF TIME."
6070  PRINT "(LIKE 60 MILES PER HOUR)"
6080 L = 10
6090  GOSUB 18000
6100  PRINT "PUSH 'RETURN' OR 'ENTER'"; REM  FOR PET PRESS ANY LET
      TER BEFORE PRESSING RETURN
6110  INPUT S$
6120  REM  SELECTION
6130  PRINT
6140  PRINT
6150 L = 24
6160  GOSUB 18000
6170  PRINT
6180  PRINT "PICK A NUMBER."
6190  PRINT "   1. GIVEN TIME AND DISTANCE,"
6200  PRINT "      FIND VELOCITY."
6210  PRINT
6220  PRINT "   2. GIVEN TIME AND VELOCITY,"
```

```
6230  PRINT "     FIND DISTANCE."
6240  PRINT
6250  PRINT "   3. GIVEN VELOCITY AND DISTANCE,"
6260  PRINT "     FIND TIME."
6270  PRINT "TYPE IN A '0' TO GO ON."
6280  INPUT SA
6290  IF SA = 0 THEN 20000
6300  ON SA GOTO 7000,7410,8000
7000  L = 24
7010  GOSUB 18000
7020  PRINT "FINDING VELOCITY GIVEN"
7030  PRINT "TIME AND DISTANCE"
7040  PRINT
7050  PRINT "WHICH UNIT FOR TIME (PICK A #)"
7060  GOSUB 9010
7070  INPUT TU
7080  PRINT "ENTER VALUE OF ";A$(TU);"."
7090  INPUT TM
7100  PRINT "WHICH UNIT FOR DISTANCE(PICK A #)"
7110  GOSUB 9100
7120  INPUT DU
7130  PRINT "ENTER VALUE OF ";B$(DU);"."
7140  INPUT DI
7150  VE = DI / TM
7160  PRINT
7170  PRINT
7180  PRINT "THE ANSWER IS ";VE;" ";B$(DU)
7190  PRINT "PER ";A$(TU);"."
7200  PRINT
7210  PRINT "WOULD YOU LIKE THE ANSWER TO BE"
7220  PRINT "CONVERTED TO OTHER UNITS?"
7230  PRINT "(YES OR NO)"
7240  INPUT S$
7250  IF S$ = "YES" THEN 7270
7260  GOTO 6120
7270  PRINT
7280  PRINT "WHAT UNITS OF TIME?"
7290  GOSUB 9010
7300  INPUT T2
7310  PRINT "WHICH UNITS OF DISTANCE"
7320  GOSUB 9100
7330  INPUT D2
7340  VX = (DI * B(DU,D2)) / (TM * A(TU,T2))
7350  PRINT VE;" ";B$(DU);" PER ";A$(TU);" EQUALS:"
7360  PRINT VX;" ";B$(D2);" PER ";A$(T2);"."
7370  PRINT
7380  PRINT "PUSH 'ENTER' OR 'RETURN'": REM  FOR PET PRESS ANY LET
      TER BEFORE PRESSING RETURN
7390  INPUT S$
7400  GOTO 6120
7410  REM  FIND DISTANCE
7420  L = 24
7430  GOSUB 18000
7440  PRINT "FINDING DISTANCE GIVEN"
7450  PRINT "TIME AND VELOCITY"
7460  PRINT
```

```
7470  PRINT "WHICH UNIT FOR TIME (PICK A #)"
7480  GOSUB 9010
7490  INPUT TU
7500  PRINT "ENTER VALUE OF ";A$(TU);"."
7510  INPUT TM
7520  PRINT "WHICH UNIT FOR DISTANCE(PICK A #)"
7530  GOSUB 9100
7540  INPUT DU
7550  PRINT "ENTER VALUE OF VELOCITY IN UNITS OF"
7560  PRINT B$(DU);" PER ";A$(TU);"."
7570  INPUT VE
7580  DI = VE * TM
7590  PRINT
7600  PRINT
7610  PRINT "THE ANSWER IS ";DI;" ";B$(DU);"."
7620  PRINT
7630  PRINT "WOULD YOU LIKE THE ANSWER TO BE"
7640  PRINT "CONVERTED TO OTHER UNITS?"
7650  PRINT "(YES OR NO)"
7660  INPUT S$
7670  IF S$ = "YES" THEN 7690
7680  GOTO 6120
7690  PRINT
7700  PRINT "WHAT UNITS OF DISTANCE?"
7710  GOSUB 9100
7720  INPUT D2
7730  DX = (DI * B(DU,D2))
7740  PRINT DI;" ";B$(DU)
7750  PRINT "EQUALS ";DX;" ";B$(D2);"."
7760  PRINT
7770  PRINT "PUSH 'ENTER' OR 'RETURN'": REM  FOR PET PRESS ANY LET
      TER BEFORE PRESSING RETURN
7780  INPUT S$
7790  GOTO 6120
8000  REM  FIND DISTANCE
8010  L = 24
8020  GOSUB 18000
8030  PRINT "FINDING TIME GIVEN"
8040  PRINT "DISTANCE AND VELOCITY"
8050  PRINT
8060  PRINT "WHICH UNIT FOR DISTANCE"
8070  PRINT "(PICK A NUMBER)"
8080  GOSUB 9100
8090  INPUT DU
8100  PRINT "ENTER VALUE OF ";B$(DU);"."
8110  INPUT DI
8120  PRINT "WHICH UNIT FOR TIME (PICK A #)"
8130  GOSUB 9010
8140  INPUT TU
8150  PRINT "ENTER VALUE OF VELOCITY IN UNITS OF"
8160  PRINT B$(DU);" PER ";A$(TU);"."
8170  INPUT VE
8180  TM = DI / VE
8190  PRINT
8200  PRINT
8210  PRINT "THE ANSWER IS ";TM;" ";A$(TU);"."
```

```
8220 PRINT
8230 PRINT "WOULD YOU LIKE THE ANSWER TO BE"
8240 PRINT "CONVERTED TO OTHER UNITS?"
8250 PRINT "(YES OR NO)"
8260 INPUT S$
8270 IF S$ = "YES" THEN 8290
8280 GOTO 6120
8290 PRINT
8300 PRINT "WHAT UNITS OF TIME?"
8310 GOSUB 9010
8320 INPUT T2
8330 TX = (TM * A(TU,T2))
8340 PRINT TM;" ";A$(TU)
8350 PRINT "EQUALS ";TX;" ";A$(T2);"."
8360 PRINT
8370 PRINT "PUSH 'ENTER' OR 'RETURN'"; REM  FOR PET PRESS ANY LET
     TER BEFORE PRESSING RETURN
8380 INPUT S$
8390 GOTO 6120
9000 REM  PRINT SUBROUTINES
9010 REM  TIME
9020 PRINT
9030 FOR I = 1 TO 5
9040 PRINT "       ";I;".  ";A$(I)
9050 NEXT I
9060 PRINT
9070 RETURN
9080 REM  DISTANCE
9090 PRINT
9100 FOR I = 1 TO 6
9110 PRINT "       ";I;".  ";B$(I)
9120 NEXT I
9130 PRINT
9140 RETURN
18000 REM  SCROLL
18010 FOR I = 1 TO L
18020 PRINT
18030 NEXT I
18040 RETURN
19000 REM  DELAY
19010 FOR K = 1 TO D
19020 NEXT K
19030 RETURN
20000 REM  CLOSING
20010 L = 24
20020 GOSUB 18000
20030 PRINT "WE'RE FINISHED, ";NA$;"!"
20040 PRINT "I HOPE YOU HAD A NICE TIME!"
20050 L = 12
20060 GOSUB 18000
20070 END
21000 DATA  1,.01667,2.778E-4,1.157E-5,3.169E-8
21010 DATA  60,1,.01667,6.944E-4,1.901E-6
21020 DATA  3600,60,1,.04167,1.141E-4
21030 DATA  86400,1440,24,1,2.738E-3
21040 DATA  31557600,525960,8766,365.25,1
```

```
21050  DATA  SECONDS,MINUTES,HOURS,DAYS,YEARS
21060  DATA  1,.1,.001,1.0E-6,3.28084E-3,6.2137E-7
21070  DATA  10,1,.01,1.0E-5,3.28084E-2,6.2137E-6
21080  DATA  1000,100,1,.001,3.28084,6.2137E-4
21090  DATA  1000000,100000,1000,1,3280.84,.62137
21100  DATA  304.8,30.48,.3048,3.048E-4,1,1.894E-4
21110  DATA  1609300,160930,1609.3,1.6093,5280,1
21120  DATA  MILLIMETERS,CENTIMETERS,METERS,KILOMETERS,FEET,MILES
```

```
           *  -->TABLE OF VARIABLES<--
```

A$(*) - TIME UNITS
1010 1080 4140 4200 4210 4230 4270 4270 7080 7190 7350
7360 7500 7560 8160 8210 8340 8350 9040

A(*,*) - TIME CONVERSIONS
1010 1040 4250 7340 8330

B$(*) - DISTANCE UNITS
1010 1160 5350 5420 5430 5450 5490 5490 7130 7180 7350
7360 7560 7610 7740 7750 8100 8160 9110

B(*,*) - DISTANCE CONVERSIONS
1010 1120 5470 7340 7730

D - DELAY
2010 2230 19010

D2 - DISTANCE UNIT CONVERTED TO
5400 5430 5470 5490 7330 7340 7360 7720 7730 7750

DI - VALUE OF DU
5460 5470 5490 7140 7150 7340 7580 7610 7730 7740 8110
8180

DU - DISTANCE UNIT STARTED WITH
5320 5330 5350 5420 5450 5470 5490 7120 7130 7180 7340
7350 7540 7560 7610 7730 7740 8090 8100 8160

DX - VALUE OF D2
5470 5490 7730 7750

I - COUNTER
1020 1040 1060 1070 1080 1090 1100 1120 1140 1150 1160
1170 2020 2030 2080 2090 2100 2150 2160 2170 2220 9030
9040 9040 9050 9100 9110 9110 9120 18010 18030

J - COUNTER
1030 1040 1050 1110 1120 1130 2030 2050 2100 2120 2170
2190

K - COUNTER
19010 19020

L - LINES FOR SCROLLING
2250 2300 2530 5010 5220 6010 6080 6150 7000 7420 8010
18010 20010 20050

NA$ - NAME
2320 2330 20030

S$ - STUDENT ANSWER
2520 5210 6110 7240 7250 7390 7660 7670 7780 8260 8270
8380

SA - STUDENT ANSWER
6280 6290 6300

T2 - TIME UNIT CONVERTED TO
4180 4210 4250 4270 7300 7340 7360 8320 8330 8350

TM - VALUE OF TU
4240 4250 4270 7090 7150 7340 7510 7580 8180 8210 8330
8340

TU - TIME UNIT STARTED WITH
4110 4120 4140 4200 4230 4250 4270 7070 7080 7190 7340
7350 7490 7500 7560 8140 8160 8210 8330 8340

TX - VALUE OF T2
4250 4270 8330 8350

VE - VELOCITY
7150 7180 7350 7570 7580 8170 8180

VX - VELOCITY AFTER CONVERSION
7340 7360

END OF VAR. LIST

SAMPLE RUN

```
]RUN
TIME DISTANCE AND VELOCITY
HI! I'M HAPPY TO SEE YOU.
WHAT IS YOUR NAME?
?MICKEY
IT'S NICE TO MEET YOU, MICKEY.
IN THIS PROGRAM WE ARE GOING TO
STUDY TIME, DISTANCE, AND
VELOCITY.
FIRST, LET'S WORK WITH TIME.
TIME CAN BE MEASURED IN A VARIETY
OF UNITS, INCLUDING SECONDS,
MINUTES, HOURS, AND SO FORTH.
WE WILL PRACTICE CONVERTING
VALUES FROM ONE TO ANOTHER FOR
A BIT JUST TO GET USED TO THEM.
PRESS THE 'RETURN' OR 'ENTER' KEY
?
TYPE IN ONE VALUE AND I WILL CONVERT
IT FOR YOU!
TYPE IN A '0' TO GO ON.
```

CHANGE FROM (PICK A NUMBER)
        1. SECONDS
        2. MINUTES
        3. HOURS
        4. DAYS
        5. YEARS
?3
CHANGE FROM HOURS TO
(PICK A NUMBER)
        1. SECONDS
        2. MINUTES
        3. HOURS
        4. DAYS
        5. YEARS
?1
CHANGE FROM HOURS TO
SECONDS.
HOW MANY HOURS?
?1.7
1.7 HOURS EQUALS 6120 SECONDS.
TYPE IN A '0' TO GO ON.
CHANGE FROM (PICK A NUMBER)
        1. SECONDS
        2. MINUTES
        3. HOURS
        4. DAYS
        5. YEARS
?0
DISTANCE IS ALSO MEASURED IN
A VARIETY OF UNITS.
AMONG THEM ARE METRIC UNITS
SUCH AS CENTIMETERS, METERS, AND
KILOMETERS. IN ADDITION, THERE
ARE ENGLISH UNITS SUCH AS FEET
AND MILES.
LET'S PRACTICE CONVERTING SOME
DISTANCES BETWEEN THE VARIOUS UNITS.
ALTHOUGH IT ISN'T TOO GOOD OF AN
IDEA TO CONVERT BETWEEN ENGLISH AND
METRIC UNITS, I WILL INCLUDE THEM BOTH
FOR YOU TO WORK WITH.
PUSH 'RETURN' OR 'ENTER'
?
TYPE IN A '0' TO GO ON.
CHANGE FROM (PICK A NUMBER)
        1. MILLIMETERS
        2. CENTIMETERS
        3. METERS
        4. KILOMETERS
        5. FEET
        6. MILES
?6
CHANGE FROM MILES TO
(PICK A NUMBER)
        1. MILLIMETERS
        2. CENTIMETERS

```
        3. METERS
        4. KILOMETERS
        5. FEET
        6. MILES
?5
CHANGE FROM MILES TO
FEET.
HOW MANY MILES?
?.5
.5 MILES EQUALS 2640 FEET.
TYPE IN A '0' TO GO ON.
CHANGE FROM (PICK A NUMBER)
        1. MILLIMETERS
        2. CENTIMETERS
        3. METERS
        4. KILOMETERS
        5. FEET
        6. MILES
?0
NOW LETS WORK WITH VELOCITY.
VELOCITY IS THE DISTANCE COVERED
IN A GIVEN UNIT OF TIME.
(LIKE 60 MILES PER HOUR)
PUSH 'RETURN' OR 'ENTER'
?
PICK A NUMBER.
    1. GIVEN TIME AND DISTANCE,
       FIND VELOCITY.
    2. GIVEN TIME AND VELOCITY,
       FIND DISTANCE.
    3. GIVEN VELOCITY AND DISTANCE,
       FIND TIME.
TYPE IN A '0' TO GO ON.
?1
FINDING VELOCITY GIVEN
TIME AND DISTANCE
WHICH UNIT FOR TIME (PICK A #)
        1. SECONDS
        2. MINUTES
        3. HOURS
        4. DAYS
        5. YEARS
?3
ENTER VALUE OF HOURS.
?3
WHICH UNIT FOR DISTANCE(PICK A #)
        1. MILLIMETERS
        2. CENTIMETERS
        3. METERS
        4. KILOMETERS
        5. FEET
        6. MILES
?6
ENTER VALUE OF MILES.
?500
```

THE ANSWER IS 166.666667 MILES
PER HOURS.
WOULD YOU LIKE THE ANSWER TO BE
CONVERTED TO OTHER UNITS?
(YES OR NO)
?YES
WHAT UNITS OF TIME?
          1. SECONDS
          2. MINUTES
          3. HOURS
          4. DAYS
          5. YEARS
?1
WHICH UNITS OF DISTANCE
          1. MILLIMETERS
          2. CENTIMETERS
          3. METERS
          4. KILOMETERS
          5. FEET
          6. MILES
?
?REENTER
?5
166.666667 MILES PER HOURS EQUALS:
244.444445 FEET PER SECONDS.
PUSH 'ENTER' OR 'RETURN'
?
PICK A NUMBER.
     1. GIVEN TIME AND DISTANCE,
        FIND VELOCITY.
     2. GIVEN TIME AND VELOCITY,
        FIND DISTANCE.
     3. GIVEN VELOCITY AND DISTANCE,
        FIND TIME.
TYPE IN A '0' TO GO ON.
?0
WE'RE FINISHED, MICKEY!
I HOPE YOU HAD A NICE TIME!
]

TOO HIGH - TOO LOW

PROGRAM DESCRIPTION

The concept of decimals with multiplication and the ability to memorize a range of numbers is exercised in this program. The computer thinks of a number and you try and guess it. Each time you guess and guess incorrectly, the computer gives you helpful hints. But be warned, not all the hints are easy, and some of them may require you to use your multiplication skills.

PROGRAM NOTES

1. Changing the "1000" in line 10010 will change the maximum number possible. A smaller number like 100 might be better for younger kids.

2. For more advanced students, consider truncating variable "D" at two decimal places, instead of just one. This would involve lines 4100, 11030, and 11060. The result would be something like: "Your answer is about 1.02 times too high."

PROGRAM LISTING

```
100  REM  TOO HIGH-TOO LOW BY GARY ORWIG
2000  REM  INTRODUCTION
2010  FOR I = 1 TO 24
2020  PRINT
2030  NEXT I
2040  PRINT "HELLO!  I'M HAPPY TO SEE YOU!"
2050  PRINT "WHAT IS YOUR NAME";
2060  INPUT NA$
```

```
2070  PRINT "I HOPE YOU HAVE A NICE TIME,"
2080  PRINT NA$;"."
2090  PRINT
2100  PRINT
2110  PRINT "THIS GAME IS VERY EASY TO EXPLAIN."
2120  PRINT "I WILL THINK OF A NUMBER,AND"
2130  PRINT "IT WILL BE YOUR JOB TO GUESS IT."
2140  PRINT
2150  PRINT
2160  FOR DE = 1 TO 5000
2170  NEXT DE
2180  PRINT "HERE WE GO!"
2190  PRINT
2200  PRINT
2210  PRINT
4000  REM  MAIN PROGRAM
4010  GOSUB 10000
4020  PRINT "I AM THINKING OF A NUMBER."
4030  PRINT "TYPE IN YOUR GUESS!"
4040  INPUT SA
4050 N = N + 1
4060  IF SA < > 0 THEN 4090
4070  PRINT "NO, I'M NOT THINKING OF 0, TRY AGAIN!"
4080  GOTO 4040
4090  GOSUB 11000
4100  IF D = 1.0 THEN 4140
4110  PRINT "YOUR GUESS IS ABOUT ";D
4120  PRINT "TIMES TOO ";RS$;"!"
4130  GOTO 4170
4140  PRINT "YOU ARE CLOSE, ";NA$;"!"
4150  PRINT "BUT YOUR GUESS IS"
4160  PRINT "A BIT TOO ";RS$;"."
4170  PRINT "GUESS AGAIN."
4180  PRINT
4190  PRINT
4200  PRINT
4210  GOTO 4030
10000  REM  RANDOMIZING - USE 'RND (0)' IN PLACE OF 'RND (1)' FOR
       TRS-80 AND PET!
10010 C = INT ( RND (1) * 1000) + 1
10020  RETURN
11000  REM  JUDGE ANSWER
11010 IF SA = C THEN 12000
11020 IF SA < C THEN 11060
11030 D = INT (SA * 10 / C) / 10
11040 RS$ = "HIGH"
11050  RETURN
11060 D = INT (C * 10 / SA) / 10
11070 RS$ = "LOW"
11080  RETURN
12000  REM  REWARD
12010  FOR I = 1 TO 11
12020  PRINT
12030  NEXT I
12040  PRINT "YOU FOUND MY NUMBER"
12050  PRINT "IN ";N;" TRIES, ";NA$;"!"
```

```
12060  FOR I = 1 TO 11
12070  PRINT
12080  NEXT I
12090  END
```

         * -->TABLE OF VARIABLES<--

C - CORRECT ANSWER
10010 11010 11020 11030 11060

D - PROPORTION
4100 4110 11030 11060

DE - DELAY
2160 2170

I - COUNTER
2010 2030 12010 12030 12060 12080

N - NUMBER OF TRIES
4050 4050 12050

NA$ - NAME
2060 2080 4140 12050

RS$ - HIGH OR LOW
4120 4160 11040 11070

SA - STUDENT ANSWER
4040 4060 11010 11020 11030 11060

END OF VAR. LIST

SAMPLE RUN

```
]RUN
TOO HIGH-TOO LOW
HELLO!  I'M HAPPY TO SEE YOU!
WHAT IS YOUR NAME?CARRA
I HOPE YOU HAVE A NICE TIME,
CARRA.
THIS GAME IS VERY EASY TO EXPLAIN.
I WILL THINK OF A NUMBER,AND
IT WILL BE YOUR JOB TO GUESS IT.
HERE WE GO!
I AM THINKING OF A NUMBER.
TYPE IN YOUR GUESS!
?50
YOUR GUESS IS ABOUT 15.2
TIMES TOO LOW!
GUESS AGAIN.
TYPE IN YOUR GUESS!
?750
YOU ARE CLOSE, CARRA!
BUT YOUR GUESS IS
A BIT TOO LOW.
GUESS AGAIN.
```

```
TYPE IN YOUR GUESS!
?760
YOU ARE CLOSE, CARRA!
BUT YOUR GUESS IS
A BIT TOO LOW.
GUESS AGAIN.
TYPE IN YOUR GUESS!
?770
YOU ARE CLOSE, CARRA!
BUT YOUR GUESS IS
A BIT TOO HIGH.
GUESS AGAIN.
TYPE IN YOUR GUESS!
?765
YOU ARE CLOSE, CARRA!
BUT YOUR GUESS IS
A BIT TOO HIGH.
GUESS AGAIN.
TYPE IN YOUR GUESS!
?762
YOU FOUND MY NUMBER
IN 6 TRIES, CARRA!
]
```

PROGRAM DESCRIPTION

Any multiple-choice quiz can be generated from this program by inputting multiple-choice questions from an instructor-made data file. The computer presents a question with multiple-choice answers, judges the answers, and provides a score at the end of the program. This is an excellent tool for testing on a variety of subjects.

PROGRAM NOTES

1. Notice that subroutine 10000 does not randomize, but instead it presents the problems in order (sequentially). You can change that if you want. Just look at line 10000 in programs which do randomize.

2. Problems which have answers less than the number 5 can get confusing. It might be better to switch to: "Type in an A, B, C, or D" if you have many of these.

PROGRAM LISTING

```
100  REM  TRIVIA QUIZ BY GARY ORWIG
1000 REM   INITIALIZATION - SET 'TL' EQUAL TO THE NUMBER OF PROBL
     EMS IN YOUR DATA SET.
1010 TL = 20
1020 DIM Q$(TL),A1$(TL),A2$(TL),A3$(TL),A4$(TL),KE(TL)
1030 FOR I = 1 TO TL
1040 READ Q$(I),A1$(I),A2$(I),A3$(I),A4$(I),KE(I)
1050 NEXT I
2000 REM  INTRODUCTION
```

```
2010  FOR I = 1 TO 50
2020  FOR J = 1 TO 50
2030  NEXT J
2040  PRINT "    TRIVIA QUIZ      ";
2050  NEXT I
2060  D = 2500
2070  GOSUB 19000
2080  L = 12
2090  GOSUB 18000
2100  PRINT "WHAT IS YOUR NAME?"
2110  GOSUB 18000
2120  INPUT NA$
2130  PRINT
2140  PRINT
2150  PRINT "I'M HAPPY TO MEET YOU, ";NA$;"."
2160  PRINT
2170  PRINT
2180  PRINT "THIS IS A QUIZ WHICH COVERS A WIDE"
2190  PRINT "VARIETY OF TOPICS.  I WILL ASK YOU"
2200  PRINT "QUESTIONS, AND YOU PICK THE NUMBER OF"
2210  PRINT "OF THE RIGHT ANSWER.
2220  L = 8
2230  GOSUB 18000
2240  PRINT "READY?  PUSH THE 'RETURN' OR 'ENTER'"
2250  PRINT "KEY TO BEGIN.": REM  FOR PET PRESS ANY LETTER BEFORE
      PRESSING RETURN
2260  INPUT S$
4000  REM  MAIN PROGRAM
4010  GOSUB 10000
4020  IF KE(NX) = 5 THEN 4060
4030  C = 0
4040  GOSUB 17000
4050  GOTO 4090
4060  C = C + 1
4070  IF C = TL + 1 THEN 20000
4080  GOTO 4010
4090  PRINT "TYPE IN A 1, 2, 3, OR 4";
4100  INPUT SA
4110  IF SA < 1 OR SA > 4 THEN 4090
4120  GOSUB 15000
4130  GOSUB 11000
4140  IF HT = 1 THEN 4200
4150  GOSUB 14000
4160  PRINT "WE WILL TRY THAT ONE AGAIN LATER!"
4170  D = 2000
4180  GOSUB 19000
4190  GOTO 4010
4200  GOSUB 12000
4210  D = 2000
4220  GOSUB 19000
4230  GOTO 4010
10000  REM  SEQUENCE QUESTIONS
10010 NX = NX + 1
10020  IF NX < TL + 1 THEN 10050
10030 NX = 0
10040  GOTO 10010
```

```
10050  RETURN
11000  REM  JUDGE ANSWER
11010  IF SA = KE(NX) THEN 11040
11020  HT = 0
11030  RETURN
11040  HT = 1
11050  KE(NX) = 5
11060  RETURN
12000  REM  REWARD
12010  PRINT
12020  PRINT "GREAT!"
12030  PRINT
12040  RETURN
14000  REM  WRONG
14010  PRINT
14020  PRINT "SORRY!"
14030  PRINT
14040  RETURN
15000  REM  SCORE KEEPING
15010  N = N + 1
15020  RETURN
17000  REM  PRINT OUT PROBLEM
17010  L = 12
17020  GOSUB 18000
17030  PRINT Q$(NX)
17040  PRINT
17050  PRINT "    1. ";A1$(NX)
17060  PRINT "    2. ";A2$(NX)
17070  PRINT "    3. ";A3$(NX)
17080  PRINT "    4. ";A4$(NX)
17090  L = 8
17100  GOSUB 18000
17110  RETURN
18000  REM  PRINT LINES
18010  FOR I = 1 TO L
18020  PRINT
18030  NEXT I
18040  RETURN
19000  REM  DELAY
19010  FOR I = 1 TO D
19020  NEXT I
19030  RETURN
20000  REM  CLOSING
20010  L = 12
20020  GOSUB 18000
20030  PRINT "IT TOOK ";N;" TRIES TO GET"
20040  PRINT TL;" PROBLEMS CORRECT!"
20050  END
21000  REM  DATA
21010  DATA "HOW MANY CALORIES IN ONE TEASPOON OF    GRANULATED SU
       GAR?"
21020  DATA  15,25,40,50,2
21030  DATA "HOW MANY BONES ARE IN THE HUMAN BODY?"
21040  DATA 150,192,206,218,3
21050  DATA  "HOW MUCH DID IT COST TO SEND A POST    CARD IN 1980
       ?"
```

```
21060   DATA  6 CENTS,8 CENTS, 10 CENTS,12 CENTS,3
21070   DATA "HOW MANY OCEANS ARE THERE?"
21080   DATA 4,5,6,7,4
21090   DATA "WHAT STATE WAS THE LAST TO JOIN THE     UNITED STATES
        ?"
21100   DATA HAWAII,ALASKA,ARIZONA,UTAH,1
21110   DATA "AT WHAT TEMPERATURE DOES WATER BOIL?"
21120   DATA  50 DEGREES C.,75 DEGREES C.,100 DGREES C.,125 DEGREES
        C.,3
21130   DATA "WHAT IS THE CLOSEST PLANET TO THE SUN?"
21140   DATA  EARTH,MERCURY,VENUS,MARS,2
21150   DATA "IF YOUR BIRTHDAY IS SEPTEMBER 16, WHAT  IS YOUR ZODIA
        C SIGN?"
21160   DATA CANCER,PISCES,ARIES,VIRGO,4
21170   DATA "HOW MANY SIDES DOES A HEXAGON HAVE?"
21180   DATA 4,5,6,8,3
21190   DATA "HOW MANY LINES MAKE A MUSICAL STAFF?"
21200   DATA 4,5,6,7,2
21210   DATA "WHAT IS THE NATIONAL ANTHEM OF THE     UNITED STATES
        ?"
21220   DATA  AMERICA,AMERICA THE BEAUTIFUL,STARS AND STRIPES FOREV
        ER,STAR SPANGLED BANNER,4
21230   DATA "WHAT IS THE REAL NAME OF THE FONZ?"
21240   DATA JAMES STEWART,HENRY WINKLER,DUSTIN HOFFMAN,JOHN DAVIDS
        ON,2
21250   DATA  "HOW MANY DAYS DOES IT TAKE FOR MARS TO  GO AROUND TH
        E SUN?"
21260   DATA 365,489.2,521.5,686.9,4
21270   DATA "WHAT IS THE CAPITAL OF ILLINOIS?
21280   DATA SPRINGFIELD,INDIANAPOLIS,AUSTIN,MADISON,1
21290   DATA "WHAT IS THE LARGEST RIVER IN THE WORLD?"
21300   DATA MISSISSIPPI,NILE,AMAZON,RHINE,3
21310   DATA "WHAT IS THE HIGHEST MOUNTAIN IN THE WORLD?"
21320   DATA MOUNT MCKINLEY,MT ST. HELENS,MOUNT DORA,MOUNT EVEREST,
        4
21330   DATA "WHEN IT IS 5:00 A.M. IN FLORIDA WHAT TIME IS IT IN CA
        LIFORNIA?"
21340   DATA "2:00 A.M.","4:00 A.M.","6:00 A.M.","8:00 A.M.",1
21350   DATA "WHAT IS THE CAPITAL OF SPAIN?"
21360   DATA  PARIS,MADRID,LISBON,BERLIN,2
21370   DATA "WHAT IS THE SQUARE ROOT OF 256?"
21380   DATA 14,15,16,18,3
21390   DATA "IN WHICH FOOD WOULD THE MOST PROTEIN BE FOUND?"
21400   DATA  APPLE,CHICKEN,BREAD,LETTUCE,2
```

          * -->TABLE OF VARIABLES<--

A1$(*) – ANSWER 1
1020 1040 17050

A2$(*) – ANSWER 2
1020 1040 17060

A3$(*) – ANSWER 3
1020 1040 17070

A4$(*) — ANSWER 4
1020 1040 17080

C — NUMBER OF PROBLEMS ANSWERED
4030 4060 4060 4070

D — DELAY
2060 4170 4210 19010

HT — HIT
4140 11020 11040

I — COUNTER
1030 1040 1040 1040 1040 1040 1040 1050 2010 2050 18010
18030 19010 19020

J — COUNTER
2020 2030

KE(*) — KEYS
1020 1040 4020 11010 11050

L — LINES OF SCROLLING
2080 2220 17010 17090 18010 20010

N — NUMBER OF TRIES
15010 15010 20030

NA$ — NAME
2120 2150

NX — NUMBER IN SEQUENCE
4020 10010 10010 10020 10030 11010 11050 17030 17050 17060
17070 17080

Q$(*) — QUESTIONS
1020 1040 17030

S$ — STUDENT ANSWER
2260

SA — STUDENT ANSWER
4100 4110 4110 11010

TL — NUMBER OF QUESTIONS IN LIST
1010 1020 1020 1020 1020 1020 1020 1030 4070 10020 20040

END OF VAR. LIST

SAMPLE RUN

]RUN
    TRIVIA QUIZ   TRIVIA QUIZ
WHAT IS YOUR NAME?
?MARLA
I'M HAPPY TO MEET YOU, MARLA.

96

THIS IS A QUIZ WHICH COVERS A WIDE
VARIETY OF TOPICS. I WILL ASK YOU
QUESTIONS, AND YOU PICK THE NUMBER OF
OF THE RIGHT ANSWER.
READY? PUSH THE 'RETURN' OR 'ENTER'
KEY TO BEGIN.
?
HOW MANY CALORIES IN ONE TEASPOON OF   GRANULATED SUGAR?
    1. 15
    2. 25
    3. 40
    4. 50
TYPE IN A 1, 2, 3, OR 4?1
SORRY!
WE WILL TRY THAT ONE AGAIN LATER!
HOW MANY BONES ARE IN THE HUMAN BODY?
    1. 150
    2. 192
    3. 206
    4. 218
TYPE IN A 1, 2, 3, OR 4?4
SORRY!
WE WILL TRY THAT ONE AGAIN LATER!
HOW MUCH DID IT COST TO SEND A POST   CARD IN 1980?
    1. 6 CENTS
    2. 8 CENTS
    3. 10 CENTS
    4. 12 CENTS
TYPE IN A 1, 2, 3, OR 4?2
SORRY!
WE WILL TRY THAT ONE AGAIN LATER!
HOW MANY OCEANS ARE THERE?
    1. 4
    2. 5
    3. 6
    4. 7
TYPE IN A 1, 2, 3, OR 4?7
TYPE IN A 1, 2, 3, OR 4?4
GREAT!
WHAT STATE WAS THE LAST TO JOIN THE   UNITED STATES?
    1. HAWAII
    2. ALASKA
    3. ARIZONA
    4. UTAH
TYPE IN A 1, 2, 3, OR 4?2
SORRY!
WE WILL TRY THAT ONE AGAIN LATER!
AT WHAT TEMPERATURE DOES WATER BOIL?
    1. 50 DEGREES C.
    2. 75 DEGREES C.
    3. 100 DGREES C.
    4. 125 DEGREES C.
TYPE IN A 1, 2, 3, OR 4?3
GREAT!
WHAT IS THE CLOSEST PLANET TO THE SUN?
    1. EARTH

```
        2. MERCURY
        3. VENUS
        4. MARS
TYPE IN A 1, 2, 3, OR 4?2
GREAT!
```

BRANCHING PROGRAMS

Branching programs allow individual learners to take different routes through the instruction, depending on how much they know and how fast they learn. The micro-computer is an ideal vehicle for these programs because it allows instant access to any part of any program. The following selection of four program listings and sample runs was chosen to demonstrate the methodology by which branching programming is used to instruct the learner in different subject areas, such as mathematics, metric conversion, and sentence grammar.

FACTOR GAME

PROGRAM DESCRIPTION

This is an interesting instructional game on factoring numbers. The computer gives you an initial quiz (pre-test) to find out if you know what factors of numbers are all about. If you obtain all of the answers correctly, then you don't need to receive instruction on factors. On the other hand, for those of you who may have wrong answers, the computer will give you a lesson on factors before you can play the game.

In the factor game you compete against the computer. To start the game, the computer displays a set of numbers. You then select a number and you add the amount of the number to your score. The computer will select all of the factors of the number you chose except the number itself. It then adds the amounts of the numbers selected to its score. The game is played until the original list of numbers selected by the computer is completed. The object of the game is to try and select numbers that do not have many factors of that number left in the list. Otherwise, the computer will gobble up all of the numbers in the list and beat you soundly!

PROGRAM NOTES

When a large maximum number is selected, the list of numbers will wrap around two or more lines. See if you can come up with a subroutine for your computer to neatly present these lines without splitting a number between the end of one line and the beginning of another.

```
100  REM  FACTOR GAME BY GARY ORWIG
2000  REM  INTRODUCTION
2010 L = 12
2020  GOSUB 18000
2030  PRINT "          FACTORS"
2040  GOSUB 18000
2050 D = 1000
2060  GOSUB 19000
2070  GOSUB 18000
2080  PRINT "WHAT IS YOUR NAME?"
2090  GOSUB 18000
2100  INPUT NA$
2110  GOSUB 18000
2120  PRINT "I'M HAPPY TO MEET YOU, ";NA$;"."
2130  GOSUB 18000
2140  GOSUB 19000
2150  GOSUB 18000
2160  PRINT "THIS IS A GAME OF FACTORS.  BEFORE WE"
2170  PRINT "GO VERY FAR, I'D BETTER CHECK TO MAKE"
2180  PRINT "SURE YOU KNOW JUST WHAT FACTORS ARE!"
2190  PRINT
2200  PRINT "WHAT NUMBER IS NOT A FACTOR OF 12?"
2210  PRINT
2220  PRINT "     1"
2230  PRINT "     3"
2240  PRINT "     4"
2250  PRINT "     6"
2260  PRINT "     8"
2270  PRINT "    12"
2280 L = 4
2290  GOSUB 18000
2300  INPUT SA
2310  IF SA = 8 THEN 2730
2320  GOSUB 18000
2330  PRINT " 1, 3, 4, 6, 8, 12"
2340  PRINT
2350  PRINT "THE NUMBER '8' IS THE ONLY NUMBER LISTED"
2360  PRINT "WHICH IS NOT A FACTOR OF 12!"
2370  PRINT
2380  PRINT "IT IS THE ONLY NUMBER IN THE SET WHICH"
2390  PRINT "HAS A REMAINDER WHEN DIVIDED INTO"
2400  PRINT "THE NUMBER '12.'  ALL OF THE OTHER"
2410  PRINT "NUMBERS IN THE SET DIVIDE INTO 12"
2420  PRINT "EVENLY."
2430  PRINT
2440  PRINT "ONE NUMBER IS A FACTOR OF ANOTHER"
2450  PRINT "NUMBER IF IT DIVIDES INTO THE NUMBER"
2460  PRINT "EVENLY."
2470  PRINT
2480  GOSUB 17000
2490 L = 12
2500  GOSUB 18000
2510  PRINT "LET'S TRY ONE MORE."
2520  PRINT
```

```
2530 PRINT "WHICH OF THE FOLLOWING IS NOT A FACTOR"
2540 PRINT "OF THE NUMBER 10?"
2550 PRINT
2560 PRINT "     1"
2570 PRINT "     2"
2580 PRINT "     3"
2590 PRINT "     5"
2600 PRINT "     10"
2610 L = 6
2620 GOSUB 18000
2630 INPUT SA
2640 IF SA = 3 THEN 2730
2650 PRINT "THE NUMBER '3' IS THE ONLY NUMBER WHICH"
2660 PRINT "DOES NOT DIVIDE INTO 10 EVENLY!"
2670 PRINT "I THINK WE BETTER BACK UP A BIT, ";NA$
2680 PRINT
2690 GOSUB 17000
2700 L = 12
2710 GOSUB 18000
2720 GOTO 2200
2730 L = 12
2740 GOSUB 18000
2750 PRINT "VERY GOOD, ";NA$;"! I THINK YOU ARE"
2760 PRINT "READY FOR THE GAME!"
2770 GOSUB 18000
2780 D = 2500
2790 GOSUB 19000
2800 GOSUB 18000
3000 REM  INSTRUCTIONS
3010 L = 12
3020 GOSUB 18000
3030 PRINT "THIS GAME IS DIFFICULT TO EXPLAIN,"
3040 PRINT "BUT YOU WILL CATCH ON QUICKLY!"
3050 PRINT
3060 PRINT "I WILL GIVE YOU A SET OF NUMBERS,"
3070 PRINT "LIKE THIS!"
3080 PRINT
3090 PRINT "1 2 3 4 5 6 7 8 9 10"
3100 PRINT
3110 PRINT "WHEN YOU PICK A NUMBER,"
3120 PRINT "LIKE '10,' YOU"
3130 PRINT "GET TO ADD IT TO YOUR SCORE."
3140 L = 5
3150 GOSUB 18000
3160 GOSUB 17000
3170 L = 12
3180 GOSUB 18000
3190 PRINT "BUT.........."
3200 PRINT
3210 PRINT "I GET TO ADD ITS REMAINING FACTORS"
3220 PRINT "(5, 2, AND 1) TO MY SCORE!"
3230 PRINT
3240 PRINT "NOW THE LIST WILL BE MISSING ALL THOSE"
3250 PRINT "NUMBERS!"
3260 PRINT
3270 PRINT "* * 3 4 * 6 7 8 9 *"
```

```
3280  PRINT
3290  PRINT "AND WE START AGAIN!"
3300  PRINT
3310  PRINT "IF YOU PICK A NUMBER WHICH HAS NO "
3320  PRINT "FACTORS LEFT IN THE LIST, I GET IT!"
3330  PRINT "ALSO, I GET ALL THE NUMBERS LEFT OVER"
3340  PRINT "WHEN ALL THE FACTORS ARE GONE!"
3350  PRINT
3360  PRINT
3370  PRINT "READY?"
3380  GOSUB 17000
3390  REM  INITIALIZATION
3400  PRINT
3410  PRINT "WHAT IS THE LARGEST NUMBER YOU WANT?"
3420  INPUT MX
3430  DIM FA(MX)
3440  PRINT
3450  PRINT "THE HIGHEST NUMBER WILL BE ";MX;"."
3460  FOR I = 1 TO MX
3470 FA(I) = I
3480  NEXT I
4000  REM  START OF MAIN PROGRAM
4010  PRINT
4020  PRINT "HERE IS THE LIST OF NUMBERS!"
4030  PRINT
4040  FOR I = 1 TO MX
4050  IF FA(I) = 0 THEN 4090
4060  PRINT FA(I);" ";
4070  NEXT I
4080  GOTO 4110
4090  PRINT "* ";
4100  NEXT I
4110  PRINT
5000  REM  INPUT NUMBER
5010  PRINT
5020  PRINT "PICK A NUMBER."
5030  INPUT N
5040  IF N > MX THEN 5070
5050  IF N < 1 THEN 5070
5060  IF FA(N) = N THEN 6000
5070  PRINT
5080  PRINT "THAT NUMBER ISN'T IN THE LIST!"
5090  PRINT "TRY AGAIN!"
5100  GOTO 5030
6000  REM  FIND FACTORS
6010 J = 0
6020  FOR I = 2 TO N
6030 F = N / I
6040  IF F < > INT (F) THEN 6110
6050  IF FA(F) = 0 THEN 6110
6060  PRINT
6070  PRINT "I GET ";F;"!"
6080 CT = CT + F
6090 FA(F) = 0
6100  GOTO 6120
6110 J = J + 1
```

```
6120  NEXT I
6130  IF J = N - 1 THEN 6170
6140 SS = SS + N
6150 FA(N) = 0
6160  GOTO 7000
6170 J = 0
6180 CT = CT + N
6190 FA(N) = 0
6200  PRINT
6210  PRINT "I GET ";N;"! IT HAD NO FACTORS!"
6220  PRINT
7000  REM  CHECK REM. #'S FOR FACTORS
7010  FOR I = 1 TO MX
7020 J = MX - I + 1
7030  FOR K = 2 TO J
7040 F = J / K
7050  IF F < > INT (F) THEN 7130
7060  IF FA(F) = 0 THEN 7130
7070  PRINT
7080  PRINT "YOUR SCORE IS: ";SS
7090  PRINT
7100  PRINT "MY SCORE IS: ";CT
7110  PRINT
7120  GOTO 4000
7130  NEXT K
7140  NEXT I
7150  PRINT
8000  REM  NO FACTORS LEFT
8010  FOR I = 1 TO MX
8020  IF FA(I) = 0 THEN 8070
8030  PRINT
8040  PRINT "I GET ";FA(I)"!"
8050 CT = CT + FA(I)
8060 FA(I) = 0
8070  NEXT I
8080  PRINT
8090  PRINT
8100  PRINT "YOUR FINAL TOTAL IS: ";SS
8110  PRINT
8120  PRINT "MY FINAL TOTAL IS: ";CT
8130  PRINT
8140  IF CT > SS THEN  PRINT "I WIN, ";NA$;"!"
8150  IF SS > CT THEN  PRINT "YOU WIN, ";NA$;"!"
8160  IF SS = CT THEN  PRINT "IT'S A TIE, ";NA$;"!"
8170  END
17000  REM  PAUSE
17010  PRINT "PUSH 'RETURN' OR 'ENTER',"; REM  FOR PET PRESS ANY L
    ETTER BEFORE PRESSING RETURN
17020  INPUT SA$
17030  RETURN
18000  REM  SCROLLING
18010  FOR S = 1 TO L
18020  PRINT
18030  NEXT S
18040  RETURN
19000  REM  DELAY
```

```
19010  FOR S = 1 TO D
19020  NEXT S
19030  RETURN
```

* -->TABLE OF VARIABLES<--

CT - COMPUTER SCORE
6080 6080 6180 6180 7100 8050 8050 8120 8140 8150 8160

D - DELAY
2050 2780 19010

F - FACTOR
6030 6040 6040 6050 6070 6080 6090 7040 7050 7050 7060

FA(*) - LIST OF NUMBERS
3430 3470 4050 4060 5060 6050 6090 6150 6190 7060 8020
8040 8050 8060

I - COUNTER
3460 3470 3470 3480 4040 4050 4060 4070 4100 6020 6030
6120 7010 7020 7140 8010 8020 8040 8050 8060 8070

J - COUNTER
6010 6110 6110 6130 6170 7020 7030 7040

K - COUNTER
7030 7040 7130

L - LINES OF SCROLLING
2010 2280 2490 2610 2700 2730 3010 3140 3170 18010

MX - HIGHEST NUMBER
3420 3430 3450 3460 4040 5040 7010 7020 8010

N - COUNTER
5030 5040 5050 5060 5060 6020 6030 6130 6140 6150 6180
6190 6210

NA$ - NAME
2100 2120 2670 2750 8140 8150 8160

S - COUNTER
18010 18030 19010 19020

SA - STUDENT ANSWER
2300 2310 2630 2640

SA$ - STUDENT ANSWER
17020

SS - STUDENT SCORE
6140 6140 7080 8100 8140 8150 8160

END OF VAR. LIST

SAMPLE RUN

```
JRUN
            FACTORS
WHAT IS YOUR NAME?
?RONDA
I'M HAPPY TO MEET YOU, RONDA.
THIS IS A GAME OF FACTORS.  BEFORE WE
GO VERY FAR, I'D BETTER CHECK TO MAKE
SURE YOU KNOW JUST WHAT FACTORS ARE!
WHAT NUMBER IS NOT A FACTOR OF 12?
        1
        3
        4
        6
        8
        12
?8

VERY GOOD, RONDA!  I THINK YOU ARE
READY FOR THE GAME!
THIS GAME IS DIFFICULT TO EXPLAIN,
BUT YOU WILL CATCH ON QUICKLY!
I WILL GIVE YOU A SET OF NUMBERS,
LIKE THIS:
1 2 3 4 5 6 7 8 9 10
WHEN YOU PICK A NUMBER,
LIKE '10,' YOU
GET TO ADD IT TO YOUR SCORE.
PUSH 'RETURN' OR 'ENTER'.
?
BUT...........
I GET TO ADD ITS REMAINING FACTORS
(5, 2, AND 1) TO MY SCORE!
NOW THE LIST WILL BE MISSING ALL THOSE
NUMBERS!
* * 3 4 * 6 7 8 9 *
AND WE START AGAIN!
IF YOU PICK A NUMBER WHICH HAS NO
FACTORS LEFT IN THE LIST, I GET IT!
ALSO, I GET ALL THE NUMBERS LEFT OVER
WHEN ALL THE FACTORS ARE GONE!
READY?
PUSH 'RETURN' OR 'ENTER'.
?
WHAT IS THE LARGEST NUMBER YOU WANT?
?10
THE HIGHEST NUMBER WILL BE 10.
HERE IS THE LIST OF NUMBERS:
1 2 3 4 5 6 7 8 9 10
PICK A NUMBER.
?5
I GET 1!
YOUR SCORE IS: 5
MY SCORE IS: 1
HERE IS THE LIST OF NUMBERS:
* 2 3 4 * 6 7 8 9 10
```

```
PICK A NUMBER.
?8
I GET 4!
I GET 2!
YOUR SCORE IS: 13
MY SCORE IS: 7
HERE IS THE LIST OF NUMBERS:
*  *  3  *  *  6  7  *  9  10
PICK A NUMBER.
?9
I GET 3!
I GET 6!
I GET 7!
I GET 10!
YOUR FINAL TOTAL IS: 22
MY FINAL TOTAL IS: 33
I WIN, RONDA!
]
```

MATH TEACHER

PROGRAM DESCRIPTION

This is an excellent program for practicing addition, subtraction, multiplication, and division on a more difficult scale than MATH TUTOR. The computer presents math problems which become more difficult as you answer the problems correctly. If you answer the questions incorrectly, the computer will adjust its math problems according to your skill level.

PROGRAM NOTES

1. Compare this program to "Math Tutor" to see how they differ. Pay close attention to the variable "MX" and see how it changes.

2. You may want to provide the answer after several tries.

PROGRAM LISTING

```
100  REM  MATH TEACHER BY GARY ORWIG
2000 REM  INTRODUCTION
2010 PRINT
2020 PRINT "*******************************************"
2030 PRINT
2040 PRINT "        MATH TEACHER"
2050 PRINT
2060 PRINT "*******************************************"
2070 FOR T = 1 TO 1000
2080 NEXT T
2090 PRINT "WHAT IS YOUR NAME";
```

```
2100  INPUT NA$
2110  PRINT
2120  PRINT
2130  PRINT "I AM HAPPY TO MEET YOU, ";NA$;"."
2140  PRINT "WE ARE GOING TO PRACTICE SOME"
2150  PRINT "MATH PROBLEMS."
2160  REM  OPERATING PARAMETERS
2170  PRINT
2180  PRINT
2190  PRINT "WOULD YOU LIKE TO PRACTICE:"
2200  PRINT "1. ADDITION"
2210  PRINT "2. SUBTRACTION"
2220  PRINT "3. MULTIPLICATION"
2230  PRINT "4. DIVISION"
2240  PRINT
2250  PRINT "(TYPE IN THE NUMBER YOU WANT)"
2260  INPUT CH$
2270  IF CH$ = "1" THEN 2350
2280  IF CH$ = "2" THEN 2350
2290  IF CH$ = "3" THEN 2350
2300  IF CH$ = "4" THEN 2350
2310  PRINT
2320  PRINT "PLEASE PAY ATTENTION, "NA$
2330  PRINT "TYPE IN ONLY A 1,2,3, OR 4!"
2340  GOTO 2200
2350  PRINT
2360  PRINT "HOW MANY PROBLEMS DO YOU"
2370  PRINT "WANT, ";NA$;
2380  INPUT NU
2390  PRINT
2400  PRINT "VERY GOOD, ";NU;" IT WILL BE!"
2410  PRINT
2420  PRINT "DO YOU KNOW WHAT LEVEL YOU WANT TO"
2430  PRINT "START AT (YES OR NO)?"
2440  INPUT SA$
2450  IF SA$ = "YES" THEN 2510
2460  PRINT "OK, I WILL START OUT EASY AND GET"
2470  PRINT "HARDER AS WE GO."
2480  MX = 10
2490  PRINT
2500  GOTO 2540
2510  PRINT "WHAT LEVEL DO YOU WANT TO START AT?"
2520  INPUT MX
2530  PRINT "OK, ";MX;" IT WILL BE!"
2540  IF CH$ = "4" THEN 2680
2550  PRINT
2560  PRINT "I AM NOW READY TO START!"
2570  PRINT
2580  FOR T = 1 TO 500
2590  NEXT T
2600  PRINT "HERE WE GO!!"
2610  FOR T = 1 TO 500
2620  NEXT T
2630  PRINT
2640  PRINT
2650  PRINT
```

```
2660  PRINT
2670  GOTO 4000
2680  PRINT
2690  PRINT "DO YOU WANT DIVISION PROBLEMS"
2700  PRINT "WITH REMAINDERS (YES OR NO)";
2710  INPUT RE$
2720  IF RE$ = "YES" THEN 2780
2730  IF RE$ = "NO" THEN 2780
2740  PRINT
2750  PRINT "JUST TYPE A 'YES' OR 'NO' PLEASE"
2760  PRINT
2770  GOTO 2680
2780  GOTO 2550
4000  REM  MAIN PROGRAM
4010  IF CH$ = "1" THEN 4730
4020  IF CH$ = "2" THEN 4570
4030  IF CH$ = "3" THEN 4470
4040  IF RE$ = "YES" THEN 4220
4050  REM  DIVISION WITHOUT REMAINDER
4060  GOSUB 10000
4070  NP = 1
4080  IF A < B THEN 4110
4090  C = A / B
4100  GOTO 4150
4110  D = B
4120  B = A
4130  A = D
4140  GOTO 4090
4150  IF C - INT (C) > 0 THEN 4060
4160  PRINT A;" DIVIDED BY ";B;" EQUALS";
4170  INPUT SA
4180  GOSUB 11000
4190  GOSUB 12000
4200  GOSUB 15000
4210  GOTO 4050
4220  REM  DIVISION WITH REMAINDER
4230  GOSUB 10000
4240  NP = 1
4250  IF A < B THEN 4290
4260  C = INT (A / B)
4270  RE = A - (C * B)
4280  GOTO 4330
4290  D = B
4300  B = A
4310  A = D
4320  GOTO 4260
4330  PRINT
4340  PRINT A;" DIVIDED BY ";B;" EQUALS?"
4350  PRINT "WHAT IS THE WHOLE NUMBER";
4360  INPUT SA
4370  GOSUB 11000
4380  GOSUB 12000
4390  PRINT "AND WHAT IS THE REMAINDER?"
4400  PRINT "TYPE IN 0 IF THERE IS NONE."
4410  INPUT SA
4420  C = RE
```

```
4430  GOSUB 11000
4440  GOSUB 12000
4450  GOSUB 15000
4460  GOTO 4220
4470  REM  MULTIPLICATION
4480  GOSUB 10000
4490 NP = 1
4500 C = A * B
4510  PRINT A;" TIMES ";B;" EQUALS";
4520  INPUT SA
4530  GOSUB 11000
4540  GOSUB 12000
4550  GOSUB 15000
4560  GOTO 4470
4570  REM  SUBTRACTION
4580  GOSUB 10000
4590 NP = 1
4600  IF A < B THEN 4630
4610 C = A - B
4620  GOTO 4670
4630 D = B
4640 B = A
4650 A = D
4660  GOTO 4610
4670  PRINT A;" MINUS ";B;" EQUALS";
4680  INPUT SA
4690  GOSUB 11000
4700  GOSUB 12000
4710  GOSUB 15000
4720  GOTO 4570
4730  REM  ADDITION
4740  GOSUB 10000
4750 NP = 1
4760 C = A + B
4770  PRINT A;" PLUS ";B;" EQUALS";
4780  INPUT SA
4790  GOSUB 11000
4800  GOSUB 12000
4810  GOSUB 15000
4820  GOTO 4730
10000  REM   RANDOMIZATION - CHANGE 'RND (1)' TO 'RND (0)' FOR TRS
   -80 AND PET!
10010 A =  INT (MX * RND (1)) + 1
10020 B =  INT (MX * RND (1)) + 1
10030  RETURN
11000  REM  JUDGE ANSWER
11010  IF SA = C THEN 11090
11020  GOSUB 14000
11030 TR = TR + 1
11040  IF TR = 3 THEN 16000
11050  PRINT
11060  PRINT "TRY AGAIN!"
11070  INPUT SA
11080  GOTO 11010
11090 HT = 1
11100  RETURN
```

```
12000  REM   REWARDS - CHANGE 'RND (1)' TO 'RND (0)' FOR TRS-80 AN
    D PET!
12010  IF HT = 0 THEN  RETURN
12020  MX = MX + 10
12030  PRINT
12040  N =  INT (5 * RND (1)) + 1
12050  ON N GOTO 12070,12090,12110,12130,12150
12060  REM  REWARDS
12070  PRINT "GREAT!"
12080  RETURN
12090  PRINT "SUPER!"
12100  RETURN
12110  PRINT "FANTASTIC!"
12120  RETURN
12130  PRINT "YOU'RE REALLY GOING NOW, ";NA$
12140  RETURN
12150  PRINT "THAT'S GREAT, ";NA$
12160  RETURN
14000  REM   WRONG - CHANGE 'RND (1)' TO 'RND (0)' FOR TRS-80 AND
    PET!
14010  PRINT
14020  IF NP = 0 THEN 14070
14030  WR = WR + 1
14040  NP = 0
14050  MX = MX - 10
14060  IF MX < 1 THEN MX = 10
14070  N =  INT (5 * RND (1)) + 1
14080  ON N GOTO 14100,14120,14140,14160,14180
14090  REM  WRONGS
14100  PRINT "OOPS!"
14110  RETURN
14120  PRINT "LOOK CLOSER, ";NA$
14130  RETURN
14140  PRINT "NO...."
14150  RETURN
14160  PRINT "ARE YOU PAYING ATTENTION, ";NA$
14170  RETURN
14180  PRINT "SORRY!"
14190  RETURN
15000  REM  SCORE KEEPING
15010  TL = TL + 1
15020  IF TL = NU THEN 20000
15030  RETURN
16000  REM  GIVE ANSWER
16010  HT = 0
16020  TR = 0
16030  PRINT "THE CORRECT ANSWER IS ";C
16040  PRINT "LET'S TRY ANOTHER!"
16050  RETURN
20000  REM  CLOSING
20010  PRINT
20020  PRINT "THAT'S ALL!"
20030  PRINT
20040  PRINT "I HOPE YOU HAD FUN, ";NA$
20050  PRINT
20060  PRINT
```

```
20070  PRINT
20080  PRINT "YOU HAD ";NU - WR;" OUT OF "
20090  PRINT NU;" PROBLEMS CORRECT!"
20100  PRINT "YOU FINISHED AT LEVEL ";MX;"!"
20110  END
```

                    * -->TABLE OF VARIABLES<--

A - ONE NUMBER
4080 4090 4120 4130 4160 4250 4260 4270 4300 4310 4340
4500 4510 4600 4610 4640 4650 4670 4760 4770 10010

B - THE OTHER NUMBER
4080 4090 4110 4120 4160 4250 4260 4270 4290 4300 4340
4500 4510 4600 4610 4630 4640 4670 4760 4770 10020

C - CORRECT ANSWER
4090 4150 4150 4260 4270 4420 4500 4610 4760 11010 16030

CH$ - STUDENT CHOICE
2260 2270 2280 2290 2300 2540 4010 4020 4030

D - TRANSFER VARIABLE
4110 4130 4290 4310 4630 4650

HT - HIT
11090 12010 16010

MX - MAXIMUM FOR A AND B
2480 2520 2530 10010 10020 12020 12020 14050 14050 14060
14060 20100

N - RANDOM NUMBER
12040 12050 14070 14080

NA$ - NAME
2100 2130 2320 2370 12130 12150 14120 14160 20040

NP - FLAG FOR WRONG ANSWER
4070 4240 4490 4590 4750 14020 14040

NU - NUMBER OF PROBLEMS
2380 2400 15020 20080 20090

RE - REMAINDER
4270 4420

RE$ - FLAG FOR DIVISION WITH REMAINDER
2710 2720 2730 4040

SA - STUDENT ANSWER
4170 4360 4410 4520 4680 4780 11010 11070

SA$ - STUDENT ANSWER
2440 2450

113

T – DELAY
2070 2080 2580 2590 2610 2620

TL – NUMBER OF PROBLEMS WORKED
15010 15010 15020

TR – NUMBER OF TRIES
11030 11030 11040 16020

WR – NUMBER WRONG
14030 14030 20080

END OF VAR. LIST

SAMPLE RUN

]RUN
****
         MATH TEACHER
****
WHAT IS YOUR NAME?JENNIFER
I AM HAPPY TO MEET YOU, JENNIFER.
WE ARE GOING TO PRACTICE SOME
MATH PROBLEMS.
WOULD YOU LIKE TO PRACTICE:
1. ADDITION
2. SUBTRACTION
3. MULTIPLICATION
4. DIVISION
(TYPE IN THE NUMBER YOU WANT)
?1
HOW MANY PROBLEMS DO YOU
WANT, JENNIFER?3
VERY GOOD, 3 IT WILL BE!
DO YOU KNOW WHAT LEVEL YOU WANT TO
START AT (YES OR NO)?
?NO
OK, I WILL START OUT EASY AND GET
HARDER AS WE GO.
I AM NOW READY TO START!
HERE WE GO!!
5 PLUS 8 EQUALS?13
GREAT!
2 PLUS 8 EQUALS?10
SUPER!
26 PLUS 18 EQUALS?42
SORRY!
TRY AGAIN!
?44
YOU'RE REALLY GOING NOW, JENNIFER
THAT'S ALL!
I HOPE YOU HAD FUN, JENNIFER
YOU HAD 2 OUT OF
3 PROBLEMS CORRECT!
YOU FINISHED AT LEVEL 30!
]

114

PROGRAM DESCRIPTION

Understanding the metric system is essential in communicating knowledge among the nations of the world as well as developing skills to work within the realms of science. In this program the computer gives you an initial quiz (pre-test) on metrics and if you get all of the answers correct you don't have to continue the program. For those of you who don't receive a perfect score on the pre-test, the computer instructs you on metrics and then gives you a test at the end of the instruction (a post-test). If you receive less than a perfect score on the post-test, the computer will send you back to the part of the instruction that you missed in the quiz at the end.

PROGRAM NOTES

1. Vary the text and questions to match your needs.

2. Notice line 4500. It allows either "1" or "2.5" to be entered as the correct answer. Consider using A, B, C, or D as the multiple choice selections.

PROGRAM LISTING

```
100  REM  METRICS BY GARY ORWIG
2000 REM  INTRODUCTION
2010 L = 12
2020 GOSUB 18000
2030 PRINT "        METRICS"
2040 GOSUB 18000
2050 D = 1000
```

```
2060  GOSUB 19000
2070  GOSUB 18000
2080  PRINT "THIS IS A PROGRAM ABOUT THE METRIC"
2090  PRINT "SYSTEM."
2100  PRINT
2110  PRINT "WOULD YOU LIKE TO TAKE A QUIZ TO SEE"
2120  PRINT "IF YOU ALREADY KNOW ABOUT THE METRIC"
2130  PRINT "SYSTEM (YES OR NO)?"
2140  L = 6
2150  GOSUB 18000
2160  INPUT SA$
2170  IF SA$ = "YES" THEN 2220
2180  PRINT "LET'S LOOK AT THE METRIC SYSTEM!"
2190  D = 1000
2200  GOSUB 19000
2210  GOTO 3000
2220  GOSUB 7000
2230  GOTO 20000
3000  REM  GUIDING PROGRAM
3010  GOSUB 4000
3020  GOSUB 5000
3030  GOSUB 6000
3040  GOSUB 7000
3050  GOTO 20000
4000  REM  DISTANCE
4010  L = 24
4020  GOSUB 18000
4030  PRINT "THE BASIC UNIT OF LENGTH IN THE METRIC"
4040  PRINT "SYSTEM IS THE 'METER.'  AT FIRST THE"
4050  PRINT "METER WAS DEFINED AS ONE TEN MILLIONTH"
4060  PRINT "THE DISTANCE FROM THE EQUATOR TO THE"
4070  PRINT "NORTH POLE.  HOWEVER, IT SOON BECAME"
4080  PRINT "EVIDENT THAT THIS DISTANCE IS VERY HARD"
4090  PRINT "TO MEASURE EVERY TIME THE STANDARD"
4100  PRINT "NEEDED TO BE CHECKED!"
4110  PRINT
4120  PRINT "PRESENTLY THE METER IS DEFINED ON THE"
4130  PRINT "BASIS OF A VERY ACCURATELY MEASURED"
4140  PRINT "WAVELENGTH OF LIGHT."
4150  L = 6
4160  GOSUB 18000
4170  GOSUB 17000
4180  L = 24
4190  GOSUB 18000
4200  PRINT "THE METRIC UNITS OF LENGTH WHICH ARE"
4210  PRINT "COMMONLY USED ARE:"
4220  PRINT
4230  PRINT "   MILLIMETER"
4240  PRINT "   CENTIMETER"
4250  PRINT "   METER"
4260  PRINT "   KILOMETER"
4270  PRINT
4280  PRINT "THE MILLIMETER IS 1/1000 OF A METER"
4290  PRINT "              1/10 OF A CENTIMETER"
4300  PRINT
4310  PRINT "THE CENTIMETER IS 1/100 OF A METER"
```

```
4320  PRINT
4330  PRINT "THE KILOMETER IS 1000 METERS."
4340 L = 6
4350  GOSUB 18000
4360  GOSUB 17000
4370 L = 24
4380  GOSUB 18000
4390  PRINT "LET'S TRY A COUPLE OF SIMPLE CONVERSION"
4400  PRINT "PROBLEMS."
4410  PRINT
4420  PRINT "25 MILLIMETERS EQUALS:"
4430  PRINT "    1.  2.5"
4440  PRINT "    2.  .25"
4450  PRINT "    3. 32."
4460  PRINT "        CENTIMETERS"
4470 L = 8
4480  GOSUB 18000
4490  INPUT SA
4500  IF SA = 2.5 THEN SA = 1
4510  ON SA GOTO 4520,4540,4570
4520  GOSUB 12000
4530  GOTO 4600
4540  PRINT "10 MILLIMETERS EQUAL 1 CENTIMETER."
4550  PRINT "25 MILLIMETERS EQUAL ? CENTIMETERS.";
4560  GOTO 4490
4570  GOSUB 11010
4580  PRINT
4590  GOTO 4410
4600  PRINT "HERE IS ANOTHER PROBLEM."
4610  PRINT
4620  PRINT ".52 KILOMETERS EQUALS:"
4630  PRINT
4640  PRINT "   1. 52 METERS
4650  PRINT "   2. 760 METERS
4660  PRINT "   3. 520 METERS
4670  PRINT
4680 L = 7
4690  GOSUB 18000
4700  INPUT SA
4710  IF SA = 520 THEN SA = 3
4720  ON SA GOTO 4730,4760,4790
4730  PRINT "1 KILOMETER EQUALS 1000 METERS"
4740  PRINT ".52 KILOMETERS EQUALS ? METERS";
4750  GOTO 4700
4760  GOSUB 11010
4770  PRINT "THINK ABOUT IT!"
4780  GOTO 4610
4790  GOSUB 12000
4800  RETURN
5000  REM  VOLUME
5010 L = 12
5020  GOSUB 18000
5030  PRINT "THE METRIC UNIT FOR VOLUME IS BASED"
5040  PRINT "UPON THE METRIC UNIT OF LENGTH."
5050  PRINT
5060  PRINT "IF A CUBE WERE CONSTRUCTED SO THAT IT"
```

```
5070  PRINT "WAS EXACTLY .1 METERS ON EACH SIDE,"
5080  PRINT "IT COULD HOLD ONE LITER OF MATERIAL."
5090  PRINT
5100  PRINT "THE LITER, THEN, IS THE BASIC METRIC"
5110  PRINT "UNIT FOR VOLUME.  THE LITER IS NOT TOO"
5120  PRINT "DIFFERENT IN SIZE FROM THE QUART."
5130  PRINT
5140  PRINT "IF A CUBE WERE FORMED EXACTLY ONE"
5150  PRINT "CENTIMETER ON A SIDE, WE WOULD CALL IT"
5160  PRINT "A 'CUBIC CENTIMETER.'  THIS VERY SMALL"
5170  PRINT "UNIT IS EXACTLY .001 LITERS, SO WE"
5180  PRINT "ALSO CALL IT A 'MILLILITER.'"
5190  PRINT
5200  PRINT "THE TERM 'CUBIC CENTIMETER' OR 'CC' AND"
5210  PRINT "THE TERM 'MILLILITER' OR 'ML' BOTH"
5220  PRINT "MEAN THE SAME AMOUNT OF VOLUME - "
5230  PRINT "ONE ONE THOUSANDTH OF A LITER."
5240  PRINT
5250  GOSUB 17000
5260 L = 12
5270  GOSUB 18000
5280  PRINT "HERE ARE A COUPLE OF QUESTIONS:"
5290  PRINT
5300  PRINT
5310  PRINT "HOW MANY CUBIC CENTIMETERS ARE IN A "
5320  PRINT "MILLITER?"
5330  PRINT
5340  PRINT "     1,  1"
5350  PRINT "     2,  2"
5360  PRINT "     3, 10"
5370 L = 9
5380  GOSUB 18000
5390  INPUT SA
5400  IF SA = 10 THEN SA = 3
5410  ON SA GOTO 5420,5450,5470
5420  GOSUB 12000
5430  PRINT "YOU ARE RIGHT!  THEY ARE THE SAME!"
5440  GOTO 5520
5450  GOSUB 11170
5460  GOTO 5290
5470  PRINT
5480  PRINT "YOU DID NOT READ VERY CLOSELY!"
5490  PRINT "THERE IS SOMETHING VERY 'UNIQUE'"
5500  PRINT "ABOUT THESE TWO UNITS!"
5510  GOTO 5290
5520  PRINT
5530  PRINT "WHAT IS THE VOLUME OF A BOX (IN LITERS)"
5540  PRINT "IF IT MEASURES .50 METERS BY .30 METERS"
5550  PRINT "BY .20 METERS?"
5560  PRINT
5570  PRINT "   1, 50 LITERS"
5580  PRINT "   2, 30 LITERS"
5590  PRINT "   3, 10 LITERS"
5600 L = 8
5610  GOSUB 18000
5620  INPUT SA
```

```
5630  IF SA = 50 THEN SA = 1
5640  IF SA = 30 THEN SA = 2
5650  IF SA = 10 THEN SA = 3
5660  ON SA GOTO 5690,5670,5690
5670  GOSUB 12000
5680  GOTO 5860
5690  PRINT
5700  PRINT
5710  PRINT "REMEMBER THAT A LITER IS DEFINED AS THE"
5720  PRINT "VOLUME OF A CUBE .10 METERS ON EACH"
5730  PRINT "SIDE. ALTHOUGH THE TERM FOR .10 METER"
5740  PRINT "ISN'T USED VERY MUCH, IT IS CALLED A"
5750  PRINT "'DECIMETER.' IF YOU CONVERT THE METER"
5760  PRINT "MEASUREMENTS TO DECIMETERS (.5 METERS"
5770  PRINT "EQUALS 5. DECIMETERS) AND MULTIPLY ALL"
5780  PRINT "THREE TOGETHER, YOU WILL END UP WITH"
5790  PRINT "THE VOLUME IN CUBIC DECIMETERS OR"
5800  PRINT "WHAT WE CALL LITERS!"
5810  PRINT
5820  GOSUB 17000
5830 L = 12
5840  GOSUB 18000
5850  GOTO 5520
5860 L = 12
5870  GOSUB 18000
5880  RETURN
6000  REM  MASS
6010 L = 12
6020  GOSUB 18000
6030  PRINT "THE METRIC UNIT FOR MASS IS THE 'GRAM.'"
6040  PRINT "ORIGINALLY THE GRAM WAS DEFINED AS THE"
6050  PRINT "MASS OF 1 CUBIC CENTIMETER OF WATER"
6060  PRINT "UNDER CONTROLLED CONDITIONS."
6070  PRINT "NOW THERE ARE MORE ACCURATE METHODS FOR"
6080  PRINT "DEFINING THE GRAM."
6090  PRINT
6100  PRINT "SINCE THE GRAM IS A SMALL UNIT OF"
6110  PRINT "MEASURE (A NICKEL HAS A MASS OF ABOUT"
6120  PRINT "5 GRAMS), A LARGER UNIT IS ALSO USED."
6130  PRINT "THE 'KILOGRAM' IS 1000 GRAMS."
6140  PRINT
6150  PRINT
6160  GOSUB 17000
6170  PRINT "HERE ARE A COUPLE OF QUESTIONS."
6180  PRINT
6190 L = 6
6200  GOSUB 18000
6210  PRINT "UNDER CONTROLLED CONDITIONS, WHAT WOULD"
6220  PRINT "BE THE MASS OF 1.0 LITER OF WATER?"
6230  PRINT "    1. 10 GRAMS"
6240  PRINT "    2. 100 GRAMS"
6250  PRINT "    3. 1000 GRAMS"
6260 L = 8
6270  GOSUB 18000
6280  INPUT SA
6290  IF SA = 10 THEN SA = 1
```

```
6300  IF SA = 100 THEN SA = 2
6310  IF SA = 1000 THEN SA = 3
6320  ON SA GOTO 6330,6330,6430
6330 L = 12
6340  GOSUB 18000
6350  PRINT "A LITER CONTAINS 1000 CUBIC CENTIMETERS."
6360  PRINT "SINCE A CUBIC CENTIMETER OF WATER HAS A"
6370  PRINT "MASS OF 1.0 GRAM, WHAT WOULD BE THE"
6380  PRINT "MASS OF 1000 CUBIC CENTIMETERS OF WATER?"
6390 L = 7
6400  GOSUB 18000
6410  GOSUB 17000
6420  GOTO 6190
6430  GOSUB 12000
6440 L = 12
6450  GOSUB 18000
6460  PRINT "HOW MANY GRAMS ARE IN .450 KILOGRAMS?"
6470  PRINT "    1. 45.0 "
6480  PRINT "    2. 450"
6490  PRINT "    3. 900"
6500 L = 9
6510  GOSUB 18000
6520  INPUT SA
6530  IF SA = 45 THEN SA = 1
6540  IF SA = 450 THEN SA = 2
6550  IF SA = 900 THEN SA = 3
6560  ON SA GOTO 6570,6640,6660
6570  GOSUB 11170
6580  PRINT
6590  PRINT "1.0 KILOGRAMS = 1000 GRAMS"
6600  PRINT ".450 KILOGRAMS = ? GRAMS"
6610  PRINT
6620 L = 6
6630  GOTO 6450
6640  GOSUB 12000
6650  GOTO 6680
6660  GOSUB 11010
6670  GOTO 6440
6680  RETURN
7000  REM  POST TEST
7010 L = 12
7020  GOSUB 18000
7030  PRINT "        QUIZ!"
7040 L = 6
7050  GOSUB 18000
7060  PRINT "WHAT IS THE METRIC UNIT FOR VOLUME?"
7070  PRINT
7080  PRINT "    1. METER"
7090  PRINT "    2. LITER"
7100  PRINT "    3. GRAM"
7110 L = 8
7120  GOSUB 18000
7130  INPUT SA
7140  ON SA GOTO 7150,7170,7150
7150 V = 0
7160  GOTO 7180
```

```
7170 V = 1
7180 L = 12
7190 GOSUB 18000
7200 PRINT "HOW MANY CENTIMETERS ARE IN 2.0 METERS?"
7210 PRINT
7220 PRINT "   1. 20"
7230 PRINT "   2. 200"
7240 PRINT "   3. 2000"
7250 L = 8
7260 GOSUB 18000
7270 INPUT SA
7280 IF SA = 20 THEN SA = 1
7290 IF SA = 200 THEN SA = 2
7300 IF SA = 2000 THEN SA = 3
7310 ON SA GOTO 7320,7340,7320
7320 DI = 0
7330 GOTO 7350
7340 DI = 1
7350 L = 12
7360 GOSUB 18000
7370 PRINT "2500 GRAMS WOULD BE HOW MANY KILOGRAMS?"
7380 PRINT
7390 PRINT "   1. 2.5"
7400 PRINT "   2. 25"
7410 PRINT "   3. 250"
7420 L = 8
7430 GOSUB 18000
7440 INPUT SA
7450 IF SA = 2.5 THEN SA = 1
7460 IF SA = 25 THEN SA = 2
7470 IF SA = 250 THEN SA = 3
7480 ON SA GOTO 7490,7510,7510
7490 MA = 1
7500 GOTO 7520
7510 MA = 0
7520 REM SUMMARY
7530 IF DI = 0 THEN GOTO 7570
7540 IF V = 0 THEN GOTO 7620
7550 IF MA = 0 THEN GOTO 7670
7560 RETURN
7570 PRINT "WE ARE GOING TO REVIEW DISTANCE."
7580 D = 1000
7590 GOSUB 19000
7600 GOSUB 4000
7610 GOTO 7540
7620 PRINT "WE ARE GOING TO REVIEW VOLUME."
7630 D = 1000
7640 GOSUB 19000
7650 GOSUB 5000
7660 GOTO 7550
7670 PRINT "WE ARE GOING TO REVIEW MASS."
7680 D = 1000
7690 GOSUB 19000
7700 GOSUB 6000
7710 GOTO 7560
11000 REM CORRECTION ROUTINES
```

```
11010  PRINT
11020  PRINT
11030  PRINT "IN THE METRIC SYSTEM, CONVERSIONS ALWAYS"
11040  PRINT "ARE SOME POWER OF TEN.  FOR EXAMPLE,"
11050  PRINT "135. CENTIMETERS BECOMES 1.35 METERS."
11060  PRINT
11070  PRINT "NOTICE HOW THE SAME DIGITS ARE IN BOTH"
11080  PRINT "ANSWERS?  ONLY THE DECIMAL POINT"
11090  PRINT "(POWERS OF TEN) CHANGES."
11100  PRINT
11110  PRINT "IN A METRIC CONVERSION, ONLY THE DECIMAL"
11120  PRINT "CHANGES POSITION!"
11130  L = 8
11140  GOSUB 18000
11150  GOSUB 17000
11160  RETURN
11170  PRINT
11180  PRINT "IN THE METRIC SYSTEM, ANY UNIT WILL"
11190  PRINT "ALWAYS BE SOME POWER OF TEN BIGGER OR"
11200  PRINT "SMALLER THAN ANOTHER UNIT."
11210  PRINT
11220  PRINT "(.001, .01, .1, 1, 10, 100, 1000)"
11230  PRINT
11240  PRINT "BOTH UNITS MUST MEASURE THE SAME"
11250  PRINT "PHYSICAL DIMENSION, THOUGH."
11260  PRINT "(DISTANCE, VOLUME, MASS, ETC.)"
11270  PRINT
11280  GOSUB 17000
11290  RETURN
12000  REM  REWARDS
12010  L = 24
12020  GOSUB 18000
12030  PRINT "VERY GOOD!"
12040  L = 12
12050  GOSUB 18000
12060  D = 1000
12070  GOSUB 19000
12080  GOSUB 18000
12090  RETURN
17000  REM  PRESS RETURN
17010  PRINT "PRESS 'RETURN' OR 'ENTER'"; REM  FOR PET PRESS ANY L
       ETTER BEFORE PRESSING RETURN
17020  INPUT SA$
17030  RETURN
18000  REM  SCROLLING
18010  FOR I = 1 TO L
18020  PRINT
18030  NEXT I
18040  RETURN
19000  REM  DELAY
19010  FOR I = 1 TO D
19020  NEXT I
19030  RETURN
20000  REM  CLOSING
20010  L = 12
20020  GOSUB 18000
```

```
20030  PRINT "WE ARE FINISHED!"
20040  PRINT "I HOPE YOU HAD A GOOD TIME!"
20050  GOSUB 18000
20060  END
```

```
         *  -->TABLE OF VARIABLES<--
```

D - DELAY
2050 2190 7580 7630 7680 12060 19010

DI - SCORE ON DISTANCE
7320 7340 7530

I - COUNTER
18010 18030 19010 19020

L - LINES OF SCROLLING
2010 2140 4010 4150 4180 4340 4370 4470 4680 5010 5260
5370 5600 5830 5860 6010 6190 6260 6330 6390 6440 6500
6620 7010 7040 7110 7180 7250 7350 7420 11130 12010 12040
18010 20010

MA - SCORE ON MASS
7490 7510 7550

SA - STUDENT ANSWER
4490 4500 4500 4510 4700 4710 4710 4720 5390 5400 5400
5410 5620 5630 5630 5640 5640 5650 5650 5660 6280 6290
6290 6300 6300 6310 6310 6320 6520 6530 6530 6540 6540
6550 6550 6560 7130 7140 7270 7280 7280 7290 7290 7300
7300 7310 7440 7450 7450 7460 7460 7470 7470 7480

SA$ - STUDENT ANSWER
2160 2170 17020

V - SCORE ON VOLUME
7150 7170 7540

END OF VAR. LIST

SAMPLE RUN

```
]RUN
        METRICS
THIS IS A PROGRAM ABOUT THE METRIC
SYSTEM.
WOULD YOU LIKE TO TAKE A QUIZ TO SEE
IF YOU ALREADY KNOW ABOUT THE METRIC
SYSTEM (YES OR NO)?
?YES
        QUIZ!
WHAT IS THE METRIC UNIT FOR VOLUME?
   1. METER
   2. LITER
   3. GRAM
?2
```

HOW MANY CENTIMETERS ARE IN 2.0 METERS?
    1. 20
    2. 200
    3. 2000
?1
2500 GRAMS WOULD BE HOW MANY KILOGRAMS?
    1. 2.5
    2. 25
    3. 250
?1
WE ARE GOING TO REVIEW DISTANCE.
THE BASIC UNIT OF LENGTH IN THE METRIC
SYSTEM IS THE 'METER.' AT FIRST THE
METER WAS DEFINED AS ONE TEN MILLIONTH
THE DISTANCE FROM THE EQUATOR TO THE
NORTH POLE. HOWEVER, IT SOON BECAME
EVIDENT THAT THIS DISTANCE IS VERY HARD
TO MEASURE EVERY TIME THE STANDARD
NEEDED TO BE CHECKED!
PRESENTLY THE METER IS DEFINED ON THE
BASIS OF A VERY ACCURATELY MEASURED
WAVELENGTH OF LIGHT.
PRESS 'RETURN' OR 'ENTER'
?
THE METRIC UNITS OF LENGTH WHICH ARE
COMMONLY USED ARE:
    MILLIMETER
    CENTIMETER
    METER
    KILOMETER
THE MILLIMETER IS 1/1000 OF A METER
                1/10 OF A CENTIMETER
THE CENTIMETER IS 1/100 OF A METER
THE KILOMETER IS 1000 METERS.
PRESS 'RETURN' OR 'ENTER'
?
LET'S TRY A COUPLE OF SIMPLE CONVERSION
PROBLEMS.
25 MILLIMETERS EQUALS:
    1. 2.5
    2. .25
    3. 32.
        CENTIMETERS
?1
VERY GOOD!
HERE IS ANOTHER PROBLEM.
.52 KILOMETERS EQUALS:
    1. 52 METERS
    2. 760 METERS
    3. 520 METERS
?1
1 KILOMETER EQUALS 1000 METERS
.52 KILOMETERS EQUALS ? METERS?520
VERY GOOD!
WE ARE FINISHED!
I HOPE YOU HAD A GOOD TIME!

]

STORY WRITER

PROGRAM DESCRIPTION

This program is an instructional game on nouns, verbs, adjectives, and adverbs as well as sentence structuring. The computer gives you an initial quiz (pre-test) on nouns, verbs, adjectives, and adverbs. If you get all of the answers correct, then the computer asks you to pick any noun, verb, adjective, and adverb and it will write sentences or stories from the words that you selected. If you do not receive a perfect score on the initial quiz, the computer will instruct you on nouns, verbs, adjectives, and adverbs. Some of the sentences or stories can be quite amusing depending on the words selected.

PROGRAM NOTES

This program should give you ideas on how to turn your computer into an author. Collections of nouns, verbs, adjectives, and adverbs can even be combined with no filler (like the new year's resolutions) to produce fundamental (although somewhat obscure) sentences. Try this order: adjective, noun, verb, noun, adverb. The result would be something like: "FAT CAT CHEW TREE SLOWLY." For activities like this you might want to enter larger lists of words in each class, then draw from them at random.

PROGRAM LISTING

```
100 REM STORY WRITER BY GARY ORWIG
2000 REM INTRODUCTION
2010 L = 12
2020 GOSUB 18000
```

```
2030  PRINT "          STORY WRITER"
2040 L = 12
2050  GOSUB 18000
2060 D = 1000
2070  GOSUB 19000
2080  GOSUB 18000
2090  PRINT "WHAT IS YOUR NAME?"
2100  GOSUB 18000
2110  INPUT NA$
2120  GOSUB 18000
2130  PRINT "I'M HAPPY TO MEET YOU, ";NA$
2140  GOSUB 18000
2150 D = 1500
2160  GOSUB 19000
2170  PRINT "THIS IS A PROGRAM WHICH WILL WRITE A"
2180  PRINT "STORY FOR YOU!"
2190  PRINT
2200  PRINT "ALL YOU HAVE TO DO IS PROVIDE ME WITH"
2210  PRINT "A FEW WORDS!"
2220  PRINT
2230  PRINT "BEFORE WE GO VERY FAR, I NEED TO CHECK"
2240  PRINT "TO SEE IF YOU KNOW WHAT A FEW LANGUAGE"
2250  PRINT "TERMS MEAN."
2260  PRINT
2270 L = 6
2280  GOSUB 18000
2290  GOSUB 17000
2300 L = 12
2310  GOSUB 18000
2320  PRINT "WHICH OF THE FOLLOWING WORDS IS A NOUN?"
2330  GOSUB 16000
2340  IF SA < > 3 THEN 2550
2350  PRINT "VERY GOOD!"
2360  PRINT "WHICH OF THE FOLLOWING WORDS IS A VERB?"
2370  GOSUB 16000
2380  IF SA < > 4 THEN 2640
2390  PRINT "GREAT!"
2400  PRINT "WHICH OF THE FOLLOWING WORDS IS"
2410  PRINT "AN ADJECTIVE?"
2420  GOSUB 16000
2430  IF SA < > 2 THEN 2740
2440  PRINT "EXCELLENT!"
2450  PRINT "WHICH OF THE FOLLOWING WORDS IS"
2460  PRINT "AN ADVERB?"
2470  GOSUB 16000
2480  IF SA < > 1 THEN 2810
2490  PRINT "VERY GOOD!"
2500  PRINT
2510  PRINT "I THINK WE ARE READY TO GO AHEAD NOW!"
2520  PRINT
2530  GOSUB 17000
2540  GOTO 3000
2550  REM  NOUN
2560  PRINT "A NOUN IS THE NAME OF A PERSON, PLACE,"
2570  PRINT "OR THING."
2580  PRINT
```

```
2590 PRINT "SIDEWALK, UMBRELLA, MAN, FLORIDA, AND"
2600 PRINT "FOOT ARE ALL NOUNS!"
2610 PRINT "NOUNS CAN BE EITHER SINGULAR"
2620 PRINT "(FOOT, MOUSE) OR PLURAL (FEET, MICE)."
2630 GOTO 2320
2640 REM VERB
2650 PRINT "A VERB IS ANY WORD WHICH EXPRESS AN"
2660 PRINT "ACTION."
2670 PRINT "YELL, RUN, JUMP, THINK, HIT, KICK,"
2680 PRINT "AND TALK ARE ALL VERBS."
2690 PRINT "A VERB CAN HAVE SEVERAL FORMS - -"
2700 PRINT "PRESENT, PAST, PAST PERFECT, ETC."
2710 PRINT "WE WILL ONLY WORK WITH PRESENT AND PAST"
2720 PRINT "TENSES (SWIM AND SWAM)."
2730 GOTO 2360
2740 REM ADJECTIVE
2750 PRINT "AN ADJECTIVE IS A WORD DESCRIBES"
2760 PRINT "SOMETHING OR SOMEBODY (A NOUN)."
2770 PRINT "SWEET, JUMPY, MODEST, ROUGH, YELLOW,"
2780 PRINT "AND STUPID ARE ALL ADJECTIVES."
2790 PRINT
2800 GOTO 2400
2810 REM ADVERB
2820 PRINT "AN ADVERB IS A WORD WHICH TELLS HOW"
2830 PRINT "SOMETHING IS DONE. IT FREQUENTLY ENDS"
2840 PRINT "IN '-LY'."
2850 PRINT "QUICKLY, SLOWLY, MODESTLY, QUIETLY,"
2860 PRINT "AND CAREFULLY ARE ALL ADVERBS."
2870 PRINT
2880 GOTO 2450
3000 REM COLLECT WORDS
3010 L = 12
3020 GOSUB 18000
3030 PRINT "FIRST I WILL NEED SOME NOUNS."
3040 PRINT "THINK OF SEVEN NOUNS (ALL SINGULAR)"
3050 PRINT "AND TYPE THEM IN ONE AT A TIME."
3060 PRINT
3070 PRINT
3080 PRINT "NOUN #1";
3090 INPUT N1$
3100 PRINT "NOUN #2";
3110 INPUT N2$
3120 PRINT "NOUN #3";
3130 INPUT N3$
3140 PRINT "NOUN #4";
3150 INPUT N4$
3160 PRINT "NOUN #5";
3170 INPUT N5$
3180 PRINT "NOUN #6";
3190 INPUT N6$
3200 PRINT "NOUN #7";
3210 INPUT N7$
3220 GOSUB 18000
3230 PRINT "GREAT! NOW I WILL NEED JUST ONE VERB."
3240 PRINT
3250 PRINT
```

```
3260  PRINT "VERB #1";
3270  INPUT V1$
3280  PRINT "NOW HOW ABOUT ONE ADJECTIVE?"
3290  PRINT
3300  PRINT
3310  PRINT "ADJECTIVE #1";
3320  INPUT J1$
3330  PRINT "NOW I NEED TWO NUMBERS."
3340  PRINT
3350  PRINT
3360  PRINT "NUMBER #1 (BETWEEN 2 AND 12)";
3370  INPUT J2$
3380  PRINT "NUMBER #2 (BETWEEN 2 AND 12)";
3390  INPUT J3$
3400  PRINT
3410  PRINT
3420  PRINT "I'M ALMOST DONE!  NOW ALL I NEED IS"
3430  PRINT "ONE ADVERB!"
3440  PRINT "ADVERB #1";
3450  INPUT AV$
4000  REM  STORY
4010  L = 12
4020  GOSUB 18000
4030  PRINT "    ";NA$;"'S NEW YEAR'S RESOLUTIONS"
4040  GOSUB 18000
4050  GOSUB 17000
4060  GOSUB 18000
4070  PRINT "I, ";NA$;", WILL STOP EATING TOO MUCH"
4080  PRINT N1$;"."
4090  GOSUB 18000
4100  GOSUB 17000
4110  GOSUB 18000
4120  PRINT "I WILL WATCH ONLY ";J1$;" TELEVISION"
4130  PRINT "SHOWS."
4140  GOSUB 18000
4150  GOSUB 17000
4160  GOSUB 18000
4170  PRINT "I WILL ";V1$;" EVERY DAY FOR "
4180  PRINT J2$;" HOURS."
4190  GOSUB 18000
4200  GOSUB 17000
4210  GOSUB 18000
4220  PRINT "I WILL MAKE MY ";N2$;" AND CLEAN"
4230  PRINT "MY ";N3$;" EVERY DAY."
4240  GOSUB 18000
4250  GOSUB 17000
4260  GOSUB 18000
4270  PRINT "I WILL TALK ";AV$;" WHILE I EAT MY"
4280  PRINT N4$;"."
4290  GOSUB 18000
4300  GOSUB 17000
4310  GOSUB 18000
4320  PRINT "I WILL GO TO BED AT ";J3$;" O'CLOCK."
4330  GOSUB 18000
4340  GOSUB 17000
4350  GOSUB 18000
```

```
4360  PRINT "I WILL TAKE GOOD CARE OF MY PET ";N5$;"."
4370  GOSUB 18000
4380  GOSUB 17000
4390  GOSUB 18000
4400  PRINT "I WILL NOT PUT ANY ";N6$;" IN MY"
4410  PRINT "MOTHER'S ";N7$;"."
4420  GOSUB 18000
4430  GOSUB 17000
4440  GOSUB 18000
4450  PRINT "I HOPE YOU CAN STICK TO YOUR"
4460  PRINT "RESOLUTIONS, ";NA$;"!"
4470  PRINT
4480  PRINT "BYE FOR NOW!"
4490  GOSUB 18000
4500  END
16000 REM  QUIZ FRAME
16010 PRINT
16020 PRINT "TYPE IN 1,2,3 OR 4."
16030 PRINT
16040 PRINT "   1. SWIFTLY"
16050 PRINT "   2. GENTLE"
16060 PRINT "   3. TREE"
16070 PRINT "   4. JUMP"
16080 PRINT
16090 L = 6
16100 GOSUB 18000
16110 INPUT SA
16120 RETURN
17000 REM  WAIT FOR PRESS RETURN
17010 PRINT "PRESS 'RETURN' OR 'ENTER'."; REM  FOR PET PRESS ANY
      LETTER BEFORE PRESSING RETURN
17020 INPUT SA$
17030 RETURN
18000 REM  SCROLLING
18010 FOR I = 1 TO L
18020 PRINT
18030 NEXT I
18040 RETURN
19000 REM  DELAY
19010 FOR I = 1 TO D
19020 NEXT I
19030 RETURN
```

                    * -->TABLE OF VARIABLES<--

AV$ - ADVERB
3450 4270

D - DELAY
2060 2150 19010

I - COUNTER
18010 18030 19010 19020

J1$ - ADJ. 1
3320 4120

J2$ - ADJ. 2
3370 4180

J3$ - ADJ. 3
3390 4320

L - LINES OF SCROLLING
2010 2040 2270 2300 3010 4010 16090 18010

N1$ - NOUN 1
3090 4080

N2$ - NOUN 2
3110 4220

N3$ - NOUN 3
3130 4230

N4$ - NOUN 4
3150 4280

N5$ - NOUN 5
3170 4360

N6$ - NOUN 6
3190 4400

N7$ - NOUN 7
3210 4410

NA$ - NAME
2110 2130 4030 4070 4460

SA - STUDENT ANSWER
2340 2380 2430 2480 16110

SA$ - STUDENT ANSWER
17020

V1$ - VERB 1
3270 4170

END OF VAR. LIST

SAMPLE RUN

]RUN
        STORY WRITER
WHAT IS YOUR NAME?
?LAURIE
I'M HAPPY TO MEET YOU, LAURIE
THIS IS A PROGRAM WHICH WILL WRITE A
STORY FOR YOU!
ALL YOU HAVE TO DO IS PROVIDE ME WITH
A FEW WORDS!
BEFORE WE GO VERY FAR, I NEED TO CHECK

TO SEE IF YOU KNOW WHAT A FEW LANGUAGE
TERMS MEAN.
PRESS 'RETURN' OR 'ENTER'.
?
WHICH OF THE FOLLOWING WORDS IS A NOUN?
TYPE IN 1,2,3 OR 4.
   1. SWIFTLY
   2. GENTLE
   3. TREE
   4. JUMP
?3
VERY GOOD!
WHICH OF THE FOLLOWING WORDS IS A VERB?
TYPE IN 1,2,3 OR 4.
   1. SWIFTLY
   2. GENTLE
   3. TREE
   4. JUMP
?4
GREAT!
WHICH OF THE FOLLOWING WORDS IS
AN ADJECTIVE?
TYPE IN 1,2,3 OR 4.
   1. SWIFTLY
   2. GENTLE
   3. TREE
   4. JUMP
?1
AN ADJECTIVE IS A WORD DESCRIBES
SOMETHING OR SOMEBODY (A NOUN).
SWEET, JUMPY, MODEST, ROUGH, YELLOW,
AND STUPID ARE ALL ADJECTIVES.
WHICH OF THE FOLLOWING WORDS IS
AN ADJECTIVE?
TYPE IN 1,2,3 OR 4.
   1. SWIFTLY
   2. GENTLE
   3. TREE
   4. JUMP
?2
EXCELLENT!
WHICH OF THE FOLLOWING WORDS IS
AN ADVERB?
TYPE IN 1,2,3 OR 4.
   1. SWIFTLY
   2. GENTLE
   3. TREE
   4. JUMP
?1
VERY GOOD!
I THINK WE ARE READY TO GO AHEAD NOW!
PRESS 'RETURN' OR 'ENTER'.
?
FIRST I WILL NEED SOME NOUNS.
THINK OF SEVEN NOUNS (ALL SINGULAR)
AND TYPE THEM IN ONE AT A TIME.

```
NOUN #1?CAT
NOUN #2?DOG
NOUN #3?TREE
NOUN #4?FROG
NOUN #5?CHICKEN
NOUN #6?HOUSE
NOUN #7?CHAIR
GREAT! NOW I WILL NEED JUST ONE VERB.
VERB #1?KICK
NOW HOW ABOUT ONE ADJECTIVE?
ADJECTIVE #1?NERVOUS
NOW I NEED TWO NUMBERS.
NUMBER #1 (BETWEEN 2 AND 12)?6
NUMBER #2 (BETWEEN 2 AND 12)?2
I'M ALMOST DONE!  NOW ALL I NEED IS
ONE ADVERB!
ADVERB #1?RAPIDLY
    LAURIE'S NEW YEAR'S RESOLUTIONS
PRESS 'RETURN' OR 'ENTER'.
?
I, LAURIE, WILL STOP EATING TOO MUCH
CAT.
PRESS 'RETURN' OR 'ENTER'.
?
I WILL WATCH ONLY NERVOUS TELEVISION
SHOWS.
PRESS 'RETURN' OR 'ENTER'.
?
I WILL KICK EVERY DAY FOR
6 HOURS.
PRESS 'RETURN' OR 'ENTER'.
?
I WILL MAKE MY DOG AND CLEAN
MY TREE EVERY DAY.
PRESS 'RETURN' OR 'ENTER'.
?
I WILL TALK RAPIDLY WHILE I EAT MY
FROG.
PRESS 'RETURN' OR 'ENTER'.
?
I WILL GO TO BED AT 2 O'CLOCK.
PRESS 'RETURN' OR 'ENTER'.
?
I WILL TAKE GOOD CARE OF MY PET CHICKEN.
PRESS 'RETURN' OR 'ENTER'.
?
I WILL NOT PUT ANY HOUSE IN MY
MOTHER'S CHAIR.
PRESS 'RETURN' OR 'ENTER'.
?
I HOPE YOU CAN STICK TO YOUR
RESOLUTIONS, LAURIE!
BYE FOR NOW!
]
```

SIMULATION PROGRAMS

Simulation programming is a form of instruction that puts the learner in a *real-life* situation and allows the learner to use decisionmaking skills to alter the situation and witness the outcome created by the decisions. Science and engineering as well as the aerospace industry use simulations for structural design and training of personnel. A great deal of enthusiasm or motivation from the learner is one good aspect of the use of simulation CAI. The six program listings and sample runs were chosen to demonstrate the use of simulation programming to teach the learner to adjust to a variety of real life situations involving such subjects as retailing, science, ballistics, and financing.

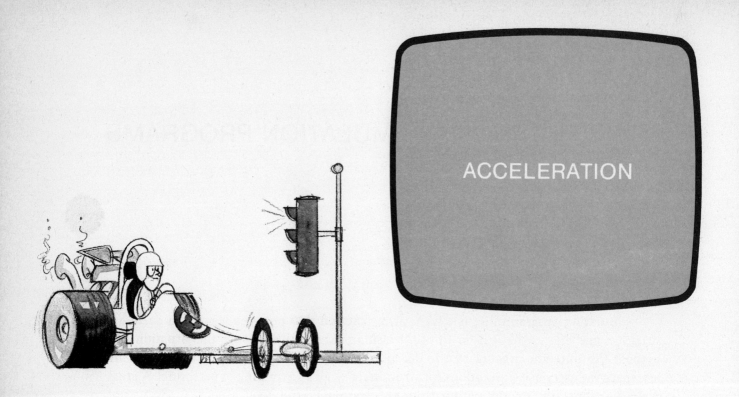

ACCELERATION

PROGRAM DESCRIPTION

This is a program which will help you to better understand what acceleration is all about. You will need to know about the relationships between time, distance, velocity, and acceleration from a science book and practice with the program Time, Distance, Velocity before you attempt to operate this simulation program.

In this program, you select any units you want to use to represent time and distance. Observe the results carefully, since the answers will be in the same units that you selected. There are two limitations to the units you input into the computer for time and distance. Do not type in "0" for a value since some of the equations would make the computer divide by "0" and as you know the equations would not operate. Also, the computer does not check to see if you have accelerated beyond the speed of light which is not a probable occurrence in the real world.

PROGRAM NOTES

1. Consider adding a "zero filter" to eliminate potential problems with division by zero.

2. How could you allow for relativity and the limitation of the speed of light? Would it be possible to check an answer to see if it approaches or exceeds the limits?

```
100  REM  ACCELERATION BY GARY ORWIG
2000  REM  INTRODUCTION
2010 L = 24
2020  GOSUB 18000
2030  FOR J = 0 TO 300 STEP 8
2040 DE = 300 - J
2050  GOSUB 19000
2060  PRINT ">>>>>>>>>>ACCELERATION>>>>>>>>>>>>>>>>>>>>>>>>>>";
2070  NEXT J
2080  FOR I = 1 TO 10
2090  PRINT ">>>>>>>>>>ACCELERATION>>>>>>>>>>>>>>>>>>>>>>>>>>";
2100  NEXT I
2110 DE = 1000
2120  GOSUB 19000
2130 L = 24
2140  GOSUB 18000
2150  PRINT "IT'S NICE TO SEE YOU!"
2160  PRINT "WHAT IS YOUR NAME?";
2170 L = 12
2180  GOSUB 18000
2190  INPUT NA$
2200  GOSUB 18000
2210  PRINT
2220  PRINT
2230  PRINT "I HOPE YOU HAVE A GOOD TIME, ";NA$;"."
2240 D = 1500
2250  GOSUB 19000
2260 L = 24
2270  GOSUB 18000
2280  PRINT "THIS IS A PROGRAM WHICH WILL HELP"
2290  PRINT "YOU TO BETTER UNDERSTAND ACCELERATION."
2300  PRINT
2310  PRINT "YOU SHOULD FIRST READ ABOUT TIME,"
2320  PRINT "DISTANCE, VELOCITY, AND ACCELERATION"
2330  PRINT "IN A SCIENCE BOOK TO GET A BASIC "
2340  PRINT "UNDERSTANDING OF THEM."
2350  PRINT
2360  PRINT "IN THIS PROGRAM, YOU CAN PICK ANY UNITS"
2370  PRINT "YOU WANT TO USE TO REPRESENT TIME AND"
2380  PRINT "DISTANCE.  THE ANSWERS WILL BE IN THOSE"
2390  PRINT "SAME UNITS."
2400  PRINT
2410  PRINT "THERE ARE TWO LIMITATIONS.............."
2420  PRINT "DON'T TYPE IN '0' FOR A VALUE!"
2430  PRINT "(SOME OF MY EQUATIONS WOULD MAKE ME TRY"
2440  PRINT "TO DIVIDE BY 0!)"
2450  PRINT "ALSO, I DON'T CHECK TO SEE IF YOU HAVE"
2460  PRINT "ACCELERATED BEYOND THE SPEED OF LIGHT!"
2470  PRINT "(SOMETHING HARD TO DO IN REAL LIFE!)"
2480  PRINT
2490  PRINT
2500  PRINT "PRESS 'RETURN' OR 'ENTER' WHEN READY.";  REM  FOR PET
      PRESS ANY LETTER BEFORE PRESSING RETURN
2510  INPUT S$
```

```
2520 L = 24
2530 GOSUB 18000
3000 REM  SET UNITS
3010 PRINT "WHAT UNIT DO YOU WANT TO USE FOR TIME?"
3020 PRINT "(SECONDS, MINUTES, HOURS, ETC.)"
3030 INPUT T$
3040 PRINT
3050 PRINT "WHAT UNIT DO YOU WANT FOR DISTANCE?"
3060 PRINT "(METERS, KILOMETERS, MILES, ETC.)"
3070 INPUT D$
3080 PRINT
3090 PRINT "TIME WILL BE IN ";T$;"."
3100 PRINT
3110 PRINT "DISTANCE WILL BE IN ";D$;"."
3120 PRINT
3130 PRINT "VELOCITY WILL BE IN"
3140 PRINT D$;" PER ";T$;"."
3150 PRINT
3160 PRINT "ACCELERATION WILL BE IN"
3170 PRINT D$;" PER ";T$;" PER ";T$;"."
3180 PRINT
3190 PRINT
3200 PRINT "PRESS 'RETURN' OR 'ENTER'": REM  FOR PET PRESS ANY L
     ETTER BEFORE PRESSING RETURN
3210 INPUT S$
3220 L = 24
3230 GOSUB 18000
4000 REM  MAIN PROGRAM
4010 PRINT "SELECT ONE AND ENTER THE NUMBER."
4020 PRINT
4030 PRINT
4040 PRINT "    1. GIVEN A & T, FIND V & D"
4050 PRINT
4060 PRINT "    2. GIVEN A & D, FIND V & T"
4070 PRINT
4080 PRINT "    3. GIVEN A & V, FIND D & T"
4090 PRINT
4100 PRINT "    4. GIVEN V & D, FIND A & T"
4110 PRINT
4120 PRINT "    5. GIVEN V & T, FIND A & D"
4130 PRINT
4140 PRINT "    6. GIVEN D & T, FIND A & V"
4150 PRINT
4160 INPUT SA
4170 IF SA < 1 OR SA > 6 THEN 4010
4180 L = 24
4190 GOSUB 18000
4200 ON SA GOTO 4210,4270,4330,4390,4450,4510
4210 PRINT "ENTER A"
4220 INPUT A
4230 PRINT "ENTER T"
4240 INPUT T
4250 GOSUB 6010
4260 GOTO 5000
4270 PRINT "ENTER A"
4280 INPUT A
```

```
4290  PRINT "ENTER D"
4300  INPUT D
4310  GOSUB 6050
4320  GOTO 5000
4330  PRINT "ENTER A"
4340  INPUT A
4350  PRINT "ENTER V"
4360  INPUT V
4370  GOSUB 6090
4380  GOTO 5000
4390  PRINT "ENTER V"
4400  INPUT V
4410  PRINT "ENTER D"
4420  INPUT D
4430  GOSUB 6130
4440  GOTO 5000
4450  PRINT "ENTER V"
4460  INPUT V
4470  PRINT "ENTER T"
4480  INPUT T
4490  GOSUB 6170
4500  GOTO 5000
4510  PRINT "ENTER D"
4520  INPUT D
4530  PRINT "ENTER T"
4540  INPUT T
4550  GOSUB 6210
4560  GOTO 5000
5000  REM  PRINT ANSWERS
5010  L = 6
5020  GOSUB 18000
5030  PRINT "ACCELERATION: ";A;" ";D$;" PER ";T$;" PER ";T$
5040  PRINT
5050  PRINT "VELOCITY:     ";V;" ";D$;" PER ";T$
5060  PRINT
5070  PRINT "DISTANCE:     ";D;" ";D$
5080  PRINT
5090  PRINT "TIME:         ";T;" ";T$
5100  PRINT
5110  PRINT
5120  PRINT "ENTER MORE VALUES (YES OR NO)"
5130  INPUT S$
5140  IF S$ = "NO" THEN 20000
5150  PRINT
5160  PRINT "SAME UNITS OF MEASUREMENT?"
5170  PRINT "(YES OR NO)"
5180  INPUT S$
5190  IF S$ = "NO" THEN 3000
5200  GOTO 4000
6000  REM  CALCULATIONS
6010  REM  A. GIVEN ACCEL. AND TIME
6020  V = A * T
6030  D = T ^ 2 * A * .5
6040  RETURN
6050  REM  B. GIVEN ACCEL. AND DISTANCE
6060  T = ((2 * D) / A) ^ .5
```

```
6070 V = (2 * A * D) ^ .5
6080  RETURN
6090  REM  C. GIVEN ACCEL. AND FINAL VEL.
6100 T = V / A
6110 D = (V ^ 2) / (2 * A)
6120  RETURN
6130  REM  D. GIVEN FINAL VELOCITY AND DISTANCE
6140 A = (V ^ 2) / (2 * D)
6150 T = (2 * D) / V
6160  RETURN
6170  REM  E. GIVEN FINAL VELOCITY AND TIME
6180 A = V / T
6190 D = (V * T) / 2
6200  RETURN
6210  REM  F. GIVEN DISTANCE AND TIME
6220 A = (2 * D) / T ^ 2
6230 V = (2 * D) / T
6240  RETURN
18000  REM  SCROLL
18010  FOR I = 1 TO L
18020  PRINT
18030  NEXT I
18040  RETURN
19000  REM  DELAY
19010  FOR I = 1 TO DE
19020  NEXT I
19030  RETURN
20000  REM  CLOSING
20010  PRINT
20020  PRINT
20030  PRINT "I HOPE YOU HAD FUN, ";NA$;"!"
20040  PRINT "BYE FOR NOW!"
20050  END
```

                    * -->TABLE OF VARIABLES<--

A - ACCELERATION
4220 4280 4340 5030 6020 6030 6060 6070 6100 6110 6140
6180 6220

D - DISTANCE
2240 4300 4420 4520 5070 6030 6060 6070 6110 6140 6150
6190 6220 6230

D$ - DISTANCE UNIT
3070 3110 3140 3170 5030 5050 5070

DE - DELAY
2040 2110 19010

I - COUNTER
2080 2100 18010 18030 19010 19020

J - COUNTER
2030 2040 2070

L - LINES OF SCROLLING
2010 2130 2170 2260 2520 3220 4180 5010 18010

NA$ - NAME
2190 2230 20030

S$ - STUDENT INPUT
2510 3210 5130 5140 5180 5190

SA - STUDENT INPUT
4160 4170 4170 4200

T - TIME
4240 4480 4540 5090 6020 6030 6060 6100 6150 6180 6190
6220 6230

T$ - TIME UNIT
3030 3090 3140 3170 3170 5030 5030 5050 5090

V - VELOCITY
4360 4400 4460 5050 6020 6070 6100 6110 6140 6150 6180
6190 6230

END OF VAR. LIST

SAMPLE RUN

]RUN
ACCELERATION
IT'S NICE TO SEE YOU!
WHAT IS YOUR NAME?
?ALLEN
I HOPE YOU HAVE A GOOD TIME, ALLEN.
THIS IS A PROGRAM WHICH WILL HELP
YOU TO BETTER UNDERSTAND ACCELERATION.
YOU SHOULD FIRST READ ABOUT TIME,
DISTANCE, VELOCITY, AND ACCELERATION
IN A SCIENCE BOOK TO GET A BASIC
UNDERSTANDING OF THEM.
IN THIS PROGRAM, YOU CAN PICK ANY UNITS
YOU WANT TO USE TO REPRESENT TIME AND
DISTANCE. THE ANSWERS WILL BE IN THOSE
SAME UNITS.
THERE ARE TWO LIMITATIONS.............
DON'T TYPE IN '0' FOR A VALUE!
(SOME OF MY EQUATIONS WOULD MAKE ME TRY
TO DIVIDE BY 0!)
ALSO, I DON'T CHECK TO SEE IF YOU HAVE
ACCELERATED BEYOND THE SPEED OF LIGHT!
(SOMETHING HARD TO DO IN REAL LIFE!)
PRESS 'RETURN' OR 'ENTER' WHEN READY.
?
WHAT UNIT DO YOU WANT TO USE FOR TIME?
(SECONDS, MINUTES, HOURS, ETC.)
?HOURS
WHAT UNIT DO YOU WANT FOR DISTANCE?

```
(METERS, KILOMETERS, MILES, ETC.)
?MILES
TIME WILL BE IN HOURS.
DISTANCE WILL BE IN MILES.
VELOCITY WILL BE IN
MILES PER HOURS.
ACCELERATION WILL BE IN
MILES PER HOURS PER HOURS.
PRESS 'RETURN' OR 'ENTER'
?
SELECT ONE AND ENTER THE NUMBER.
     1. GIVEN A & T, FIND V & D
     2. GIVEN A & D, FIND V & T
     3. GIVEN A & V, FIND D & T
     4. GIVEN V & D, FIND A & T
     5. GIVEN V & T, FIND A & D
     6. GIVEN D & T, FIND A & V
?6
ENTER D
?1000
ENTER T
?1
ACCELERATION: 2000 MILES PER HOURS PER HOURS
VELOCITY:    2000 MILES PER HOURS
DISTANCE:    1000 MILES
TIME:        1 HOURS
ENTER MORE VALUES (YES OR NO)
?YES
SAME UNITS OF MEASUREMENT?
(YES OR NO)
?NO
WHAT UNIT DO YOU WANT TO USE FOR TIME?
(SECONDS, MINUTES, HOURS, ETC.)
?SECONDS
WHAT UNIT DO YOU WANT FOR DISTANCE?
(METERS, KILOMETERS, MILES, ETC.)
?MILES
TIME WILL BE IN SECONDS.
DISTANCE WILL BE IN MILES.
VELOCITY WILL BE IN
MILES PER SECONDS.
ACCELERATION WILL BE IN
MILES PER SECONDS PER SECONDS.
PRESS 'RETURN' OR 'ENTER'
?
SELECT ONE AND ENTER THE NUMBER.
     1. GIVEN A & T, FIND V & D
     2. GIVEN A & D, FIND V & T
     3. GIVEN A & V, FIND D & T
     4. GIVEN V & D, FIND A & T
     5. GIVEN V & T, FIND A & D
     6. GIVEN D & T, FIND A & V
?1
ENTER A
?250
ENTER T
```

```
?300
ACCELERATION: 250 MILES PER SECONDS PER SECONDS
VELOCITY:    75000 MILES PER SECONDS
DISTANCE:    11250000 MILES
TIME:       300 SECONDS
ENTER MORE VALUES (YES OR NO)
?NO
I HOPE YOU HAD FUN, ALLEN!
BYE FOR NOW!
]
```

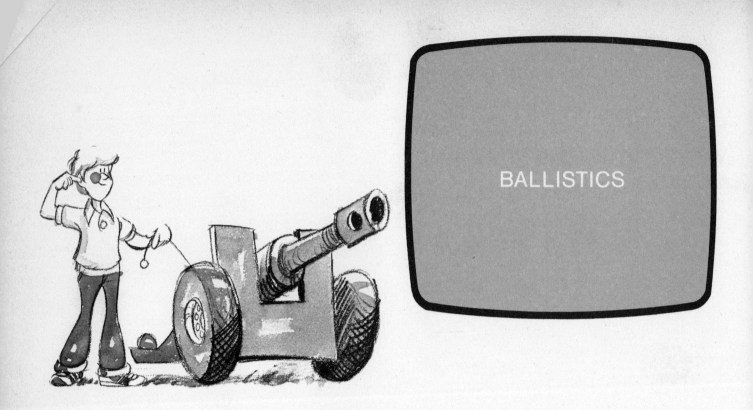

BALLISTICS

PROGRAM DESCRIPTION

The science of ballistics is demonstrated in this program. The computer simulates the flight of a cannon ball. You must supply the angle at which the cannon is to be fired. This angle is expressed in a range of "0" to "90" degrees. In addition, you will have to decide on the velocity of the cannon ball since you can vary the amount of the gunpowder in the cannon. As a helpful hint, usually velocities in the range of 200 to 300 meters per second are very effective. The object is to hit the target in as few tries as possible.

This program calculates the "pure" parabolic path of the projectile. It does not consider wind resistance.

PROGRAM NOTES

1. This is a program for the graphics enthusiast! If you have graphics ability, you can plot the trajectory by incrementing time (figure altitude and range every 0.5 seconds of flight time). Then plot appropriate values of X and Y on the screen.

2. The screen printout is currently set up for a 40-character-per-line screen. It may take a bit of adjusting for other screens.

3. Depending on the level of the students, you might want to add prompting, like "Try a slightly lower angle," etc.

```
100  REM  BALLISTICS BY GARY ORWIG
1000 REM  INITILIZATION
1010 G = 9.80
2000 REM  INTRODUCTION
2010 FOR I = 1 TO 10
2020 FOR J = 1 TO I
2030 PRINT "BALLISTICS    ";
2040 NEXT J
2050 PRINT
2060 PRINT
2070 NEXT I
2080 DE = 1000
2090 GOSUB 19000
2100 L = 24
2110 GOSUB 18000
2120 PRINT "WHAT IS YOUR NAME?"
2130 L = 12
2140 GOSUB 18000
2150 INPUT NA$
2160 PRINT
2170 PRINT "NICE TO MEET YOU, ";NA$;"."
2180 L = 3
2190 GOSUB 18000
2200 PRINT "THIS IS A PROGRAM WHICH SIMULATES THE"
2210 PRINT "FLIGHT OF A CANNON BALL."
2220 PRINT
2230 PRINT "YOU MUST SUPPLY THE ANGLE AT WHICH"
2240 PRINT "THE GUN IS TO BE FIRED.  THIS IS AN"
2250 PRINT "ANGLE EXPRESSED IN A RANGE OF "
2260 PRINT "0 TO 90 DEGREES."
2270 PRINT
2280 PRINT "IN ADDITION, YOU WILL HAVE TO DECIDE"
2290 PRINT "ON THE VELOCITY OF THE CANNON BALL."
2300 PRINT "SINCE YOU CAN VARY THE AMOUNT OF "
2310 PRINT "GUNPOWDER IN THE CANNON, THIS IS NOT"
2320 PRINT "A PROBLEM.  USUALLY VELOCITIES IN THE"
2330 PRINT "RANGE OF 200 TO 300 METERS PER SECOND"
2340 PRINT "ARE EFFECTIVE."
2350 PRINT
2360 PRINT "PRESS 'RETURN' OR 'ENTER'": REM  FOR PET PRESS ANY LE
     TTER BEFORE PRESSING RETURN
2370 INPUT S$
2380 L = 13
2390 GOSUB 18000
2400 PRINT "    HERE WE GO!"
2410 GOSUB 18000
2420 DE = 1000
2430 GOSUB 19000
4000 REM  MAIN PROGRAM
4010 GOSUB 10000
4020 L = 24
4030 GOSUB 18000
4040 PRINT "TARGET RANGE IS ";RX;" METERS."
4050 PRINT "ENTER ELEVATION ANGLE IN DEGREES:";
```

```
4060  INPUT ED
4070  IF ED < 90 THEN 4100
4080  PRINT "YOU'RE SHOOTING THE WRONG WAY, ";NA$;"!"
4090  GOTO 4050
4100  PRINT "ENTER VELOCITY IN M/S:";
4110  INPUT VI
4120  GOSUB 6000
4130  GOSUB 18000
4140  PRINT "          BOOM!"
4150  GOSUB 18000
4160  PRINT
4170  PRINT "ELEVATION:         ";ED;" DEGREES"
4180  PRINT
4190  PRINT "INIT. VELOCITY:     ";VI;" M/S"
4200  PRINT
4210  PRINT "TOTAL DISTANCE:     ";D;" METERS"
4220  PRINT
4230  PRINT "MAXIMUM ELEVATION: ";H;" METERS"
4240  PRINT
4250  PRINT "TOTAL TIME IN AIR: ";T;" SEC."
4260  PRINT
4270  PRINT
4280  GOSUB 7000
4290  GOSUB 11000
4300  IF HT = 2 THEN 12000
4310  IF HT = 1 THEN  GOSUB 12500
4320  IF HT = 0 THEN  GOSUB 14000
4330  GOTO 4040
6000  REM  CALULATIONS
6010  ER = ED * .0174533
6020  H = (VI *  SIN (ER)) ^ 2 / (2 * G)
6030  H =  INT (H)
6040  T = (2 * VI *  SIN (ER)) / G
6050  D =  COS (ER) * VI * T
6060  T =  INT (T)
6070  D =  INT (D)
6080  DB =  INT ((D / 200) + .5)
6090  RETURN
7000  REM  PLOT RESULTS
7010  PRINT
7020  PRINT
7030  IF DB < 41 THEN 7070
7040  PRINT "       OUT OF SIGHT!"
7050  PRINT "                          >>>"
7060  GOTO 7150
7070  FOR I = 1 TO DB - 3
7080  PRINT " ";
7090  NEXT I
7100  PRINT "CRASH"
7110  FOR I = 1 TO DB - 1
7120  PRINT " ";
7130  NEXT I
7140  PRINT "#"
7150  PRINT "X/";
7160  FOR I = 1 TO DT - 4
7170  PRINT " ";
```

```
7180  NEXT I
7190  PRINT "^^^"
7200  FOR I = 1 TO 40
7210  PRINT "*";
7220  NEXT I
7230  FOR I = 1 TO DT - 1
7240  PRINT " ";
7250  NEXT I
7260  PRINT "^"
7270  FOR I = 1 TO DT - 3
7280  PRINT " ";
7290  NEXT I
7300  PRINT RX
7310  RETURN
10000  REM    RANDOMIZATION OF RANGE - CHANGE 'RND (1)' TO 'RND (0
    )' FOR TRS-80 AND PET!
10010 R =  INT ( RND (1) * 11)
10020 RX = 5000 + (200 * R)
10030 DT =  INT ((RX / 200) + .5)
10040  RETURN
11000  REM  JUDGE RESULTS
11010 HT = 0
11020  IF DB = DT THEN HT = 2
11030  IF DB = DT + 1 THEN HT = 1
11040  IF DB = DT - 1 THEN HT = 1
11050  RETURN
12000  REM  REWARD
12010  FOR I = 1 TO 60
12020  PRINT "   KAPOW!!  ";
12030  NEXT I
12040  PRINT
12050  PRINT
12060  PRINT "DIRECT HIT!"
12070 DE = 1000
12080  GOSUB 19000
12090 L = 24
12100  GOSUB 18000
12110  GOTO 20000
12500  REM  CLOSE HIT
12510  PRINT "OUCH!! DAMAGED, BUT NOT OUT!"
12520  RETURN
14000  REM  MISS
14010  PRINT "HA HA!  MISSED ME!!"
14020  RETURN
18000  REM  SCROLLING
18010  FOR I = 1 TO L
18020  PRINT
18030  NEXT I
18040  RETURN
19000  REM  DELAY
19010  FOR I = 1 TO DE
19020  NEXT I
19030  RETURN
20000  REM  CLOSING
20010  PRINT "WANT TO TRY AGAIN?"
20020  PRINT "TYPE IN 'YES' OR 'NO'"
```

```
20030  INPUT S$
20040  IF S$ = "YES" THEN 4000
20050  PRINT "BYE FOR NOW, ";NA$;"!"
```

```
         * -->TABLE OF VARIABLES<--
```

D - TOTAL DISTANCE
4210 6050 6070 6070 6080

DB - DISTANCE IN SCALE
6080 7030 7070 7110 11020 11030 11040

DE - DELAY
2080 2420 12070 19010

DT - DISTANCE TO TARGET IN SCALE
7160 7230 7270 10030 11020 11030 11040

ED - ELEVATION IN DEGREES
4060 4070 4170 6010

ER - ELEVATION IN RADIANS
6010 6020 6040 6050

G - ACCELERATION OF GRAVITY
1010 6020 6040

H - MAXIMUM ELEVATION,
4230 6020 6030 6030

HT - HIT
4300 4310 4320 11010 11020 11030 11040

I - COUNTER
2010 2020 2070 7070 7090 7110 7130 7160 7180 7200 7220
7230 7250 7270 7290 12010 12030 18010 18030 19010 19020

J - COUNTER
2020 2040

L - SCROLLING LINES
2100 2130 2180 2380 4020 12090 18010

NA$ - NAME
2150 2170 4080 20050

R - RANDOM NUMBER
10010 10020

RX - TARGET RANGE IN METERS
4040 7300 10020 10030

S$ - STUDENT INPUT
2370 20030 20040

T - TIME IN AIR IN SECONDS
4250 6040 6050 6060 6060

VI - INITIAL VELOCITY
4110 4190 6020 6040 6050

END OF VAR. LIST

SAMPLE RUN

]RUN
BALLISTICS
WHAT IS YOUR NAME?
?JUDY
NICE TO MEET YOU, JUDY.
THIS IS A PROGRAM WHICH SIMULATES THE
FLIGHT OF A CANNON BALL.
YOU MUST SUPPLY THE ANGLE AT WHICH
THE GUN IS TO BE FIRED. THIS IS AN
ANGLE EXPRESSED IN A RANGE OF
0 TO 90 DEGREES.
IN ADDITION, YOU WILL HAVE TO DECIDE
ON THE VELOCITY OF THE CANNON BALL.
SINCE YOU CAN VARY THE AMOUNT OF
GUNPOWDER IN THE CANNON, THIS IS NOT
A PROBLEM. USUALLY VELOCITIES IN THE
RANGE OF 200 TO 300 METERS PER SECOND
ARE EFFECTIVE.
PRESS 'RETURN' OR 'ENTER'
?
      HERE WE GO!
TARGET RANGE IS 5600 METERS.
ENTER ELEVATION ANGLE IN DEGREES:?45
ENTER VELOCITY IN M/S:?250
         BOOM!
ELEVATION: 45 DEGREES
INIT. VELOCITY: 250 M/S
TOTAL DISTANCE: 6377 METERS
MAXIMUM ELEVATION: 1594 METERS
TOTAL TIME IN AIR: 36 SEC.

                              CRASH
                                #
X/   ^^^
****
                       5600

HA HA! MISSED ME!!
TARGET RANGE IS 5600 METERS.
ENTER ELEVATION ANGLE IN DEGREES:?35
ENTER VELOCITY IN M/S:?250
         BOOM!
ELEVATION: 35 DEGREES
INIT. VELOCITY: 250 M/S
TOTAL DISTANCE: 5992 METERS
MAXIMUM ELEVATION: 1049 METERS
TOTAL TIME IN AIR: 29 SEC.

```
                              CRASH
                               ╬
X/                            ^^^
*******************************************
                            5600


HA HA!  MISSED ME!!
TARGET RANGE IS 5600 METERS.
ENTER ELEVATION ANGLE IN DEGREES:?35
ENTER VELOCITY IN M/S:?245
         BOOM!
ELEVATION:        35 DEGREES
INIT. VELOCITY:   245 M/S
TOTAL DISTANCE:    5755 METERS
MAXIMUM ELEVATION: 1007 METERS
TOTAL TIME IN AIR: 28 SEC.


                              CRASH
                               ╬
X/                            ^^^
*******************************************
                            5600


OUCH!! DAMAGED, BUT NOT OUT!
TARGET RANGE IS 5600 METERS.
ENTER ELEVATION ANGLE IN DEGREES:?35
ENTER VELOCITY IN M/S:?240
         BOOM!
ELEVATION:        35 DEGREES
INIT. VELOCITY:   240 M/S
TOTAL DISTANCE:    5523 METERS
MAXIMUM ELEVATION: 966 METERS
TOTAL TIME IN AIR: 28 SEC.


                              CRASH
                               ╬
X/                            ^^^
*******************************************
                            5600


    KAPOW!!     KAPOW!!     KAPOW!!     KAPOW!!
DIRECT HIT!
WANT TO TRY AGAIN?
TYPE IN 'YES' OR 'NO'
?NO
BYE FOR NOW, JUDY!
]
```

CAR WASH

PROGRAM DESCRIPTION

This program simulates the planning and operation of a typical Saturday car wash. You operate a car wash for five days with the sole objective of making as much money as you possibly can obtain. You have a total of five helpers, each of whom can wash a maximum of 20 cars during the day. One important hint: Pay careful attention to the weather forecasts, since rainy days can cause you to lose a great deal of money!

The main variables in this program are as follows:

A. Price per wash

B. Weather

C. Amount of advertising

D. Traffic

E. Number of helpers

PROGRAM NOTES

1. You can vary the weather by changing variables A, B, C, and D in lines 6400 - 6620. These four variables represent the odds given to the four outcomes by any of the four predictions.

2. Consider adding other factors such as: A. Gas station owner demands 10 dollars per day rent. B. Sunburn strikes down 2 workers!

PROGRAM LISTING

```
100  REM  CAR WASH BY GARY ORWIG
1000  REM  INITIALIZATION
1010 BA = 25.00
1020 WA = 5
2000  REM  INTRODUCTION
2010 L = 24
2020  GOSUB 18000
2030  PRINT "          CAR WASH!"
2040 L = 12
2050  GOSUB 18000
2060 DE = 1500
2070  GOSUB 19000
2080 L = 24
2090  GOSUB 18000
2100  PRINT "YOU ARE GOING TO START A CAR WASH!"
2110  PRINT
2120  PRINT "YOU WILL RUN IT FOR FIVE DAYS"
2130  PRINT "WITH THE SOLE OBJECT BEING TO MAKE"
2140  PRINT "AS MUCH MONEY AS POSSIBLE!"
2150  PRINT
2160  PRINT "YOU WILL HAVE A TOTAL OF 5 WORKERS,"
2170  PRINT "EACH OF WHOM CAN WASH A MAXIMUM OF"
2180  PRINT "20 CARS DURING THE DAY."
2190  PRINT
2200  PRINT "AS YOU WILL SEE, THERE ARE A"
2210  PRINT "NUMBER OF FACTORS YOU MUST CONSIDER,"
2220  PRINT "BUT BY ALL MEANS, YOU NEED TO WATCH"
2230  PRINT "THE WEATHER FORECASTS, SINCE RAINY"
2240  PRINT "WEATHER WILL DO YOU IN!"
2250  PRINT
2260  PRINT "THE ONLY WAY TO LEARN IS BY DOING,SO"
2270  PRINT "WHEN YOU ARE READY, PUSH THE 'RETURN'"
2280  PRINT "OR 'ENTER' KEY."
2290 L = 3
2300  GOSUB 18000
2310  INPUT S$
4000  REM  MAIN PROGRAM
4010 DA = DA + 1
4020  IF DA = 6 THEN 20000
4030 WA = 5
4040 L = 24
4050  GOSUB 18000
4060  PRINT "TODAY IS DAY NUMBER ";DA;"."
4070 L = 6
4080  GOSUB 18000
4090 DE = 1500
4100  GOSUB 19000
4110  GOSUB 6320
4120  PRINT
4130  PRINT "THE WEATHER FORECAST IS:"
4140  PRINT WP$
4150 L = 12
4160  GOSUB 18000
4170 DE = 2000
```

```
4180  GOSUB 19000
4190  GOSUB 18000
4200  PRINT "YOU HAVE A BALANCE OF ";BA;" DOLLARS."
4210  PRINT
4220  PRINT "WHAT PRICE ARE YOU GOING TO CHARGE";
4230  INPUT P
4240  GOSUB 6010
4250  IF P < .26 OR P > 4.49 THEN 4220
4260  PRINT
4270  PRINT "IT COSTS ABOUT .25 PER CAR FOR MATERIALS"
4280  PRINT "PRESENTLY YOU HAVE ";MM;" DOLLARS"
4290  PRINT "WORTH OF SOAP,SPONGES,RAGS,ETC."
4300  PRINT "DO YOU WISH TO ADD TO THIS (YES OR NO)"
4310  INPUT S$
4320  IF S$ = "NO" THEN 4400
4330  PRINT
4340  PRINT "ENTER THE AMOUNT YOU WANT TO ADD."
4350  INPUT SA
4360  GOSUB 7000
4370  IF SA > 0 THEN 4340
4380  PRINT "YOU NOW HAVE $";MM;" WORTH OF MATERIALS."
4390  PRINT "AND A BALANCE OF $";BA
4400  PRINT
4410  REM
4420  PRINT "BALANCE = $";BA
4430  PRINT "AMOUNT SPENT ON ADVERTISING = $";TT
4440  PRINT "YOU HAVE A CHOICE OF THE FOLLOWING"
4450  PRINT "FORMS OF ADVERTISING:"
4460  PRINT
4470  PRINT "  MEDIUM    COST PER UNIT"
4480  PRINT
4490  PRINT "1. RADIO       $20.00"
4500  PRINT "2. NEWSPAPER    $5.00"
4510  PRINT "3. POSTERS      $1.00"
4520  PRINT "4. KIDS AT CURB  $1.00"
4530  PRINT
4540  PRINT "PICK A NUMBER (OR 0 FOR NONE)."
4550  INPUT SA
4560  IF SA = 0 THEN 4750
4570  IF SA = 4 THEN 4610
4580  PRINT "HOW MANY UNITS?"
4590  INPUT UN
4600  GOSUB 4710
4610  PRINT "YOU NOW HAVE ";WA;" KIDS TO WASH CARS"
4620  PRINT "AND ";5 - WA;" KIDS AT THE CURB"
4630  PRINT "WAVING CARS IN.  EACH KID AT THE CURB"
4640  PRINT "HAS A POSTER ($1.00) AND A BIG SMILE."
4650  PRINT "********BUT THEY CAN'T WASH CARS !******"
4660  PRINT
4670  PRINT "HOW MANY OF YOUR 5 KIDS DO YOU WANT AT"
4680  PRINT "THE CURB?"
4690  WA = 5
4700  INPUT UN
4710  GOSUB 6130
4720  TT = TT + TL
4730  BA = BA - TL
```

```
4740  GOTO 4410
4750  REM
5000  REM  LIST VARIABLES
5010 L = 24
5020  GOSUB 18000
5030  PRINT " SUMMARY FOR START OF DAY ";DA
5040  PRINT
5050  PRINT "WEATHER FORECAST: ";WP$
5060  PRINT
5070  PRINT "CASH ON HAND : $";BA
5080  PRINT
5090  PRINT "CASH VALUE OF CAR WASH SUPPLIES : $";MM
5100  PRINT
5110  PRINT "ADVERTISING BUDGET FOR TODAY: $";TT
5120  PRINT
5130  PRINT "NUMBER OF 'CURB KIDS': ";5 - WA
5140  PRINT
5150  PRINT "NUMBER OF CAR WASHERS: ";WA
5160  PRINT
5170  PRINT "PRICE PER CAR: $";P
5180  PRINT
5190  PRINT "PRESS 'RETURN' OR 'ENTER'": REM  FOR PET PRESS ANY LE
      TTER BEFORE PRESSING RETURN
5200  PRINT "TO GET THE DAY GOING!"
5210 L = 3
5220  GOSUB 18000
5230  INPUT S$
5500  REM  WASH CARS!
5510  GOSUB 6640
5520  GOSUB 6750
5530  GOSUB 6850
5540 IC = P * VW
5550 BA = BA + IC
5560  PRINT "WEATHER: ";WF$
5570  PRINT "TRAFFIC: ";SF$
5580  PRINT "VEHICLES WASHED: ";VW
5590  PRINT "VEHICLES NOT WASHED: ";VI - VW
5600  PRINT "INCOME: $";IC
5610  PRINT "COST OF MATERIALS USED: $";VW * .25
5620  PRINT "MATERIALS STARTED WITH: $";MM
5630  PRINT "BALANCE ON HAND: $";BA
5640 MM = MM - (VW * .25)
5650 TT = 0
5660  PRINT
5670  IF VI > WA * 20 THEN  PRINT "TOO MANY CARS FOR ";WA;" WASHER
      S!"
5680  IF MM < .25 THEN  PRINT "OUT OF SUPPLIES!"
5690  PRINT
5700  PRINT "PRESS 'RETURN' OR 'ENTER'": REM  FOR PET PRESS ANY LE
      TTER BEFORE PRESSING RETURN
5710 L = 6
5720  GOSUB 18000
5730  INPUT S$
5740  GOTO 4000
6000  REM  CALCULATIONS
6010  REM  PRICE FACTOR
```

```
6020  IF P < 4.50 THEN 6040
6030  PRINT "YOUR PRICE IS TOO HIGH!"
6040  IF P > .25 THEN 6060
6050  PRINT "YOUR PRICE IS TOO LOW!"
6060  IF P < .76 THEN PF = 2.0
6070  IF P > .75 AND P < 1.26 THEN PF = 1.5
6080  IF P > 1.25 AND P < 1.76 THEN PF = 1.0
6090  IF P > 1.75 AND P < 2.51 THEN PF = .75
6100  IF P > 2.50 AND P < 3.51 THEN PF = .50
6110  IF P > 3.50 THEN PF = .25
6120  RETURN
6130  REM  ADVERTISING FACTOR
6140  ON SA GOTO 6150,6190,6230,6270
6150 TL = 20 * UN
6160  GOSUB 11000
6170 AF = AF + .10 * UN
6180  RETURN
6190 TL = 5 * UN
6200  GOSUB 11000
6210 AF = AF + .05 * UN
6220  RETURN
6230 TL = 1 * UN
6240  GOSUB 11000
6250 AF = AF + .02 * UN
6260  RETURN
6270 TL = 1 * UN
6280 WA = WA - UN
6290  GOSUB 11000
6300 AF = AF + .2 * UN
6310  RETURN
6320  REM  WEATHER PREDICTION
6330 N = 100
6340  GOSUB 10000
6350  IF R < 31 THEN WP = 1
6360  IF R > 30 AND R < 61 THEN WP = 2
6370  IF R > 60 AND R < 86 THEN WP = 3
6380  IF R > 85 THEN WP = 4
6390  ON WP GOTO 6400,6460,6520,6580
6400 WP$ = "10% CHANCE OF RAIN"
6410 A = 50
6420 B = 30
6430 C = 10
6440 D = 10
6450  RETURN
6460 WP$ = "25% CHANCE OF RAIN"
6470 A = 30
6480 B = 35
6490 C = 20
6500 D = 15
6510  RETURN
6520 WP$ = "50% CHANCE OF RAIN"
6530 A = 15
6540 B = 20
6550 C = 30
6560 D = 35
6570  RETURN
```

```
6580 WP$ = "90% CHANCE OF RAIN"
6590 A = 5
6600 B = 10
6610 C = 20
6620 D = 65
6630 RETURN
6640 REM  ACTUAL WEATHER
6650 GOSUB 10000
6660 IF R < A + 1 THEN WF = 1.5
6670 IF R > A AND R < A + B + 1 THEN WF = 1
6680 IF R > A + B AND R < A + B + C + 1 THEN WF = .5
6690 IF R > A + B + C THEN WF = .001
6700 IF WF = 1.5 THEN WF$ = "HOT AND SUNNY"
6710 IF WF = 1 THEN WF$ = "PARTLY SUNNY"
6720 IF WF = .5 THEN WF$ = "CLOUDY"
6730 IF WF = .001 THEN WF$ = "RAIN!"
6740 RETURN
6750 REM  STREET FACTOR
6760 N = 10
6770 GOSUB 10000
6780 IF R < 4 THEN SF = 1.3
6790 IF R > 3 AND R < 10 THEN SF = 1
6800 IF R = 10 THEN SF = .5
6810 IF SF = 1.3 THEN SF$ = "HEAVY TRAFFIC"
6820 IF SF = 1 THEN SF$ = "AVERAGE TRAFFIC"
6830 IF SF = .5 THEN SF$ = "STREET REPAIRS!"
6840 RETURN
6850 REM  BUSINESS FOR DAY
6860 VI =  INT (50 * PF * (AF + 1) * WF * SF)
6870 VM = WA * 20
6880 ML = MM / .25
6890 IF VI < VM THEN 6920
6900 VW = VM
6910 GOTO 6950
6920 VW = VI
6930 IF VW < ML THEN 6950
6940 VW = ML
6950 RETURN
7000 REM  ADD TO MATERIALS
7010 IF SA > BA GOTO 7060
7020 BA = BA - SA
7030 MM = MM + SA
7040 SA = 0
7050 RETURN
7060 PRINT "THAT'S MORE THAN YOU HAVE!"
7070 RETURN
10000 REM   RANDOMIZATION - CHANGE 'RND (1)' TO 'RND (0)' FOR TR
    S-80 AND PET!
10010 R =  INT ( RND (1) * N) + 1
10020 RETURN
11000 REM  CHECK BALANCE
11010 IF TL > BA OR WA < 1 THEN 11030
11020 RETURN
11030 IF TL > BA GOTO 11050
11040 GOTO 11080
11050 PRINT "YOU DON'T HAVE $";TL;"!"
```

```
11060  TL = 0
11070  GOTO 4400
11080  PRINT "THERE'S NO ONE LEFT TO WASH CARS!"
11090  GOTO 4610
18000  REM  SCROLLING
18010  FOR I = 1 TO L
18020  PRINT
18030  NEXT I
18040  RETURN
19000  REM  DELAY
19010  FOR I = 1 TO DE
19020  NEXT I
19030  RETURN
20000  REM  CLOSING
20010  L = 24
20020  GOSUB 18000
20030  PRINT "YOUR 5 DAYS ARE OVER!"
20040  PRINT
20050  PRINT "YOU HAVE ACCUMULATED A TOTAL OF "
20060  PRINT BA;" DOLLARS!"
20070  PRINT "DIVIDED 5 WAYS (REMEMBER YOUR 4"
20080  PRINT "PARTNERS), THAT MAKES ";BA / 5;" DOLLARS"
20090  PRINT "PER PERSON!"
20100  L = 6
20110  GOSUB 18000
20120  END
```

```
        *  -->TABLE OF VARIABLES<--
```

A - WEATHER FACTOR
6410 6470 6530 6590 6660 6670 6670 6680 6680 6690

AF - ADVERTISING FACTOR
6170 6170 6210 6210 6250 6250 6300 6300 6860

B - WEATHER FACTOR
6420 6480 6540 6600 6670 6680 6680 6690

BA - BALANCE ON HAND
1010 4200 4390 4420 4730 4730 5070 5550 5550 5630 7010
7020 7020 11010 11030 20060 20080

C - WEATHER FACTOR
6430 6490 6550 6610 6680 6690

D - WEATHER FACTOR
6440 6500 6560 6620

DA - DAY NUMBER
4010 4010 4020 4060 5030

DE - DELAY
2060 4090 4170 19010

I - COUNTER
18010 18030 19010 19020

IC - INCOME
5540 5550 5600

L - LINES FOR SCROLLING
2010 2040 2080 2290 4040 4070 4150 5010 5210 5710 18010
20010 20100

ML - MATERIALS LIMIT
6880 6930 6940

MM - MATERIALS STARTED WITH
4280 4380 5090 5620 5640 5640 5680 6880 7030 7030

N - MAXIMUM RANDOM NUMBER
6330 6760 10010

P - PRICE PER WASH
4230 4250 4250 5170 5540 6020 6040 6060 6070 6070 6080
6080 6090 6090 6100 6100 6110

PF - PRICE FACTOR
6060 6070 6080 6090 6100 6110 6860

R - RANDOM NUMBER
6350 6360 6360 6370 6370 6380 6660 6670 6670 6680 6680
6690 6780 6790 6790 6800 10010

S$ - STUDENT ANSWER
2310 4310 4320 5230 5730

SA - STUDENT ANSWER
4350 4370 4550 4560 4570 6140 7010 7020 7030 7040

SF - STREET (TRAFFIC) FACTOR
6780 6790 6800 6810 6820 6830 6860

SF$ - STREET MESSAGE
5570 6810 6820 6830

TL - COST OF ADVERTISING AS SELECTED
4720 4730 6150 6190 6230 6270 11010 11030 11050 11060

TT - TOTAL ADVERTISING BUDGET FOR DAY
4430 4720 4720 5110 5650

UN - UNITS OF EACH AD TECHNIQUE
4590 4700 6150 6170 6190 6210 6230 6250 6270 6280 6300

VI - VEHICLES ENTERING
5590 5670 6860 6890 6920

VM - MAXIMUM NO. OF VEHICLES WHICH COULD BE WASHED
6870 6890 6900

VW - VEHICLES ACTUALLY WASHED
5540 5580 5590 5610 5640 6900 6920 6930 6940

WA - NUMBER OF CAR WASHERS
1020 4030 4610 4620 4690 5130 5150 5670 5670 6280 6280
6870 11010

WF - ACTUAL WEATHER FACTOR
6660 6670 6680 6690 6700 6710 6720 6730 6860

WF$ - WEATHER MESSAGE
5560 6700 6710 6720 6730

WP - WEATHER PREDICTION
6350 6360 6370 6380 6390

WP$ - WEATHER PREDICTION MESSAGE
4140 5050 6400 6460 6520 6580

END OF VAR. LIST

SAMPLE RUN

```
]RUN
          CAR WASH!
YOU ARE GOING TO START A CAR WASH!
YOU WILL RUN IT FOR FIVE DAYS
WITH THE SOLE OBJECT BEING TO MAKE
AS MUCH MONEY AS POSSIBLE!
YOU WILL HAVE A TOTAL OF 5 WORKERS,
EACH OF WHOM CAN WASH A MAXIMUM OF
20 CARS DURING THE DAY.
AS YOU WILL SEE, THERE ARE A
NUMBER OF FACTORS YOU MUST CONSIDER,
BUT BY ALL MEANS, YOU NEED TO WATCH
THE WEATHER FORECASTS, SINCE RAINY
WEATHER WILL DO YOU IN!
THE ONLY WAY TO LEARN IS BY DOING,SO
WHEN YOU ARE READY, PUSH THE 'RETURN'
OR 'ENTER' KEY.
?
TODAY IS DAY NUMBER 1.
THE WEATHER FORECAST IS:
10% CHANCE OF RAIN
YOU HAVE A BALANCE OF 25 DOLLARS.
WHAT PRICE ARE YOU GOING TO CHARGE?2.00
IT COSTS ABOUT .25 PER CAR FOR MATERIALS
PRESENTLY YOU HAVE 0 DOLLARS
WORTH OF SOAP,SPONGES,RAGS,ETC.
DO YOU WISH TO ADD TO THIS (YES OR NO)
?YES
ENTER THE AMOUNT YOU WANT TO ADD.
?15.00
YOU NOW HAVE $15 WORTH OF MATERIALS.
AND A BALANCE OF $10
BALANCE = $10
AMOUNT SPENT ON ADVERTISING = $0
YOU HAVE A CHOICE OF THE FOLLOWING
```

FORMS OF ADVERTISING:
    MEDIUM   COST PER UNIT
1. RADIO $20.00
2. NEWSPAPER $5.00
3. POSTERS $1.00
4. KIDS AT CURB $1.00
PICK A NUMBER (OR 0 FOR NONE).
?2
HOW MANY UNITS?
?1
BALANCE = $5
AMOUNT SPENT ON ADVERTISING = $5
YOU HAVE A CHOICE OF THE FOLLOWING
FORMS OF ADVERTISING:
    MEDIUM   COST PER UNIT
1. RADIO $20.00
2. NEWSPAPER $5.00
3. POSTERS $1.00
4. KIDS AT CURB $1.00
PICK A NUMBER (OR 0 FOR NONE).
?4
YOU NOW HAVE 5 KIDS TO WASH CARS
AND 0 KIDS AT THE CURB
WAVING CARS IN. EACH KID AT THE CURB
HAS A POSTER ($1.00) AND A BIG SMILE,
********BUT THEY CAN'T WASH CARS !******
HOW MANY OF YOUR 5 KIDS DO YOU WANT AT
THE CURB?
?1
BALANCE = $4
AMOUNT SPENT ON ADVERTISING = $6
YOU HAVE A CHOICE OF THE FOLLOWING
FORMS OF ADVERTISING:
    MEDIUM   COST PER UNIT
1. RADIO $20.00
2. NEWSPAPER $5.00
3. POSTERS $1.00
4. KIDS AT CURB $1.00
PICK A NUMBER (OR 0 FOR NONE).
?3
HOW MANY UNITS?
?3
BALANCE = $1
AMOUNT SPENT ON ADVERTISING = $9
YOU HAVE A CHOICE OF THE FOLLOWING
FORMS OF ADVERTISING:
    MEDIUM   COST PER UNIT
1. RADIO $20.00
2. NEWSPAPER $5.00
3. POSTERS $1.00
4. KIDS AT CURB $1.00
PICK A NUMBER (OR 0 FOR NONE).
?0
 SUMMARY FOR START OF DAY 1
WEATHER FORECAST: 10% CHANCE OF RAIN
CASH ON HAND : $1

```
CASH VALUE OF CAR WASH SUPPLIES : $15
ADVERTISING BUDGET FOR TODAY: $9
NUMBER OF 'CURB KIDS': 1
NUMBER OF CAR WASHERS: 4
PRICE PER CAR: $2
PRESS 'RETURN' OR 'ENTER'
TO GET THE DAY GOING!
?
WEATHER: PARTLY SUNNY
TRAFFIC: AVERAGE TRAFFIC
VEHICLES WASHED: 49
VEHICLES NOT WASHED: 0
INCOME: $98
COST OF MATERIALS USED: $12.25
MATERIALS STARTED WITH: $15
BALANCE ON HAND: $99
PRESS 'RETURN' OR 'ENTER'
?
```

CHECK-OUT COUNTER

PROGRAM DESCRIPTION

This program roughly simulates some of the things you would do in a department store check-out counter. The computer scrolls a number of prices and you must simulate the operation of a cash register by entering the prices into the computer one at a time. You must enter in correct prices and give the right amount of change at the end of the check-out or you will have a great number of customers angry with you! As you proceed, the prices will move faster and faster to help you increase your efficiency. The faster you can go without making any errors the higher your pay will be!

PROGRAM NOTES

1. It would be best to "flash" the prices, rather than to scroll them if your computer will allow it.

2. Computers usually do a terrible job of sticking to only 2 decimal places, as is required in money matters. While this program has several counter measures scattered through it, you might try to pull together the "Mighty Money Maker" subroutine which all money values would be passed through during the operation of the program. The two problem areas are: (A) printing 3.4 dollars instead of 3.40 dollars, and (B) printing 3.4000001 dollars instead of 3.40 dollars! Good luck!

```
100  REM  CHECK-OUT COUNTER BY GARY ORWIG
1000  REM  INITIALIZATION - 'MX' IS MAXIMUM OF VALUES DISPLAYED.
1010 MX = 10
2000  REM  INTRODUCTION
2010 L = 24
2020  GOSUB 18000
2030  FOR J = 1 TO 10
2040  PRINT "        CHECK - OUT COUNTER"
2050 L = 12
2060  GOSUB 18000
2070 D = 250
2080  GOSUB 19000
2090  NEXT J
2100  PRINT "THIS PROGRAM ROUGHLY SIMULATES SOME OF"
2110  PRINT "THE THINGS YOU WOULD DO AT A DEPARTMENT"
2120  PRINT "STORE CHECK OUT COUNTER."
2130  PRINT
2140  PRINT "YOU WILL SEE A BUNCH OF PRICES, AND"
2150  PRINT "TYPE THEM ONE AT A TIME INTO THE "
2160  PRINT "COMPUTER.  YOU MUST TYPE THEM IN"
2170  PRINT "ACCURATELY, OR YOU WILL HAVE ANGRY"
2180  PRINT "CUSTOMERS AFTER YOU!"
2190  PRINT
2200  PRINT "AFTER TYPING IN ALL THE PRICES, YOU"
2210  PRINT "WILL RING UP A TOTAL, BE GIVEN CASH,"
2220  PRINT "AND MAKE THE CORRECT CHANGE."
2230  PRINT "ONCE AGAIN, YOU MUST BE ACCURATE!"
2240  PRINT
2250  PRINT "AS YOU PROCEED, THE PRICES WILL MOVE"
2260  PRINT "FASTER AND FASTER.  THE FASTER YOU CAN"
2270  PRINT "GO WITHOUT MISTAKES, THE HIGHER YOUR"
2280  PRINT "PAY WILL BE!"
2290  PRINT
2300  PRINT "PUSH 'ENTER' OR 'RETURN' TO START.": REM  FOR PET PRE
      SS ANY LETTER BEFORE PRESSING RETURN
2310  INPUT SA$
3000  REM  EXAMPLE
3010  GOSUB 18000
3020  PRINT "YOU WILL SEE A PRICE, LIKE THIS:"
3030  GOSUB 18000
3040 D = 1000
3050  GOSUB 19000
3060  GOSUB 18000
3070  GOSUB 10000
3080  PRINT "              ";R$
3090  GOSUB 18000
3100 D = 200
3110  GOSUB 19000
3120 L = 24
3130  GOSUB 18000
3140  PRINT "AS SOON AS THE PRICE DISAPPEARS, TYPE"
3150  PRINT "IT IN AND PUSH 'RETURN' OR 'ENTER'."
3160  INPUT SA$
3170  IF SA$ = R$ THEN  PRINT "VERY GOOD!"
```

```
3180 D = 1000
3190  GOSUB 19000
3200  GOSUB 18000
3210  PRINT "       HERE WE GO!"
3220 L = 12
3230  GOSUB 18000
3240  GOSUB 19000
3250 D = 300
3260 MX = 10
4000  REM  MAIN PROGRAM
4010  IF D < 50 THEN 20000
4020  GOSUB 10000
4030 L = 12
4040  GOSUB 18000
4050  PRINT "              ";R$
4060  GOSUB 18000
4070  GOSUB 19000
4080  GOSUB 18000
4090  INPUT SA
4100  GOSUB 11000
4110  GOTO 4000
4120  PRINT "PUSH 'RETURN' OR 'ENTER' TO GET"
4130  PRINT "THE TOTAL."; REM  FOR PET PRESS ANY LETTER BEFORE PRE
     SSING RETURN
4140  INPUT SA$
4150  PRINT "YOUR TOTAL IS ";SS
4160  REM  CALCULATE PAYMENT
4170 PA = PA + 10
4180  IF PA > SS THEN 4200
4190  GOTO 4170
4200  PRINT
4210  PRINT
4220  PRINT "THE CUSTOMER PAYS YOU WITH ";PA
4230  PRINT "DOLLARS."
4240  PRINT
4250 CC = PA - SS
4260 CC =  INT (CC * 100 + .5) / 100
4270  PRINT "THE REQUIRED CHANGE IS ";CC
4280  PRINT "DOLLARS."
4290  PRINT
4300  PRINT
4310  PRINT "CHANGE BACK!"
4320  PRINT
4330  PRINT "HOW MANY 'FIVES'?"
4340  INPUT SA
4350 SC = SA * 5 + SC
4360  PRINT "HOW MANY 'ONES'?"
4370  INPUT SA
4380 SC = SA + SC
4390  PRINT "HOW MANY 'QUARTERS'?"
4400  INPUT SA
4410 SC = SA * .25 + SC
4420  PRINT "HOW MANY 'DIMES'?"
4430  INPUT SA
4440 SC = SA * .10 + SC
4450  PRINT "HOW MAY 'NICKLES'?"
```

```
4460  INPUT SA
4470 SC = SA * .05 + SC
4480  PRINT "HOW MANY 'PENNIES'?"
4490  INPUT SA
4500 SC = SA * .01 + SC
4510  PRINT
4520  PRINT "YOU GAVE THE CUSTOMER ";SC
4530  PRINT "DOLLARS CHANGE."
4540 CC =  INT (CC * 100 + .5) / 100
4550 SC =  INT (SC * 100 + .5) / 100
4560  IF CC = SC THEN 4710
4570  PRINT "THE CASH REGISTER SHOWS THAT YOU SHOULD"
4580  PRINT "HAVE PAID BACK ";CC;" DOLLARS!"
4590  IF CC > SC THEN 4650
4600  PRINT "CUSTOMER GOES AWAY HAPPY!!"
4610  PRINT "BUT YOUR PAY WILL BE DOCKED!"
4620 D = D + 50
4630  PRINT
4640  GOTO 5000
4650  PRINT "ANGRY CUSTOMER WANTS MANAGER!!"
4660  PRINT
4670  PRINT "MANAGER SMOOTHS THINGS OUT, BUT HE"
4680  PRINT "IS SURE MAD AT YOU!"
4690 D = D + 50
4700  GOTO 5000
4710  PRINT "GOOD GOING!"
4720 D = D - 50
5000  REM  SPOT CHECK TOTAL
5010  PRINT " A SPOT CHECK OF THE PURCHASES"
5020  PRINT "SHOWS THE CORRECT TOTAL IS: ";CT
5030  PRINT "DOLLARS."
5040  PRINT "YOUR TOTAL WAS: ";SS
5050  PRINT "DOLLARS."
5060 CT =  INT (CT * 100 + .5) / 100
5070 SS =  INT (SS * 100 + .5) / 100
5080  IF CT = SS THEN 5220
5090  IF CT > SS THEN 5160
5100  PRINT "YOU OVER CHARGED THE CUSTOMER "
5110 DF =  INT ((SS - CT) * 100 + .5) / 100
5120  PRINT DF;" DOLLARS"
5130  PRINT "BECAUSE YOU KEYED IN THE PRICES WRONG!"
5140 D = D + 50
5150  GOTO 6000
5160  PRINT "THE STORE LOST"
5170 DF =  INT ((CT - SS) * 100 + .5) / 100
5180  PRINT DF;" DOLLARS BECAUSE"
5190  PRINT "YOU KEYED IN THE PRICES WRONG!"
5200 D = D + 50
5210  GOTO 6000
5220  PRINT "GOOD GOING!"
5230 D = D - 50
6000  REM  GO AGAIN?
6010 PA =  INT (600 - D) / 100
6020  PRINT
6030  PRINT "YOUR PRESENT PAY IS ";PA
6040  PRINT "DOLLARS PER HOUR."
```

```
6050 PRINT
6060 PRINT "WOULD YOU LIKE TO GO AGAIN?"
6070 PRINT "(YES OR NO)"
6080 INPUT SA$
6090 IF SA$ = "NO" THEN 20060
6100 REM  RESET
6110 PA = 0
6120 CT = 0
6130 SS = 0
6140 SA = 0
6150 CC = 0
6160 SC = 0
6170 DF = 0
6180 PB = 0
6190 PRINT
6200 PRINT "PRESS 'RETURN' OR 'ENTER' TO START!": REM  FOR PET PR
     ESS ANY LETTER BEFORE PRESSING RETURN
6210 INPUT SA$
6220 GOTO 4000
10000 REM   RANDOMIZATION - CHANGE 'RND (1)' TO 'RND (0)' FOR TR
      S-80 AND PET!
10010 R =  RND (1) * MX
10020 R$ =  STR$ (R)
10030 FOR I = 1 TO  LEN (R$)
10040 IF  MID$ (R$,I,1) < > "." THEN  NEXT I
10050 IF I + 2 >  LEN (R$) THEN 10000
10060 R$ =  MID$ (R$,1,I + 2)
10070 RETURN
11000 REM  JUDGE ANSWER
11010 CT = CT +  VAL (R$)
11020 SS = SS + SA
11030 PB = PB + 1
11040 IF PB = 11 THEN 4120
11050 RETURN
18000 REM  SCROLLING
18010 FOR I = 1 TO L
18020 PRINT
18030 NEXT I
18040 RETURN
19000 REM  DELAY
19010 FOR I = 1 TO D
19020 NEXT I
19030 RETURN
20000 REM  CLOSE
20010 PRINT "YOU ARE A SUPER WHIZ AT THE CHECKOUT"
20020 PRINT "COUNTER! YOU MAY RETIRE WITH FULL"
20030 PRINT "BENIFITS!"
20040 PRINT
20050 PRINT "BYE!"
20060 END
```

            * -->TABLE OF VARIABLES<--

CC - REQUIRED CHANGE
4250 4260 4260 4270 4540 4540 4560 4580 4590 6150

CT - CORRECT TOTAL
5020 5060 5060 5080 5090 5110 5170 6120 11010 11010

D - DELAY
2070 3040 3100 3180 3250 4010 4620 4620 4690 4690 4720
4720 5140 5140 5200 5200 5230 5230 6010 19010

DF - DEFICIT FROM WRONG KEY IN
5110 5120 5170 5180 6170

I - COUNTER
10030 10040 10040 10050 10060 18010 18030 19010 19020

J - COUNTER
2030 2090

L - LINES OF SCROLLING
2010 2050 3120 3220 4030 18010

MX - MAXIMUM VALUES DISPLAYED
1010 3260 10010

PA - CUSTOMER PAYS THIS AMOUNT
4170 4170 4180 4220 4250 6010 6030 6110

PB - NO. OF PRICES DISPLAYED
6180 11030 11030 11040

R - RANDOM NUMBER
10010 10020

R$ - RANDOM NUMBER AS STRING (NEEDED FOR TRAILING ZEROS)
3080 3170 4050 10020 10030 10040 10050 10060 10060 11010

SA - STUDENT ANSWER
4090 4340 4350 4370 4380 4400 4410 4430 4440 4460 4470
4490 4500 6140 11020

SA$ - STUDENT ANSWER
2310 3160 3170 4140 6080 6090 6210

SC - CHANGE RETURNED BY STUDENT
4350 4350 4380 4380 4410 4410 4440 4440 4470 4470 4500
4500 4520 4550 4550 4560 4590 6160

SS
4150 4180 4250 5040 5070 5070 5080 5090 5110 5170 6130
11020 11020

END OF VAR. LIST

SAMPLE RUN

]RUN
CHECK-OUT COUNTER
THIS PROGRAM ROUGHLY SIMULATES SOME OF
THE THINGS YOU WOULD DO AT A DEPARTMENT

STORE CHECK OUT COUNTER.
YOU WILL SEE A BUNCH OF PRICES, AND
TYPE THEM ONE AT A TIME INTO THE
COMPUTER. YOU MUST TYPE THEM IN
ACCURATELY, OR YOU WILL HAVE ANGRY
CUSTOMERS AFTER YOU!
AFTER TYPING IN ALL THE PRICES, YOU
WILL RING UP A TOTAL, BE GIVEN CASH,
AND MAKE THE CORRECT CHANGE.
ONCE AGAIN, YOU MUST BE ACCURATE!
AS YOU PROCEED, THE PRICES WILL MOVE
FASTER AND FASTER. THE FASTER YOU CAN
GO WITHOUT MISTAKES, THE HIGHER YOUR
PAY WILL BE!
PUSH 'ENTER' OR 'RETURN' TO START.
?
YOU WILL SEE A PRICE, LIKE THIS:
            6.71
AS SOON AS THE PRICE DISAPPEARS, TYPE
IT IN AND PUSH 'RETURN' OR 'ENTER'.
?6.71
VERY GOOD!
        HERE WE GO!
            3.02
?3.02
            2.40
?2.40
            6.84
?6.48
            .43
?.43
            4.95
?4.95
            2.79
?2.79
            7.48
?7.48
            7.56
?7.56
            6.13
?6.13
            .84
?.84
            6.95
?6.95
PUSH 'RETURN' OR 'ENTER' TO GET
THE TOTAL.
?
YOUR TOTAL IS 49.03
THE CUSTOMER PAYS YOU WITH 50
DOLLARS.
THE REQUIRED CHANGE IS .97
DOLLARS.
CHANGE BACK:
HOW MANY 'FIVES'?
?0

```
HOW MANY 'ONES'?
?0
HOW MANY 'QUARTERS'?
?3
HOW MANY 'DIMES'?
?2
HOW MAY 'NICKLES'?
?0
HOW MANY 'PENNIES'?
?2
YOU GAVE THE CUSTOMER .97
DOLLARS CHANGE.
GOOD GOING!
 A SPOT CHECK OF THE PURCHASES
SHOWS THE CORRECT TOTAL IS: 49.39
DOLLARS.
YOUR TOTAL WAS: 49.03
DOLLARS.
THE STORE LOST
.36 DOLLARS BECAUSE
YOU KEYED IN THE PRICES WRONG!
YOUR PRESENT PAY IS 3
DOLLARS PER HOUR.
WOULD YOU LIKE TO GO AGAIN?
(YES OR NO)
?NO
]
```

STOCK MARKET

PROGRAM DESCRIPTION

This program is a simulation of some of the events which take place during the buying and selling of stock in companies traded on a stock exchange. The program enables you to place orders with the computer just as you would by phoning a stockbroker from your own home. You may choose to buy and sell stock from a limited portfolio of stocks based upon newspaper headlines relevant to those companies that own the shares of stock.

You start with $10,000 and your main objective is to increase that value as much as possible in six buying and selling sessions. Do watch the newspaper headlines carefully. They are your only hints to guide you toward success or failure in the market. The computer creates more havoc because many times the newspaper headlines are not always true statements. You have to read "between the lines." A computer printer would be very valuable in this simulation program by making it easier to refer back to your past stock transations.

PROGRAM NOTES

This is a very simple introduction to the stock market. Consider adding complicating factors (dividends, mergers, etc.) as your group can handle them. Although it rarely is this simple, additional subroutines might fit right into the "gosubs" in the main program (starting on line 4000).

```
100  REM   STOCK MARKET BY GARY ORWIG
1000 REM  INITIALIZE
1010 REM   THE FOLLOWING LINE DEFINES A FUNCTION WHICH ROUNDS NUM
     BERS TO TWO DECIMAL PLACES.  IT IS USED IN SUBROUTINE 16000.
      IF YOU CAN'T DEFINE FUNCTIONS IN YOUR BASIC, DELETE THE FOLL
     OWING LINE, SUBROUTINE 16000, AND LINE 6050.
1020 DEF  FN RD(X) =  INT (X * 100 + .5) * .01
1030 DIM G$(6),GF(6),N$(6),N1(6),N2(6),N3(6),N4(6),N5(6),N6(6),S$
     (6),SY(6),SN(6),OD(6),SM$(6)
1040 DIM C(6),S(6),N(6)
1050 FOR I = 1 TO 6
1060 READ G$(I),GF(I)
1070 NEXT I
1080 FOR I = 1 TO 6
1090 READ N$(I),N1(I),N2(I),N3(I),N4(I),N5(I),N6(I)
1100 NEXT I
1110 FOR I = 1 TO 6
1120 READ S$(I),SY(I),SN(I),OD(I),SM$(I)
1130 NEXT I
1140 CA = 10000: REM  CASH TO START WITH
1150 C(1) = 20: REM  THESE 6 VALUES ARE STARTING PRICES OF STOCK.
1160 C(2) = 30
1170 C(3) = 70
1180 C(4) = 40
1190 C(5) = 50
1200 C(6) = 40
2000 REM  INTRODUCTION
2010 FOR I = 1 TO 50
2020 PRINT "STOCK MARKET    ";
2030 NEXT I
2040 PRINT
2050 PRINT
2060 PRINT
2070 FOR I = 1 TO 1000
2080 NEXT I
2090 PRINT "THIS IS A SIMULATION OF SOME OF THE"
2100 PRINT "EVENTS WHICH TAKE PLACE IN THE"
2110 PRINT "BUYING AND SELLING OF STOCK."
2120 PRINT
2130 PRINT "YOU GET TO BUY AND SELL FROM A LIMITED"
2140 PRINT "PORTFOLIO OF STOCKS BASED UPON NEWS"
2150 PRINT "HEADLINES RELEVANT TO THOSE COMPANIES."
2160 PRINT
2170 PRINT "YOU START WITH 10000 DOLLARS, AND YOUR"
2180 PRINT "SOLE MISSION IS TO INCREASE THAT VALUE"
2190 PRINT "AS MUCH AS POSSIBLE IN 6 BUYING/SELLING"
2200 PRINT "SESSIONS."
2210 PRINT "DO WATCH THE HEADLINES CAREFULLY."
2220 PRINT "THEY ARE YOUR ONLY HINTS FOR SUCCESS."
2230 PRINT "BE CAREFUL, THOUGH BECAUSE NOT ALL"
2240 PRINT "HEADLINES ALWAYS TURN OUT TO BE TRUE!"
2250 PRINT
2260 PRINT
2270 PRINT
```

```
2280  PRINT
2290  PRINT "PRESS 'RETURN' OR 'ENTER'": REM  FOR PET PRESS ANY LE
      TTER BEFORE PRESSING RETURN
2300  INPUT SA$
2310  PRINT
2320  PRINT
2330  PRINT "HERE ARE THE COMPANIES:"
2340  PRINT
2350  PRINT "MIDNIGHT OIL COMPANY"
2360  PRINT "A COMPANY KNOWN FOR TAKING BIG RISKS."
2370  PRINT "SOMETIMES THEY WIN, BUT OFTEN THEY LOSE!"
2380  PRINT
2390  PRINT "SOLAR SEEKERS, INC."
2400  PRINT "A NEW COMPANY JUST GETTING ESTABLISHED."
2410  PRINT "APPEAR TO EMPLOY A NUMBER OF HIGH"
2420  PRINT "TECHNOLOGY EXPERTS."
2430  PRINT
2440  PRINT "MCDANIEL AIRCRAFT"
2450  PRINT "A WELL ESTABLISHED MILITARY/INDUSTRIAL"
2460  PRINT "ORIENTED AERONAUTICS COMPANY."
2470  PRINT
2480  PRINT
2490  PRINT
2500  PRINT "PRESS 'RETURN' OR 'ENTER'": REM  FOR PET PRESS ANY LE
      TTER BEFORE PRESSING RETURN
2510  INPUT SA$
2520  PRINT
2530  PRINT
2540  PRINT
2550  PRINT "HAPPY DAYS SOUTHERN MOTELS"
2560  PRINT "A LARGE CHAIN OF SOUTH UNITED STATES"
2570  PRINT "MOTELS, LARGELY DEPENDENT UPON TOURISM."
2580  PRINT "COMMUNITY PHONE COMPANY"
2590  PRINT "A TYPICAL UTILITY - - CONSERVATIVE AND"
2600  PRINT "FAIRLY IMMUNE TO WORLD PROBLEMS."
2610  PRINT
2620  PRINT "FRIENDLY ELECTRIC COMPANY"
2630  PRINT "A VERY PROGRESSIVE UTILITY, HEAVY INTO"
2640  PRINT "NUCLEAR POWER, WITH QUITE A BIT OF"
2650  PRINT "COMMUNITY OPPOSITION."
2660  PRINT
2670  PRINT
2680  PRINT "PRESS 'RETURN' OR 'ENTER'": REM  FOR PET PRESS ANY LE
      TTER BEFOR PRESSING RETURN
2690  INPUT SA$
2700  PRINT
2710  PRINT
2720  PRINT
2730  PRINT "HERE WE GO!"
2740  PRINT
2750  PRINT
2760  PRINT
2770  FOR I = 1 TO 1500
2780  NEXT I
4000  REM  MAIN PROGRAM
4010  DA = DA + 1
```

```
4020  IF DA = 7 THEN 20000
4030  GOSUB 5000
4040  GOSUB 6000
4050  GOSUB 8000
4060  GOSUB 7000
4070  IF SF = SN THEN  PRINT SM$(C)
4080  GOTO 4000
5000  REM  PRINT HEADLINES
5010  GOSUB 10000
5020  IF G$(R) = "*" THEN 5010
5030  PRINT G$(R)
5040  G$(R) = "*"
5050  GF = GF(R)
5060  GOSUB 10000
5070  IF N$(R) = "*" THEN 5060
5080  PRINT N$(R)
5090  N$(R) = "*"
5100  N(1) = N1(R)
5110  N(2) = N2(R)
5120  N(3) = N3(R)
5130  N(4) = N4(R)
5140  N(5) = N5(R)
5150  N(6) = N6(R)
5160  GOSUB 10000
5170  IF S$(R) = "*" THEN 5160
5180  PRINT S$(R)
5190  S$(R) = "*"
5200  SY = SY(R)
5210  SN = SN(R)
5220  OD = OD(R)
5230  SM$ = SM$(R)
5240  C = R
5250  RETURN
6000  REM  MENU
6010  VA = 0
6020  FOR I = 1 TO 6
6030  VA = VA + S(I) * C(I)
6040  NEXT I
6050  GOSUB 16000
6060  PRINT "COMPANY        SHARES       VALUE"
6070  PRINT
6080  PRINT "1. MID. OIL   ","  ";S(1),C(1)
6090  PRINT "2. SOL SEE    ","  ";S(2),C(2)
6100  PRINT "3. MC AIR     ","  ";S(3),C(3)
6110  PRINT "4. HAP MO     ","  ";S(4),C(4)
6120  PRINT "5. COM PHO    ","  ";S(5),C(5)
6130  PRINT "6. FRI ELEC   ","  ";S(6),C(6)
6140  PRINT "CASH ON HAND: ";CA
6150  PRINT "VALUE OF STOCK: ";VA
6160  PRINT "TOTAL WORTH: ";CA + VA
6170  RETURN
7000  REM  CALCULATE STOCK VALUE
7010  FOR I = 1 TO 6
7020  C(I) = C(I) * GF * N(I)
7030  NEXT I
7040  GOSUB 10500
```

```
7050  IF R > OD GOTO 7080
7060 SF = SY
7070  GOTO 7090
7080 SF = SN
7090 C(C) = C(C) * SF
7100  RETURN
8000  REM  PURCHASE,SELL
8010  PRINT "DO YOU WISH TO: "
8020  PRINT "   1. PURCHASE"
8030  PRINT "   2. SELL"
8040  PRINT "   3. NEITHER"
8050  PRINT "ENTER 1, 2, OR 3"
8060  INPUT Z
8070  IF Z < 1 OR Z > 3 THEN 8050
8080  IF Z = 2 THEN 8210
8090  IF Z = 3 THEN  RETURN
8100  PRINT "BUY WHICH NUMBER?"
8110  PRINT "ENTER A NUMBER 1 THROUGH 6."
8120  INPUT Z
8130  PRINT "HOW MANY SHARES?"
8140  INPUT Z2
8150  IF C(Z) * Z2 > CA GOTO 8190
8160 S(Z) = S(Z) + Z2
8170 CA = CA - (C(Z) * Z2)
8180  GOTO 4040
8190  PRINT "YOU DON'T HAVE ENOUGH MONEY!"
8200  GOTO 8000
8210  PRINT "SELL WHICH NUMBER?"
8220  PRINT "ENTER A NUMBER 1 THROUGH 6"
8230  INPUT Z
8240  IF Z < 1 OR Z > 6 THEN 8220
8250  PRINT "HOW MANY SHARES?"
8260  INPUT Z2
8270  IF Z2 > S(Z) THEN 8310
8280 S(Z) = S(Z) - Z2
8290 CA = CA + Z2 * C(Z)
8300  GOTO 4040
8310  PRINT "YOU DON'T HAVE THAT MANY SHARES!"
8320  GOTO 8000
10000  REM   RANDOMIZATION - CHANGE 'RND (1)' TO 'RND (0)' FOR TR
    S-80 AND PET!
10010 R =  INT ( RND (1) * 6) + 1
10020  RETURN
10500 R =  INT ( RND (1) * 4) + 1
10510  RETURN
16000  REM  ROUNDING ROUTINE
16010  FOR I = 1 TO 6
16020 S(I) =  FN RD(S(I))
16030 C(I) =  FN RD(C(I))
16040  NEXT I
16050 CA =  FN RD(CA)
16060 VA =  FN RD(VA)
16070  RETURN
20000  REM  CLOSING
20010  GOSUB 6000
20020  PRINT "YOU HAVE COMPLETED THE SIX CYCLES!"
```

```
20030  PRINT "YOU STARTED WITH 10000 DOLLARS."
20040  PRINT "YOU NOW HAVE ";CA;" DOLLARS CASH."
20050  PRINT "AND ";VA;" DOLLARS WORTH OF STOCK."
20060  PRINT "THIS IS A TOTAL VALUE OF ";CA + VA;" DOLLARS."
20070  END
20080  PRINT "BYE FOR NOW!"
20090  END
21000  REM  DATA
21010  DATA "DOLLAR LOSES VALUE OVERSEAS!",.90
21020  DATA "DOLLAR GAINS VALUE OVERSEAS!",1.10
21030  DATA "WORSENING RELATIONS WITH COMMUNIST     COUNTRIES!",.
       85
21040  DATA "KEY CABINET MEMBER CAUGHT TAKING BRIBES",.95
21050  DATA "INFLATION TAPERING OFF.",1.10
21060  DATA "SERIOUS RECESSIONS LOOMS!",.80
21070  DATA "STEEL STRIKE!",.85,.95,.80,1.0,1.0,1.0
21080  DATA "SERIOUS GASOLINE SHORTAGE, PRICES     SKYROCKET!",1
       .4,1.2,.95,.75,1.0,1.0
21090  DATA "WAR IN MID EAST!",1.2,1.0,1.4,1.0,1.0,1.0
21100  DATA "SAFE DISPOSAL OF ATOMIC WASTE FOUND!",.80,.90,1.0,1.0
       ,1.0,1.2
21110  DATA "HUGE NEW COAL FIELD FOUND IN U.S.!",.75,.80,1.1,1.0,1
       .0,1.1
21120  DATA "RECORD COLD WINTER HITS!",1.2,1.2,1.0,1.7,1.0,1.0
21130  DATA "RUMOR OF NEW OIL FIELD DISCOVERY BY     MIDNIGHT OIL!
       ",2.5,.1,1
21140  DATA "OIL FIELD A BUST, MIDNIGHT OIL DOWN    THE TUBES!"
21150  DATA "NEW, INEXPENSIVE ELECTRIC CELL FOUND    BY SOLAR SEEK
       ERS!",2.0,.75,3
21160  DATA "SOLAR CELL NOT YET PERFECTED - IT MELTS"
21170  DATA "MCDANIEL AIRCRAFT SELLS 100 JETS TO     MIDEAST.",1.5
       ,.75,3
21180  DATA "GOVERNMENT ACCUSSES MCDANIEL AIRCRAFT  OF WAR - MONG
       ERING!"
21190  DATA "HAPPY DAYS SOUTHERN MOTELS ANNOUNCES    GRAND OPENING
        OF NEW LUXURY RETREAT AT  KEY WEST.",2.0,.2,3
21200  DATA "HURRICANE HITS KEY WEST, NEW RESORT     DESTROYED!"
21210  DATA  "PHONE RATES FROZEN BY CONSUMERS' GROUP",.8,1.0,2
21220  DATA  "COURT OVER - RULES PHONE RATE FREEZE."
21230  DATA  "FRIENDLY ELECTRIC COMPANY LOSES MAIN    ATOMIC REACT
       OR!",.75,1.0,2
21240  DATA  "REACTOR DAMAGE MINOR, BACK IN OPERATION"
```

* -->TABLE OF VARIABLES<--

*RD(*) - ROUNDING FUNCTION
1020 16020 16030 16050 16060

C - BUFFER FOR RANDOM NUMBER
4070 5240 7090 7090

C(*) - VALUE OF STOCKS
1040 1150 1160 1170 1180 1190 1200 6030 6080 6090 6100
6110 6120 6130 7020 7020 7090 7090 8150 8170 8290 16030
16030

CA – CASH ON HAND
1140 6140 6160 8150 8170 8170 8290 8290 16050 16050 20040
20060

DA – DAY NUMBER
4010 4010 4020

G$(*) – GENERAL INTEREST HEADLINES LIST
1030 1060 5020 5030 5040

GF – GENERAL HEADLINE FACTOR
5050 7020

GF(*) – GENERAL HEADLINES FACTORS LIST
1030 1060 5050

I – COUNTER
1050 1060 1060 1070 1080 1090 1090 1090 1090 1090 1090
1090 1100 1110 1120 1120 1120 1120 1120 1130 2010 2030
2070 2080 2770 2780 6020 6030 6030 6040 7010 7020 7020
7020 7030 16010 16020 16020 16030 16030 16040

N$(*) – SPECIFIC HEADLINES LIST
1030 1090 5070 5080 5090

N(*) – SPECIFIC HEADLINE FACTOR
1040 5100 5110 5120 5130 5140 5150 7020

N1(*) – SPEC HEAD FACT LIST
1030 1090 5100

N2(*) – """"
1030 1090 5110

N3(*) – """"
1030 1090 5120

N4(*) – """"
1030 1090 5130

N5(*) – """"
1030 1090 5140

N6(*) – """"
1030 1090 5150

OD – ODDS
5220 7050

OD(*) – ODDS LIST
1030 1120 5220

R – RANDOM NUMBER
5020 5030 5040 5050 5070 5080 5090 5100 5110 5120 5130
5140 5150 5170 5180 5190 5200 5210 5220 5230 5240 7050
10010 10500

S$(*) – POSITIVE NEWS LIST
1030 1120 5170 5180 5190

S(*) – SHARES OF EACH STOCK
1040 6030 6080 6090 6100 6110 6120 6130 8160 8160 8270
8280 8280 16020 16020

SA$ – STUDENT ANSWER
2300 2510 2690

SF – STOCK FACTOR
4070 7060 7080 7090

SM$ – SPECIFIC BAD NEWS
5230

SM$(*) – SPECIFIC BAD NEWS LIST
1030 1120 4070 5230

SN – FACTOR ON NEGATIVE NEWS
4070 5210 7080

SN(*) – FACTOR ON NEGATIVE NEWS LIST
1030 1120 5210

SY – FACTOR ON POSITIVE NEWS
5200 7060

SY(*) – FACTOR ON POSITIVE NEWS LIST
1030 1120 5200

VA – VALUE OF STOCK
6010 6030 6030 6150 6160 16060 16060 20050 20060

X – DEFINE ROUNDING FUNCTION
1020 1020

Z – STUDENT INPUT SELECTION
8060 8070 8070 8080 8090 8120 8150 8160 8160 8170 8230
8240 8240 8270 8280 8280 8290

ZZ – STUDENT INPUT SHARES
8140 8150 8160 8170 8260 8270 8280 8290

END OF VAR. LIST

SAMPLE RUN

]RUN
STOCK MARKET   STOCK MARKET   STOCK MARKET   STOCK MARKET
THIS IS A SIMULATION OF SOME OF THE
EVENTS WHICH TAKE PLACE IN THE
BUYING AND SELLING OF STOCK.
YOU GET TO BUY AND SELL FROM A LIMITED
PORTFOLIO OF STOCKS BASED UPON NEWS
HEADLINES RELEVANT TO THOSE COMPANIES.

YOU START WITH 10000 DOLLARS, AND YOUR
SOLE MISSION IS TO INCREASE THAT VALUE
AS MUCH AS POSSIBLE IN 6 BUYING/SELLING
SESSIONS.
DO WATCH THE HEADLINES CAREFULLY.
THEY ARE YOUR ONLY HINTS FOR SUCCESS.
BE CAREFUL, THOUGH BECAUSE NOT ALL
HEADLINES ALWAYS TURN OUT TO BE TRUE!
PRESS 'RETURN' OR 'ENTER'
?

HERE ARE THE COMPANIES:
MIDNIGHT OIL COMPANY
A COMPANY KNOWN FOR TAKING BIG RISKS.
SOMETIMES THEY WIN, BUT OFTEN THEY LOSE!
SOLAR SEEKERS, INC.
A NEW COMPANY JUST GETTING ESTABLISHED.
APPEAR TO EMPLOY A NUMBER OF HIGH
TECHNOLOGY EXPERTS.
MCDANIEL AIRCRAFT
A WELL ESTABLISHED MILITARY/INDUSTRIAL
ORIENTED AERONAUTICS COMPANY.
PRESS 'RETURN' OR 'ENTER'
?

HAPPY DAYS SOUTHERN MOTELS
A LARGE CHAIN OF SOUTH UNITED STATES
MOTELS. LARGELY DEPENDENT UPON TOURISM.
COMMUNITY PHONE COMPANY
A TYPICAL UTILITY - - CONSERVATIVE AND
FAIRLY IMMUNE TO WORLD PROBLEMS.
FRIENDLY ELECTRIC COMPANY
A VERY PROGRESSIVE UTILITY, HEAVY INTO
NUCLEAR POWER, WITH QUITE A BIT OF
COMMUNITY OPPOSITION.
PRESS 'RETURN' OR 'ENTER'
?

HERE WE GO!
INFLATION TAPERING OFF.
WAR IN MID EAST!
MCDANIEL AIRCRAFT SELLS 100 JETS TO   MIDEAST.

COMPANY	SHARES	VALUE
1. MID. OIL	0	20
2. SOL SEE	0	30
3. MC AIR	0	70
4. HAP MO	0	40
5. COM PHO	0	50
6. FRI ELEC	0	40

CASH ON HAND: 10000
VALUE OF STOCK: 0
TOTAL WORTH: 10000
DO YOU WISH TO:
    1. PURCHASE
    2. SELL
    3. NEITHER
ENTER 1, 2, OR 3
?1
BUY WHICH NUMBER?

```
ENTER A NUMBER 1 THROUGH 6.
?3
HOW MANY SHARES?
?100
COMPANY        SHARES      VALUE
1. MID. OIL      0         20
2. SOL SEE       0         30
3. MC AIR      100         70
4. HAP MO        0         40
5. COM PHO       0         50
6. FRI ELEC      0         40
CASH ON HAND: 3000
VALUE OF STOCK: 7000
TOTAL WORTH: 10000
DO YOU WISH TO:
    1. PURCHASE
    2. SELL
    3. NEITHER
ENTER 1, 2, OR 3
?3
WORSENING RELATIONS WITH COMMUNIST    COUNTRIES!
STEEL STRIKE!
FRIENDLY ELECTRIC COMPANY LOSES MAIN    ATOMIC REACTOR!
COMPANY        SHARES      VALUE
1. MID. OIL      0         26.4
2. SOL SEE       0         33
3. MC AIR      100         161.7
4. HAP MO        0         44
5. COM PHO       0         55
6. FRI ELEC      0         44
CASH ON HAND: 3000
VALUE OF STOCK: 16170
TOTAL WORTH: 19170
DO YOU WISH TO:
    1. PURCHASE
    2. SELL
    3. NEITHER
ENTER 1, 2, OR 3
?1
BUY WHICH NUMBER?
ENTER A NUMBER 1 THROUGH 6.
?1
HOW MANY SHARES?
?100
COMPANY        SHARES      VALUE
1. MID. OIL    100         26.4
2. SOL SEE       0         33
3. MC AIR      100         161.7
4. HAP MO        0         44
5. COM PHO       0         55
6. FRI ELEC      0         44
CASH ON HAND: 360
VALUE OF STOCK: 18810
TOTAL WORTH: 19170
```

```
DO YOU WISH TO:
    1. PURCHASE
    2. SELL
    3. NEITHER
ENTER 1, 2, OR 3
?2
SELL WHICH NUMBER?
ENTER A NUMBER 1 THROUGH 6
?3
HOW MANY SHARES?
?100
COMPANY       SHARES      VALUE
1. MID. OIL    100        26.4
2. SOL SEE     0          33
3. MC AIR      0          161.7
4. HAP MO      0          44
5. COM PHO     0          55
6. FRI ELEC    0          44
CASH ON HAND: 16530
VALUE OF STOCK: 2640
TOTAL WORTH: 19170
DO YOU WISH TO:
    1. PURCHASE
    2. SELL
    3. NEITHER
ENTER 1, 2, OR 3
?3
REACTOR DAMAGE MINOR, BACK IN OPERATION
DOLLAR LOSES VALUE OVERSEAS!
HUGE NEW COAL FIELD FOUND IN U.S.!
RUMOR OF NEW OIL FIELD DISCOVERY BY     MIDNIGHT OIL!
COMPANY       SHARES      VALUE
1. MID. OIL    100        19.07
2. SOL SEE     0          26.65
3. MC AIR      0          109.96
4. HAP MO      0          37.4
5. COM PHO     0          46.75
6. FRI ELEC    0          37.4
CASH ON HAND: 16530
VALUE OF STOCK: 1907.4
TOTAL WORTH: 18437.4
DO YOU WISH TO:
    1. PURCHASE
    2. SELL
    3. NEITHER
ENTER 1, 2, OR 3
?1
BUY WHICH NUMBER?
ENTER A NUMBER 1 THROUGH 6.
?1
HOW MANY SHARES?
?200
COMPANY       SHARES      VALUE
1. MID. OIL    300        19.07
2. SOL SEE     0          26.65
3. MC AIR      0          109.96
```

```
4. HAP MO        0        37.4
5. COM PHO       0        46.75
6. FRI ELEC      0        37.4
CASH ON HAND: 12716
VALUE OF STOCK: 5721
TOTAL WORTH: 18437
DO YOU WISH TO:
   1. PURCHASE
   2. SELL
   3. NEITHER
ENTER 1, 2, OR 3
?2
SELL WHICH NUMBER?
ENTER A NUMBER 1 THROUGH 6
?3
HOW MANY SHARES?
?100
YOU DON'T HAVE THAT MANY SHARES!
DO YOU WISH TO:
   1. PURCHASE
   2. SELL
   3. NEITHER
ENTER 1, 2, OR 3
?3
OIL FIELD A BUST, MIDNIGHT OIL DOWN    THE TUBES!
SERIOUS RECESSIONS LOOMS!
SERIOUS GASOLINE SHORTAGE, PRICES      SKYROCKET!
NEW, INEXPENSIVE ELECTRIC CELL FOUND   BY SOLAR SEEKERS!
COMPANY          SHARES       VALUE
1. MID. OIL      300          1.29
2. SOL SEE       0            19.19
3. MC AIR        0            108.86
4. HAP MO        0            33.66
5. COM PHO       0            42.08
6. FRI ELEC      0            37.03
CASH ON HAND: 12716
VALUE OF STOCK: 386.17
TOTAL WORTH: 13102.17
DO YOU WISH TO:
   1. PURCHASE
   2. SELL
   3. NEITHER
ENTER 1, 2, OR 3
?
```

TEACH ME

PROGRAM DESCRIPTION

A fundamental demonstration of computer logic or "intelligence" is demonstrated in this program. The computer's memory is expanded by inputting questions and correct answers into the computer. You start with one question and the computer gradually builds its memory from one question to the next.

There is only one restriction in that the question must be answered with a "YES" or "NO". In order to see the logic "tree" being developed, type in "LIST" at the beginning of each sequence. You can stop the building sequence by entering "STOP".

PROGRAM NOTES

This program has been around in many versions for quite some time. Although actual techniques vary, the result is always the construction of a "decision tree." With careful construction, the decision tree will make the computer appear to be learning. Whether or not this is true intelligence can be debated, but it is fun!

You might want to develop a method for saving the string array F$() and reading it back in again at some other time. This would let you continue an interesting "training" session.

PROGRAM LISTING

```
100  REM  TEACH ME BY GARY ORWIG
1000 REM   INITIALIZATION - MX DETERMINES MAXIMUM FILE SIZE - - M
     AY INCREASE IF MEMORY PERMITS.
1010 MX = 200
```

```
1020  DIM F$(MX)
1030  F$(1) = "YES"
1040  F$(2) = "ON"
1050  F$(4) = "YES"
1060  F$(6) = "NO"
1070  F$(8) = "EOD"
2000  REM  INTRODUCTION
2010  LI = 24
2020  GOSUB 18000
2030  FOR I = 1 TO 75
2040  PRINT "   TEACH ME!";
2050  NEXT I
2060  DE = 1500
2070  GOSUB 19000
2080  GOSUB 18000
2090  PRINT "THIS IS A PROGRAM WHICH ALLOWS YOU"
2100  PRINT "TO TEACH THE COMPUTER!"
2110  PRINT
2120  PRINT "THE COMPUTER STARTS WITH A QUESTION,"
2130  PRINT "AND GRADUALLY BUILDS FROM IT."
2140  PRINT
2150  PRINT "THERE IS ONLY ONE RESTRICTION IN THAT"
2160  PRINT "THE QUESTION MUST BE ANSWERED WITH"
2170  PRINT "A 'YES' OR 'NO', NOTHING IN BETWEEN"
2180  PRINT "IS ALLOWED!"
2190  PRINT
2200  PRINT "TO SEE THE LOGIC TREE WHICH IS"
2210  PRINT "BEING DEVELOPED, TYPE IN 'LIST'"
2220  PRINT "AT THE BEGINNING OF A SEQUENCE."
2230  PRINT
2240  PRINT "TO STOP, TYPE IN 'STOP' AT THE"
2250  PRINT "BEGINNING OF A SEQUENCE."
2260  PRINT
2270  PRINT "PUSH 'RETURN' OR 'ENTER' TO START.": REM  FOR PET PRE
      SS ANY LETTER BEFORE PRESSING RETURN
2280  INPUT SA$
2290  GOSUB 18000
2300  I = 0
3000  REM  INPUT OPERATING PARAMETERS
3010  PRINT "GIVE ME A QUESTION TO START WITH."
3020  PRINT "LIKE 'DOES IT SWIM?'"
3030  INPUT F$(3)
3040  PRINT "GIVE ME THE NAME OF SOMETHING WHICH DOES"
3050  INPUT F$(5)
3060  PRINT "GIVE ME THE NAME OF SOMETHING WHICH"
3070  PRINT "DOESN'T."
3080  INPUT F$(7)
4000  REM  MAIN PROGRAM
4010  LI = 6
4020  GOSUB 18000
4030  PRINT "TEACH ME!"
4040  LI = 6
4050  GOSUB 18000
4060  B = 0
4070  A = 0
4080  I = 1
```

```
4090 I = I + 1
4100  IF F$(I) = "ON" THEN 4140
4110  IF F$(I - 1) = "YES" THEN 4360
4120  IF F$(I - 1) = "NO" THEN 4360
4130  GOTO 4090
4140 L = I + 1
4150  FOR I = L TO MX
4160 J = I
4170  IF F$(I) = "YES" THEN 4220
4180  PRINT
4190  PRINT F$(I)
4200  PRINT
4210  NEXT I
4220  INPUT SA$
4230  IF SA$ = "YES" THEN 4090
4240  IF SA$ = "LIST" THEN 7020
4250  IF SA$ = "STOP" THEN 20000
4260  FOR I = J TO MX
4270  IF F$(I) = "YES" THEN 4290
4280  GOTO 4310
4290 B = B + 1
4300  GOTO 4340
4310  IF F$(I) = "NO" THEN 4330
4320  GOTO 4340
4330 A = A + 1
4340  IF B = A THEN 4090
4350  NEXT I
4360  PRINT
4370  PRINT "ARE YOU THINKING OF A ";F$(I);"?"
4380  INPUT SA$
4390  PRINT
4400  IF SA$ = "NO" THEN 4430
4410  GOSUB 12000
4420  GOTO 4030
4430  PRINT
4440  PRINT "OK, I GIVE UP!  WHAT WERE"
4450  PRINT "YOU THINKING OF?"
4460  INPUT SA$
4470  PRINT
4480  PRINT "TYPE IN A QUESTION,"
4490  PRINT "WHICH WHEN ANSWERED 'YES'"
4500  PRINT "WILL INDICATE YOU ARE THINKING OF THE"
4510  PRINT SA$
4520  PRINT
4530 I$ = "ON"
4540  GOSUB 6010
4550 S$ = SA$
4560 L = I
4570 L = L + 1
4580  INPUT SA$
4590 I$ = SA$
4600  PRINT
4610 I = L
4620  GOSUB 6010
4630 I = L + 1
4640 I$ = "YES"
```

```
4650  GOSUB 6010
4660 SA$ = S$
4670 I = L + 2
4680 I$ = SA$
4690  GOSUB 6010
4700 I = L + 3
4710 I$ = "NO"
4720  GOSUB 6010
4730  GOTO 4030
6000  REM  SHUFFLE STACK
6010 M = I - 1
6020 M = M + 1
6030  IF F$(M) = "EOD" THEN 6050
6040  GOTO 6020
6050  IF M = MX THEN 20500
6060  FOR N = M + 1 TO I STEP - 1
6070 F$(N) = F$(N - 1)
6080  NEXT N
6090 F$(I) = I$
6100  RETURN
7000  REM  PRINT THE STACK
7010  PRINT
7020 D = 1
7030  FOR H = D TO D + 15
7040  PRINT F$(H)
7050  NEXT H
7060 D = D + 16
7070  PRINT
7080  PRINT "PRESS 'RETURN' OR 'ENTER' TO"; REM  FOR PET PRESS ANY
      LETTER BEFORE PRESSING RETURN
7090  PRINT "CONTINUE LIST."
7100  PRINT "TYPE IN 'RETURN' TO RETURN TO PROGRAM."
7110  INPUT SA$
7120  IF SA$ < > "RETURN" THEN 7030
7130  GOTO 4030
12000  REM  REWARD
12010 LI = 12
12020  GOSUB 18000
12030  PRINT "         I GOT ONE RIGHT!"
12040  GOSUB 18000
12050 DE = 1000
12060  GOSUB 19000
12070  GOSUB 18000
12080  RETURN
18000  REM  SCROLLING
18010  FOR K = 1 TO LI
18020  PRINT
18030  NEXT K
18040  RETURN
19000  REM  DELAY
19010  FOR K = 1 TO DE
19020  NEXT K
19030  RETURN
20000  REM  CLOSING
20010  PRINT " I HOPE YOU HAD FUN!"
20020  PRINT " BYE FOR NOW!"
```

```
20030 END
20500 REM  OUT OF SPACE IN STACK
20510 PRINT "YOU HAVE FILLED UP MY MEMORY!"
20520 PRINT "I'M AFRAID I HAVE TO STOP NOW."
20530 PRINT "BYE!  COME BACK AGAIN!"
20540 END
```

                 * -->TABLE OF VARIABLES<--

A - NO COUNTER
4070 4330 4330 4340

B - YES COUNTER
4060 4290 4290 4340

D - PRINT 16 LINES COUNTER
7020 7030 7030 7060 7060

DE - DELAY
2060 12050 19010

F$(*) - INFORMATION FILE
1020 1030 1040 1050 1060 1070 3030 3050 3080 4100 4110
4120 4170 4190 4270 4310 4370 6030 6070 6070 6090 7040

H - PRINT 16 LINES COUNTER
7030 7040 7050

I - COUNTER
2030 2050 2300 4080 4090 4090 4100 4110 4120 4140 4150
4160 4170 4190 4210 4260 4270 4310 4350 4370 4560 4610
4630 4670 4700 6010 6060 6090

I$ - WORD VARIABLE
4530 4590 4640 4680 4710 6090

J - COUNTER
4160 4260

K - COUNTER
18010 18030 19010 19020

L - COUNTER
4140 4150 4560 4570 4570 4610 4630 4670 4700

LI - SCROLLING LINES
2010 4010 4040 12010 18010

M - COUNTER
6010 6020 6020 6030 6050 6060

MX - FILE MAXIMUM SIZE
1010 1020 4150 4260 6050

N - COUNTER
6060 6070 6070 6080

S$ - STUDENT INPUT BUFFER
4550 4660

SA$ - STUDENT INPUT
2280 4220 4230 4240 4250 4380 4400 4460 4510 4550 4580
4590 4660 4680 7110 7120

END OF VAR. LIST

SAMPLE RUN

```
]RUN
    TEACH ME!    TEACH ME!
THIS IS A PROGRAM WHICH ALLOWS YOU
TO TEACH THE COMPUTER!
THE COMPUTER STARTS WITH A QUESTION,
AND GRADUALLY BUILDS FROM IT.
THERE IS ONLY ONE RESTRICTION IN THAT
THE QUESTION MUST BE ANSWERED WITH
A 'YES' OR 'NO'. NOTHING IN BETWEEN
IS ALLOWED!
TO SEE THE LOGIC TREE WHICH IS
BEING DEVELOPED, TYPE IN 'LIST'
AT THE BEGINNING OF A SEQUENCE.
TO STOP, TYPE IN 'STOP' AT THE
BEGINNING OF A SEQUENCE.
PUSH 'RETURN' OR 'ENTER' TO START.
?
GIVE ME A QUESTION TO START WITH.
LIKE 'DOES IT SWIM?'
?DOES IT FLY?
GIVE ME THE NAME OF SOMETHING WHICH DOES
?BIRD
GIVE ME THE NAME OF SOMETHING WHICH
DOESN'T.
?COW
TEACH ME!
DOES IT FLY?
?YES
ARE YOU THINKING OF A BIRD?
?NO
OK, I GIVE UP! WHAT WERE
YOU THINKING OF?
?AIRPLANE
TYPE IN A QUESTION,
WHICH WHEN ANSWERED 'YES'
WILL INDICATE YOU ARE THINKING OF THE
AIRPLANE
?DOES IT HAVE A MOTOR?
TEACH ME!
DOES IT FLY?
?NO
ARE YOU THINKING OF A COW?
?NO
OK, I GIVE UP! WHAT WERE
YOU THINKING OF?
```

```
?CAT
TYPE IN A QUESTION,
WHICH WHEN ANSWERED 'YES'
WILL INDICATE YOU ARE THINKING OF THE
CAT
?DOES IT MEOW?
TEACH ME!
DOES IT FLY?
?YES
DOES IT HAVE A MOTOR?
?NO
ARE YOU THINKING OF A BIRD?
?YES
          I GOT ONE RIGHT!
TEACH ME!
DOES IT FLY?
?NO
DOES IT MEOW?
?NO
ARE YOU THINKING OF A COW?
?NO
OK, I GIVE UP!  WHAT WERE
YOU THINKING OF?
?DOG
TYPE IN A QUESTION,
WHICH WHEN ANSWERED 'YES'
WILL INDICATE YOU ARE THINKING OF THE
DOG
?DOES IT BARK?
TEACH ME!
DOES IT FLY?
?NO
DOES IT MEOW?
?NO
DOES IT BARK?
?YES
ARE YOU THINKING OF A DOG?
?YES
          I GOT ONE RIGHT!
TEACH ME!
DOES IT FLY?
?LIST
YES
ON
DOES IT FLY?
YES
ON
DOES IT HAVE A MOTOR?
YES
AIRPLANE
NO
BIRD
NO
ON
DOES IT MEOW?
YES
```

```
CAT
NO
PRESS 'RETURN' OR 'ENTER' TO
CONTINUE LIST.
TYPE IN 'RETURN' TO RETURN TO PROGRAM.
?
ON
DOES IT BARK?
YES
DOG
NO
COW
EOD
PRESS 'RETURN' OR 'ENTER' TO
CONTINUE LIST.
TYPE IN 'RETURN' TO RETURN TO PROGRAM.
?STOP
PRESS 'RETURN' OR 'ENTER' TO
CONTINUE LIST.
TYPE IN 'RETURN' TO RETURN TO PROGRAM.
?
PRESS 'RETURN' OR 'ENTER' TO
CONTINUE LIST.
TYPE IN 'RETURN' TO RETURN TO PROGRAM.
?RETURN
TEACH ME!
DOES IT FLY?
?STOP
 I HOPE YOU HAD FUN!
 BYE FOR NOW!
 ]
```

Appendix A
GRAPHIC SUBROUTINES

One of the most exciting attributes of microcomputers is their ability to generate video graphics. Unfortunately, one of the most frustrating weaknesses of microcomputers is the total lack of uniformity in the manner in which graphics are created. For this reason, the only real help for a new computer user lies in the documentation for his or her particular machine.

However, since the use of graphics is so important in computer-assisted instruction, the authors of this book felt it important to encourage the use of graphics, and to provide a few basic programs to start on. Graphics are most easily added to the reward and wrong answer routines. In these areas they provide motivation and variety as the program advances. Several simple examples of such graphics routines are included in this appendix. These examples will work only on the computers specified, and they should be considered strictly as building blocks for more widely varied routines.

APPLE II COMPUTER

```
]LIST
50 REM  HAPPY FACE – LEAVE OFF THE FIRST THREE LINES!
100  GOSUB 12000
110  END
12000  REM  REWARD
12010  GR
12020  COLOR= 13
12030  FOR A = 1 TO 7.5 STEP .05
12040  PLOT (20 +  SIN (A) * 13),(20 +  COS (A) * 15)
12050  NEXT A
12060  PLOT 14,14: PLOT 15,14: PLOT 24,14: PLOT 25,14
12070  PLOT 19,20: PLOT 20,20: PLOT 14,24: PLOT 15,24: PLOT 24,24:
    PLOT 25,24
12080  PLOT 16,26: PLOT 17,26: PLOT 22,26: PLOT 23,26
12090  PLOT 18,28: PLOT 19,28: PLOT 20,28: PLOT 21,28
12100  FOR I = 1 TO 1000
12110  NEXT I
12120  TEXT
12130  CALL - 936
12140  RETURN
]
```

```
]LIST
50  REM  SAD FACE - LEAVE OFF THE FIRST THREE LINES!
100  GOSUB 14000
110  END
14000  REM  WRONG ANSWER
14010  GR
14020  COLOR= 13
14030  FOR A = 1 TO 7.5 STEP .05
14040  PLOT (20 +  SIN (A) * 13),(20 +  COS (A) * 15)
14050  NEXT A
14060  PLOT 14,14: PLOT 15,14: PLOT 24,14: PLOT 25,14
14070  PLOT 19,20: PLOT 20,20: PLOT 14,28: PLOT 15,28: PLOT 24,28:
     PLOT 25,28
14080  PLOT 16,27: PLOT 17,27: PLOT 22,27: PLOT 23,27
14090  PLOT 18,26: PLOT 19,26: PLOT 20,26: PLOT 21,26
14100  FOR I = 1 TO 1000
14110  NEXT I
14120  TEXT
14130  CALL - 936
14140  RETURN
]

]LIST
50  REM  KALEIDOSCOPE - LEAVE OFF THE FIRST THREE LINES!
100  GOSUB 12000
110  END
12000  REM  REWARD
12010  GR
12020  I =  INT ( RND (1) * 40)
12030  W =  INT ( RND (1) * 48) + 3
12040  FOR K = 38 TO 0 STEP - 1
12050  GOSUB 12130
12060  NEXT K
12070  FOR K = 0 TO 38
12080  GOSUB 12130
12090  NEXT K
12100  TEXT
12110  CALL - 936
12120  RETURN
12130  COLOR= W / 8 + I * 3 + K / 4
12140  J = K - I
12150  J =  ABS (J)
12160  S =  INT (J / 19)
12170  J = J - (S * 19)
12180  HLIN 19 - J,19 + J AT K
12190  HLIN 19 - J,19 + J AT 38 - K
12200  VLIN 19 - J,19 + J AT K
12210  VLIN 19 - J,19 + J AT 38 - K
12220  IF K > 19 THEN 12270
12230  HLIN 19 - J,19 + J AT 19 - K
12240  HLIN 19 - J,19 + J AT K + 19
12250  VLIN 19 - J,19 + J AT 19 - K
12260  VLIN 19 - J,19 + J AT K + 19
12270  RETURN
]
```

TRS-80 COMPUTER

```
]LIST
50  REM  TRS-80 HAPPY FACE - LEAVE OFF THE FIRST THREE LINES!
100  GOSUB 12000
110  END
12000  REM  REWARD
12010 CLS
12020  FOR I = 1 TO 7.5 STEP .05
12030 SET( SIN (I) * 27 + 64, COS (I) * 12 + 24)
12040  NEXT I
12050 SET(51,18):SET(74,18)
12060 SET(64,24)
12070 SET(50,29):SET(75,29)
12080 SET(51,30):SET(74,30)
12090 SET(52,31):SET(73,31)
12100  FOR I = 53 TO 72
12110 SET(I,32)
12120  NEXT I
12130  RETURN
]

]LIST
50  REM  TRS-80 SAD FACE - LEAVE OFF THE FIRST THREE LINES!
100  GOSUB 12000
110  END
14000  REM   WRONG ANSWER
14010 CLS
14020  FOR I = 1 TO 7.5 STEP .05
14030 SET( SIN (I) * 27 + 64, COS (I) * 12 + 24)
14040  NEXT I
14050 SET(51,18):SET(74,18)
14060 SET(64,24)
14070 SET(50,32):SET(75,32)
14080 SET(51,31):SET(74,31)
14090 SET(52,30):SET(73,30)
14100  FOR I = 53 TO 72
14110 SET(I,29)
14120  NEXT I
14130  FOR I = 1 TO 1000
14140  NEXT I
14150 CLS
14160  RETURN
]
```

```
12000 REM REWARD
12010 PRINT"⬛"
12020 PRINT"
12030 PRINT"
12040 PRINT"
12050 PRINT"
12060 PRINT"
12070 PRINT"
12080 PRINT"
12090 PRINT"
12100 PRINT"
12110 PRINT"
12120 FOR I=1 TO 1000
12130 NEXT I
12140 FOR I=1 TO 40
12150 PRINT
12160 NEXT I
12170 END
13000 PRINT
13010 PRINT
13020 PRINT
13030 PRINT
13040 PRINT
13050 PRINT
14000 REM WRONG ANSWER
14010 PRINT"⬛"
14020 PRINT"
14030 PRINT"
14040 PRINT"
14050 PRINT"
14060 PRINT"
14070 PRINT"
14080 PRINT"
14090 PRINT"
14100 PRINT"
14110 PRINT"
14120 FOR I=1 TO 1000
14130 NEXT I
14140 FOR I=1 TO 40
14150 PRINT
14160 NEXT I
14170 END
READY.


READY.

12000 REM REWARD - ROCKET BLAST OFF!
12010 PRINT"⬛"
12020 FORZ=1TO20:PRINT:NEXTZ
12030 XX$="▨▨▨▨▨▨▨▨▨▨▨▨▨▨▨▨▨▨▨▨▨"
12040 YY$="▛▛▛▛▛▛▛▛▛▛▛▛▛▛▛▛▛▛▛▛▛▛"
12050 AA$="▞  ▛▛▛▛▛▛▛▛▛▛▛▛▛▛▛▛▛▛___▟▙/▟▙/▟▙▙▙"
12060 BB$="▙  ▜▙ ▜▙ ▜▙ ▜▙   ▜▙   ▟▟▟▟▟▟▙▙▙"
```

```
12070 PRINT"░░░░░░░░░░░░░░░"SPC(16)"░░░░    ░░░ ░░░ U░░░ S░░░ A";
12080 PRINT"░░░░     ░░░░░| | ░░░░░░░░"AA$;
12090 FORI=1TO1000:NEXT
12100 FORI=1TO11
12110 PRINTBB$AA$;
12120 FORJ=1TO50:NEXT:NEXT
12130 PRINTBB$"░":FORI=1TO21:FORJ=1TO(22-I)/5
12140 PRINTSPC(16)"░░░░░░░T]"
12150 PRINTSPC(16)"░░░░░░░T]"
12160 NEXT:PRINTLEFT$(XX$,I+3)RIGHT$(YY$,I+4)
12170 NEXT:PRINT"░"
12180 FORZ=1TO500:NEXT
12190 END
13000 PRINT
13010 PRINT
13020 PRINT
13030 PRINT
13040 PRINT
13050 PRINT

READY.
```

Address. A number that designates a location where information is stored in a memory device.

Algorithm. A statement of mathematical and/or logical steps to be followed in the solution of a problem.

ASCII. American Standard Code for Information Interchange. A standard set of binary codes which represent letters, numbers, and symbols.

BASIC. Beginners All-Purpose Symbolic Instruction Code. A high-level conversational programming language in widespread use. Incorporates simple English words and common mathematical symbols.

Baud. A rate of data transfer, given in bits per second. Alphabetic characters usually require about 10 bits per character, so a baud rate of 300 corresponds to about 30 characters per second.

Binary Code. The most fundamental of codes, using only 0's and 1's to represent data. Can be represented by the presence or absence of electrical current within key parts of a computer.

Branching Programmed Instruction. The material to be learned is presented in a sequence of small steps or frames similar to linear programmed instruction. The learner is presented a paragraph or so of information and asked questions concerning the paragraph. A correct answer advances or branches the program to the next step, where the learner's correct answer is verified and further information in paragraph form is presented. If the answer is incorrect or a near miss, the learner is transferred to a frame which explains the point in elementary or remedial terms. The learner is then sent back to the original point or frame to begin the advancement or branching process once again.

Bus. The set of electrical lines connecting the various parts of the computer. Data and control signals are sent along these lines.

Byte. A basic unit of information in a computer. A byte usually represents one character and is normally eight bits in length.

CAI. Computer-Assisted (Aided or Administered) Instruction. Many times CAI can be also referred to as CAL (computer-assisted learning) or CBL (computer-based learning). An *extrinsic* programming technique for individual instruction using computer hardware and software.

Character. Letters, numbers, and symbols which can be arranged into information. A character can usually be defined as one byte of information.

Computer Literacy. Knowledge or awareness of how computers are operated, programmed, and applied as an object of instruction.

Courseware. The terms *course* and *software* combined. The material to be learned is written in a computer programming language such as BASIC or PILOT.

CPU. Central Processing Unit. The "brain" of the computer. Directs all functions of the computer.

CRT. Cathode Ray Tube. The tube which makes the television screen perform. Used to display text and graphics created by a computer. Frequently linked with a keyboard to create a CRT terminal.

Cursor. A movable spot on the face of a CRT which indicates where the next character will be displayed.

Data. Information transferred to or from a computer.

Debug. The process of locating and eliminating errors in a program listing.

Dialog. A type of computer-assisted instruction (CAI) that is least used. Software is complex and requires a great deal of data storage capability. Instruction begins with the learner submitting questions or data to the computer. The computer replies with correct answers and additional information on the subject(s) and even provides practice problems Dialog CAI is not very practical with present microcomputers because of the lack of data storage capability.

Diagnostic Routine. A form of programming which lets the computer test itself for internal hardware malfunctions.

Disc (Disk). A mass storage device capable of high storage and retrieval speeds. Similar in appearance to a magnetic oxide coated record. Can be either *floppy* (flexible) or *hard*, depending upon performance requirements.

Dot Matrix. A technique of using an array of dots to create characters. A 5 x 7 array of dots is the bare minimum for alphanumeric characters, while larger arrays, such as 7 x 9, will allow upper and lower case letters, and underlining.

Drill and Practice. A type of computer-assisted instruction (CAI) that is used most widely by educators. Material is presented in form of practice problems and exercises for the purpose of learning reinforcement. Computer provides studen reward and recognition for correct answers and remedial information for wrong answers. Excellent for present microcomputer hardware.

Duplex (Full Duplex). An interface which allows simultaneous two-way communication between a computer and a peripheral device.

EPROM. Erasable Programmable Read Only Memory. A long-term memory which, under special conditions, can be erased and rewritten.

File. A set of data which has some specified relationship.

Firmware. Programs which are stored in ROM. They are immediately available for execution; there is no need to load them from a storage device.

Floating Point BASIC. A full-sized BASIC programming language capable of handling a complete range of mathematic computations. It also includes sophisticated methods for manipulating words or "strings" of non-numeric characters.

GIGO. Garbage In, Garbage Out. Any errors which enter a computer will result in errors in the output.

Graphics. The ability of the computer to construct line drawings, graphs, charts, etc. on a CRT or a printer.

Graphic Subroutine. A small segment of a program listing that performs a specific graphic function. Graphic subroutines can substitute word subroutines in order to draw or plot a graphic design to depict the meaning of the word.

Hardware. The equipment which makes up a computer system.

High-Level Language. A computer language with characteristics of English words, decimal arithmetic, and common mathematics symbols. Each instruction usually represents many individual computer operations.

Input. Information (or data) entering a computer or peripheral device. The same information may be *output* from some other part of the computer system.

Interface. A hardware and/or software device used to connect a computer to peripheral equipment such as printers.

I/O. Input/Output of information. The two terms are frequently used together because they often involve the same communication lines.

K or Kilo. Symbol or prefix for 1,000. In computer language, 1 K actually stands for 2 to the tenth power or 1,024.

Linear Programmed Instruction. Material to be learned is presented in a logical (fixed) sequence of small steps or frames. Immediate confirmation of correct or incorrect answers is given and student progresses onto the next frame at his or her own rate. Correct answer must be given before the learner advances onto the next step or frame.

Machine Language. A language which can be executed directly by the computer. Usually a series of binary or hexadecimal numbers. Very difficult for humans to work with.

Memory. The high speed electronic components in a computer which store information often in RAM or ROM.

Modem. Modulator-Demodulator. An interface which allows the computer to send (receive) digital signals over analog signal telecommunication lines or satellites.

Output. Information or data coming from a computer.

Peripheral Device. Equipment which links to a computer by means of an interface. Printers, CRT's, tape and disc drives are examples.

PILOT. A high-level programming language using interaction and conversation techniques. Developed by Dr. John Starkweather at the University of California, San Francisco.

Programmed Instruction (PI). Material to be learned is presented in short sequential steps or frames. Each frame represents a fact to be learned. A dialog in the form of questions and answers is set up between a single tutor and a single learner.

PROM. Programmable Read Only Memory. Permanently recorded data stored on special RAM memory. Once programmed the data cannot be altered by computer or man. Useful for storing frequently utilized instructions.

RAM. Random Access Memory. The "working" memory of the computer. This memory can be accessed and altered (programmed) by the computer or man as needed.

REM. A REMarks statement in a program listing. It is used to explain a portion of the program and does not have to be entered into the computer's memory.

ROM. Read Only Memory. About the same as PROM, except that ROM is usually programmed at the time of manufacture. Many times in the form of cassette or cartridge tapes. ROM cannot be altered (programmed) by the computer or man.

Simulation Programmed Instruction. A type of programmed instruction (PI) and computer-assisted instruction (CAI) that puts the learner in a real-life physical or social situation. Simulations are designed to allow the learner to use decision-making skills to alter the situation and witness the outcome created by the decisions. Personal, educational growth derives from the parallel effect of the various inputs to real-life conditions. A great deal of enthusiasm or motivation from the learner is one good aspect of the use of simulation CAI. Many computer games (for example, Space War games) are simulations. Science and engineering as well the aerospace industry use simulations for structural design and the training of personnel. Simulations are difficult to create, but they have tremendous potential for use on present microcomputers.

Software. Programs and necessary documentation which are needed to make a computer operate.

Testing. A type of computer-assisted instruction (CAI) that educators first used on a computer. Computer gives a "test" by asking questions while the learner responds with the correct or incorrect answer. A score is recorded by the computer and a grade is displayed at the end of the test. Microcomputers are good application for this type of CAI.

Tutorial. A type of computer-assisted instruction (CAI) that is the second most widely used application by educators. Linear, branching, or simulation programmed instruction is implemented on a computer. Microcomputers are widely used for this type of CAI.

Terminal. A peripheral device which usually consists of a printer or a CRT, a keyboard, and sometimes a floppy or hard disc device.

Appendix C
REFERENCES

BOOKS

1. Atkinson, R. C., and Wilson, H. A., eds. *Computer-Assisted Instruction: A Book of Readings.* Academic Press, New York, 1969.

2. Barnes, O. Dennis, and Schrieber, Deborah B. *Computer-Assisted Instruction, A Selected Bibliography.* Association For Educational Communications and Technology, Washington, D.C., 1972.

3. Bassler, Richard A., and Joslin, Edward O. *Applications of Computer Systems.* College Readings, Inc., Arlington, VA, 1974.

4. Blishen, Edward. *The Encyclopedia of Education.* Philosophical Library, Inc., New York, 1970.

5. Bullock, Donald H. *Programmed Instruction.* Educational Technology Publications, Inc., Englewood Cliffs, NJ, 1978.

6. Edwards, J. B., Ellis, A. S., Richardson, D. E., Holznagel, D., and Klassen, D. *Computer Applications in Instruction: A Teacher's Guide to Selection and Use.* Time Share Corporation, Hanover, NH, 1978.

7. Kurshan, Barbara. *Computer Literacy: Practical Ways to Teach the Basic Mathematic Skills.* Virginia Council of Teachers of Mathematics, Richmond, VA, 1978.

8. Lange, Philip C., ed. *Programmed Instruction Part II.* University of Chicago Press, 1967.

9. McKenzie, John, ed. *Interactive Computer Graphics in Science Teaching.* Halstead Press, New York, 1978.

10. Nahigian, J. Victor, and Hodges, William S. *Computer Games For Businesses, Schools, and Homes.* Winthrop Publishers, Inc., Cambridge, MA, 1979.

11. Raphael, Bertram. *The Thinking Computer.* W. H. Freeman, San Francisco, 1976.

12. Reese, Jay. *Simulation Games and Learning Activities Kit For The Elementary School.* Parker Publishing Company, Inc. West Nyack, NY, 1977.

PERIODICALS

1. Ahl, David H. "Computer Simulation Games." *Teacher*, February 1980, pp. 60-61.

2. Aiken, Robert M. and Braun, Ludwig. "Into the 80's with Microcomputer-Based Learning." *Computer*, July 1980, pp. 11-16.

3. Allee, Jr., John G., and Williams, Robert L. "A Challenge for the Language Arts CAI Developer." *Creative Computing*, September 1980, pp. 120-125.

4. Barnett, Bruce D. "Grading Made Easy." *Creative Computing*, September 1980, pp. 146-149.

5. Bejar, Isaac I. "Milliken Math Sequences." *Creative Computing*, September 1980, pp. 56-57.

6. Bell, Fred. "Classroom Computers: Beyond the 3R's." *Creative Computing*, September 1979, pp. 68-70.

7. Billings, Karen. "Microcomputers in Education: Now and in the Future." *Kilobaud MICROCOMPUTING*, June 1980, pp. 100-102.

8. Blaschke, Charles L. "Microcomputer Software Development for Schools: What, Who, How?" *Educational Technology*, October 1979, pp. 26-28.

9. Bork, Alfred, and Franklin, Stephen. "Personal Computers in Learning." *Educational Technology*, October 1979, pp. 7-12.

10. Campbell, J. Olin. "Personal Computers In The Classroom." *Interface Age*, October 1979, pp. 60-62.

11. Carlson, Ronald. "Complements and Supplements." *Creative Computing*, September 1980, pp. 140-142.

12. Carlstrom, Geraldine. "Operating a Microcomputer Convinced Me—and My Second Graders—To Use It Again. . .and Again. . ." *Teacher*, February 1980, pp. 54-55.

13. Carpenter, Chuck. "Chem Lab Simulations From High Technology." *Creative Computing*, September 1980, pp. 58-59.

14. Carr, Everett Q., "Computer Survival Course for Kids." *Kilobaud MICROCOMPUTING*, June 1980, pp. 122-123.

15. Cohen, Michael R. "Improving Teachers' Conceptions of Computer-Assisted Instruction." *Educational Technology*, August 1978, pp. 41-42.

16. Cook, William H. "Math Teacher." *Kilobaud MICROCOMPUTING*, June 1980, pp. 134-136.

17. Derner, Robert R. "A Teacher for Your Apple." *Personal Computing*, August 1980, pp. 48-49.

18. D'Ignazio, S. Frederick. "The World Inside The Computer." *Creative Computing*, September 1980, pp. 40-44.

19. Dwyer, Tom. "Books as an Antidote to the CAI Blues, Or Take a Publisher to Lunch." *BYTE*, July 1980, pp. 74-84.

20. Fincher, Jack. "Computers Are Kid Stuff." *Next*, March/April 1980, pp. 38-41 ff.

21. Fink, Robert K. "Living Off the Land." *Personal Computing*, August 1980, pp. 50-51.

22. Frann, Steven. "Computers and Education: Views of Seymour Papert." *Technology Review*, November 1979, pp. 77-78.

23. Frenzel, Lou, "The Personal Computer—Last Chance for CAI?" *BYTE*, July 1980, pp. 86-96.

24. Friel, Susan, and Roberts, Nancy. "Computer Literacy Bibliography." *Creative Computing*, September 1980, pp. 92-97.

25. Gilder, Jules H. "Radio Electronics Buyer's Guide To Home Computers." *Radio Electronics*, October 1980, pp. 45-84.

26. Heines, Jesse M. "Courseware Development and the NSF." *Computer*, July 1980, pp. 31-34.

27. Huntington, John F. "Microcomputers and Computer-Assisted Instruction." *Educational Technology*, May 1979, pp. 32-37.

28. Inman, Don, "Apples, Computers and Teachers," *Interface Age*, October 1979, pp. 68-70.

29. Kahn, Henry F. "Needed: An Alternative for Mathematics Textbooks." *School Science and Mathematics*, October 1979, pp. 472-477.

30. Knight, Anne H. "Computer Anxiety: One Way to Handle It." *Creative Computing*, September 1979, pp. 74-75.

31. Larsen, Sally Greenwood. "Kids and Computers: The Future Is Today." *Creative Computing*, September 1979, pp. 58-60.

32. Lehman, James D. "Nich, A BASIC Game of Ecology." *Creative Computing*, July 1979, pp. 87-91.

33. Lichtman, David. "Survey of Educators' Attitudes Toward Computers." *Creative Computing*, January 1979, pp. 48-50.

34. Lipson, Joseph I. "Technology In Science Education: The Next 10 Years." *Computer*, July 1980, pp. 21-28.

35. Lubar, David. "Educational Software." *Creative Computing*, September 1980, pp. 64-72.

36. Luehrmann, Arthur. "Computer Illiteracy—A National Crisis and a Solution For It." *BYTE*, July 1980, pp. 98-102.

37. March, Paul W. "The Microcomputer Goes to School." *Audiovisual Instruction*, May 1978, pp. 38-40.

38. Martellaro, Helena C. "Why Don't They Adopt Us?" *Creative Computing*, September 1980, pp. 104-105.

39. Mazur, Ken. "Grow Old Along with Me! The Best Is Yet to Be. . ." *Personal Computing*, August 1980, pp. 39-41.

40. McGowan, Francis. "The Micro In A Small School." *Interface Age*, October 1979, pp. 64, 99 ff.

41. Miller, Inabeth. "The Micros Are Coming." *Media and Methods*, April 1980, pp. 31-34 ff.

42. Miller, W. R., and Randolph, James E. "Occupational Information Through Computer Simulation." *Journal of Educational Research,* March/April, 1977, pp. 199-204.

43. Molnar, Andrew. "The Next Great Crisis in American Education—Computer Literacy." *EDUCOM Bulletin,* Spring 1979.

44. Mourer, Donald E. "The Computer vs. the Professor." *Creative Computing.* September 1979, pp. 78-81.

45. Noddings, Nel. "Word Problems Made Painless." *Creative Computing,* September 1980, pp. 108-113.

46. Piele, Donald T. "How To Solve It—with the Computer." *Creative Computing,* September 1980, pp. 126-131.

47. Piele, Donald T. "Micros 'GOTO' School." *Creative Computing,* September 1979, pp. 132-134.

48. Potts, Michael. "Smart Programs, Dumb Programs." *Creative Computing,* September 1980, pp. 100-102.

49. Ropes, George. "Bringing Microcomputers Into Schools." *Kilobaud MICROCOMPUTING,* June 1980, pp. 104-105.

50. Schwartz, Marc D. "Intergrating CAI and Videotape." *Creative Computing,* September 1980, pp. 116-117.

51. Sorlie, William E., and Essex, Diane L. "So You Want to Develop A Computer-Based Instruction Project? Some Recommendations to Consider First," *Educational Technology,* March 1979, pp. 53-57.

52. Souviney, Randall. "There's a Microcomputer in Your Future," *Teacher,* February 1980, pp. 53-58.

53. Spivak, Howard, and Varden, Stuart. "Classrooms Make Friends with Computers." *Instructor,* February 1980, pp. 52-58 and Part II March 1980, pp. 84-90.

54. Stark, Peter A. "Computer Education and Vocations." *Kilobaud MICROCOMPUTING,* June 1980, pp. 150-156.

55. Stone, Deborah. "Computers at an Alternative School." *Creative Computing,* September 1980, pp. 46-47

56. Strickland, A. W. "Metric Instruction in Elementary Science Methods Using Computer-Managed Instruction." *Educational Technology,* August 1979, pp. 31-32.

57. Viacant, William J. "The Briefcase-size Computer and Its Impact on Education." *Computers and People,* May 1978, pp. 24-25.

58. Victor, John Eric. "Rudimentary Computer Teaching Aid." *Kilobaud MICROCOMPUTING,* June 1980, pp. 162-163.

59. Wexler, Henrietta. "Computer Literacy." *American Education,* June 1979, pp. 41 ff.

60. Woolley, Robert D. "Microcomputers and Videodiscs: New Dimensions for Computer Based Education." *Interface Age,* December 1979, pp. 78-82.

61. Zinn, Karl L. "Personal Computers at the University of Michigan: An Assessment of Potential Impact." *Creative Computing,* September 1978, pp. 84 ff.

62. "Getting Started With Microcomputers." *Instructional Innovator*, September 1980 Vol. 25, No. 26.